Dharma

कम तोलने का फल
अधिक बोझा लादने का फल
गर्भ गिराने का फल
लालच का फल
धर्म सभा
रिश्वत लेने का फल
वैतरणी नदी
हिंसा का फल
पर स्त्री गमन का फल

Dharma

ALF HILTEBEITEL

Dimensions of Asian Spirituality

UNIVERSITY OF HAWAI'I PRESS
Honolulu

DIMENSIONS OF ASIAN SPIRITUALITY
Henry Rosemont, Jr., General Editor

This series makes available short but comprehensive works on specific Asian philosophical and religious schools of thought, works focused on a specific region, and works devoted to the full articulation of a concept central to one or more of Asia's spiritual traditions. Series volumes are written by distinguished scholars in the field who not only present their subject matter in historical context for the non-specialist reader, but also express their own views of the contemporary spiritual relevance of their subject matter for global citizens of the twenty-first century.

Printed in the United States of America
15 14 13 12 11 10 6 5 4 3 2 1

Library of Congress Cataloging-in-Publication Data
Hiltebeitel, Alf.
Dharma / Alf Hiltebeitel.
p. cm. — (Dimensions of Asian spirituality)
Includes bibliographical references and index.
ISBN 978-0-8248-3466-1 (hardcover : alk. paper) —
ISBN 978-0-8248-3486-9 (pbk. : alk. paper)
1. Dharma. I. Title. II. Series: Dimensions of Asian spirituality.

B132.D5H55 2010
294.3'4—dc22
2010010614

University of Hawai'i Press books are printed on acid-free Paper and meet the guidelines for permanence and durability of the Council on Library Resources.

Series design by Rich Hendel
Printed by The Maple-Vail Book Manufacturing Group

Frontis art: An Indian poster depicts, at center, Yama Dharmarāja as king of the dead in his Hall of Yama. The other panels all pair modern earthly sins with otherworldly punishments and are captioned in Hindi: the fruits of cheating with weights *(upper left)*, of overburdening animals *(upper center)*, of poisoning *(upper right)*, of killing *(lower left)*, of adultery by women *(lower center)*, and of theft *(lower right)*. The fruits of greed are shown in the set to the left of the central image, and, to the right, the results of taking bribes.

Contents

Editor's Preface

ABOUT THIS SERIES

The University of Hawai'i Press has long been noted for its scholarly publications in, and commitment to, the field of Asian Studies. The present volume is the fifth in a series initiated by the press in keeping with that commitment, Dimensions of Asian Spirituality.

It is a most appropriate time for such a series. A number of the world's religions—major and minor—originated in Asia, continue to influence significantly the lives of almost half of the world's peoples, and should now be seen as global in scope, reach, and impact, with rich and varied resources for every citizen of the twenty-first century to explore.

Religion is at the heart of every culture. To be sure, cultures have also been influenced by climate, geology, and the consequent patterns of economic activity they have developed for the production and distribution of goods. Only a very minimal knowledge of physical geography is necessary to understand why African sculptors largely employed wood as their medium while their Italian Renaissance brethren usually worked with marble. But while necessary for understanding cultures—not least our own—matters of geography and economics will not be sufficient. Wood and marble are also found in China, yet Chinese sculptors carved Confucian sages, Daoist immortals, and bodhisattvas from their materials, not *chiwaras* or *pietas*.

In the same way, a mosque, synagogue, cathedral, *stūpa*, and pagoda may be equally beautiful, but they are beautiful in different ways, and the differences cannot be accounted for merely on the basis of the materials used in their construction; their beauty, their ability to inspire awe and to invite contemplation, rests largely on the religious view of the world—and the place of human beings in that world—that inspired and is expressed in their architecture.

Thus the spiritual dimensions of a culture are reflected significantly not only in art and architecture, but in music, myths, poetry, rituals, customs, and patterns of social behavior as well; it follows that if we wish to understand why and how members of other cultures live as they do, we must understand the religious beliefs and practices to which they adhere.

In the first instance, such understanding of the "other" leads to tolerance, which is surely a good thing; much of the pain and suffering in the world today is attributable to intolerance, a fear and hatred of those who look, think, and act differently. But as technological changes in communication, production, and transportation shrink the world, more and more people must confront the fact of human diversity in multiply diverse forms—both between and within nation–states—and hence there is a growing need to go beyond mere tolerance of difference to an appreciation and celebration of it. Tolerance alone cannot contribute substantively to making the world a better—and sustainable—place for human beings to live, the evils attendant on intolerance notwithstanding and not to be minimized. But in an important sense, mere tolerance is easy because it is passive: I can fully respect your right to believe and worship as you wish, associate with whomever, and say what you will simply by ignoring you; you assuredly have a right to speak but not to make me listen.

Yet for most of us who live in economically developed societies or are among the affluent in developing nations, tolerance is not enough; ignoring the poverty, disease, and gross inequalities that afflict fully a third of the human race will only exacerbate, not alleviate, the conditions responsible for the misery that generates the violence becoming ever more commonplace throughout the world today.

Some would have us believe that religion is—as it supposedly always has been—the root cause of the violence and therefore should be done away with. This negative view is reinforced by invoking distorted accounts of the cosmologies of the world's religious heritages and pointing out that they are incompatible with much that we know of the world today from science. These negative accounts, now increasing quantitatively as their quality declines, also suffer from a continued use of the Abrahamic monotheistic religions of the West as a template for all religions, one ill-suited to the particularities of the several Asian spiritual traditions.

Despite the attacks on religion today, it should be clear that they are not going to go away; nor should they. Those who see only the untoward influences—influences not to be ignored—are taking "a printed bill of fare as the equivalent for a solid meal," to quote William James. Worse than that, to point the finger at religion as responsible for most of the violence worldwide today is to obscure a far more important root cause: poverty. In this view, the violence will cease only when the more fortunate among the peoples of the world become active, not passive; take up the plight of the less fortunate; and resolve to create and maintain a more just world—a resolve that requires a full appreciation of the co-humanity of everyone, significant differences in religious beliefs and practices notwithstanding.

Such appreciation should not, of course, oblige everyone to endorse all of the beliefs and practices followed by adherents of other religions, just as one may object to certain beliefs and practices within one's own faith. A growing number of Catholics, for instance, support a married clergy, the ordination of women, recognition of rights for gays and lesbians, and full reproductive rights for women. Yet they remain Catholics, believing that the tenets of their faith have the conceptual resources to bring about and justify these changes.

In the same way, we can also believe—as a number of Muslim women do—that the Quran and other Islamic theological writings contain the conceptual resources to overcome the inferior status of women in many Muslim countries. And indeed we can believe that every spiritual tradition has within it the resources to counter older practices inimical to the full flourishing of all the faithful—and of the faithful of other traditions as well.

Another reason to go beyond mere tolerance to appreciation and celebration of the many and varied forms of spiritual expression is virtually a truism: the more we look through a window on another culture's beliefs and practices, the more it becomes a mirror of our own (even for those who follow no religious tradition). We must look very carefully and charitably, however, else the reflections become distorted. When studying other religions, most people are strongly inclined to focus on cosmological and ontological questions, asking, What do these people believe about how the world came to be, is, and where it is heading? Do they believe in ghosts? Immortal souls? A creator god?

Answering these and related metaphysical questions is, of course, necessary for understanding and appreciating fully the specific forms and content of the art, music, architecture, rituals, and traditions inspired by the specific religion under study. But the sensitive—and sensible—student will bracket the further question of whether the metaphysical pronouncements are literally true; we must attend carefully to the metaphysics (and theologies) of the religions we study, but questions of their literal truth should be set aside to concentrate on a different question: How could a thoughtful, thoroughly decent human being subscribe to and follow these beliefs and attendant practices?

We may come to see and appreciate how each religious tradition, studied in this light, provides a coherent account of a world not fully amenable to human manipulation, nor perhaps even to full human understanding. The metaphysical pronouncements of the world's religions of course differ measurably from faith to faith, and each has had a significant influence on the physical expressions of the respective faith in synagogues, *stūpas,* mosques, pagodas, and cathedrals. Despite these differences among the buildings, however, the careful and sensitive observer can see the spiritual dimensions of human life that these sacred structures share and express, and in the same way we can come to see and appreciate the common spiritual dimensions of each religion's differing metaphysics and theology. While the several religious traditions give different answers to the question of the meaning of life, they all provide a multiplicity of similar guidelines and spiritual disciplines to enable everyone to find meaning *in* life, in this world.

By plumbing the spiritual depths of other religious traditions, then, we may come to more deeply explore the spiritual resources of our own and at the same time diminish the otherness of the other and create a more peaceable and just world in which all can find meaning in their all-too-human lives.

About this Book

Against this background we may turn more directly to the present volume, the first in the Dimensions of Asian Spirituality series to focus specifically on South Asia, and on India in particular (which earlier encompassed what is now Pakistan and Bangladesh as well as Nepal). *Dharma* is unique in the series in another way, being the first to deal solely with a single spiritual concept—an unusual and highly challenging scholarly undertaking.

Readers will agree, I believe, that Alf Hiltebeitel has met the challenge in exemplary fashion. He has a thorough command of the several and varied texts of early Buddhism and the Brahmanical traditions that collectively come under the heading of Hinduism that allows him to trace clearly the evolution and development of the concept of *dharma/dhamma* over a period of many centuries and through schools of religious thought. His translations are lucid and lively, and in his own narrative he has a distinctive voice that invites the reader to enter into dialogue with him no less than with the ancient texts.

Dharma is a most timely volume for us. Various conceptual aspects of South Asian spirituality have been increasingly penetrating the ethos and worldview(s) of all modern industrial societies. This is especially the case in the United States today: *Yoga* in one form or another is now a very common (and very useful) form of exercise (although it is much more than that); many people speak easily of "good" or "bad" *karma; nirvāṇa* became a well-known term in its popular sense of "bliss," even before a rock band with that name became famous; everyone knows that a *guru* is a special kind of teacher; and more.

So, too, for *dharma,* which we have come to think we might understand from programs like "Dharma and Gregg," and Jack Kerouac's well-known novel *The Dharma Bums.* Hiltebeitel makes clear, however, that *dharma* denotes more than a single, simple concept; rather, it has had distinctive meanings to practitioners of various faiths at the same time, and equally distinctive meanings within the same faith over lengthier periods of time (as with the other terms listed above). Derived from the Sanskritic root √*dhṛ*, which originally meant "to hold," Hiltebeitel shows how the concept changed greatly over the centuries but never entirely lost the sense of holding, even when, for example, one meaning of *dharma* came to be "the Buddha's teachings" (only for Buddhists, of course!). We can still see the basic definition working, as the Buddha's teachings are surely something we should want to hold onto, and firmly.

Alf Hiltebeitel follows this root meaning of *dharma* through its manifold transformations in the ten texts he has selected for examination, which, as he says, may correctly be called "*dharma* texts" because the concept occupies such a prominent place in each one of them, from the Edicts of Aśoka and the *Laws of Manu* to the *Rāmāyaṇa* and the *Mahābhārata,* with a special chapter devoted to that portion of the latter epic we know as the *Bhagavad Gītā,* wherein the god Vishnu in human form (Krishna) lectures on *dharma* to the warrior prince Arjuna.

The present work is not, however, solely or even largely an etymological and/or philological treatise, nor is it a lengthy excursion in literary criticism—even though elements of all three are included in it at times, appropriately, when necessary. *Dharma* is found in the secular world of South Asia past and present, but its home is in the sacred, and it is thus the spiritual dimensions of *dharma* that should engage readers as they begin to come to terms—pun not intended—with the ancient civilization that gave birth to two of the major religious faiths in the world, whose adherents make up almost a third of the human race today.

Acknowledgments

A series editor may take on many tasks, including seeing a text through serial lives. This work has gone through at least seven drafts. Through each incarnation Henry Rosemont has been its midwife. To paraphrase the Buddha, this birth will be its last. My thanks to Henry for helping ensure the book's improvement in each incarnation. To Bill Harman, now revealed as the University of Hawai'i Press's anonymous reader of the last two drafts, thanks for his solid appreciation and many good ideas that helped enhance the book's accessibility. I was also fortunate to get constructive input from Patricia Crosby, executive editor at the University of Hawai'i Press, who encouraged me in my work on this book. And thanks to Jackie Doyle for the fine-tuning she did as the press's copy editor. Finally, thanks to the following conversation partners for making memorable contributions: Vishwa Adluri, Eyal Aviv, Greg Bailey, Madeleine Biardeau, Brian Black, Adam Bowles, Simon Brodbeck, Ane Kunga Chodron, Gurcharan Das, Donald Davis, James L. Fitzgerald, Elena Garcés, Stephanie Jamison, Randy Kloetzli, Meghan Lisicich, Tim Lubin, T. P. Mahadevan, Tom Michael, Jan Nattier, Patrick Olivelle, Laurie Patton, Dan Rudmann, Perundevi Srinivasan, and Jarrod Whittaker.

CHAPTER 1

Dharma and South Asian Spirituality

Readers, here are many of the terms I am going to use in this book on *dharma,* in Sanskrit and their Pāli variants (Sanskrit and Pāli are two of the major Indo-Aryan languages of classical South Asia). Starting with their Sanskrit forms, we have *dharma* itself, meaning that which "holds," or "upholds." The classical term *dharma* also has a precursor in older Vedic Sanskrit, where you will find the form *dhárman. Dhárman* can be translated as "foundation," in that a foundation is something that "holds." Both derive from the verbal root √*dhṛ,* "to hold." Among other Sanskrit terms you will meet are *nirvāṇa* and *mokṣa,* both of which describe the goal of liberation. Liberation usually has to do not with "holding" but with "letting go." In that *dharma* is concerned with things that "hold," you can expect that it has to do with things that are *worth* holding *to,* even if they must ultimately be "let go" if one is to attain *nirvāṇa* or *mokṣa.*

Here you will meet a linguistic feature of *dharma* that has to do with the way it is used to speak of things worth holding to in what is known as *saṃsāra,* the "world in flux." You might think of *saṃsāra*'s hold, and thus *dharma*'s, too, as "the ties that bind." This linguistic feature is that *dharma* is prominently used in compounds with other words. When it appears as the first member, it can refer to something being "virtuous," "lawful," "just," or "righteous," as with *dharma-yuddha,* a "just war," or *dharma-rāja,* a "righteous king." When it appears as the second member, it can refer to the "law" or "duty" that pertains to the person or group mentioned before it, as with *sva-dharma,* "one's own duty," or *vara-dharma,* "the laws of class" or "caste." You will also hear of "the laws of life-stages," called *āśramas.* Be forewarned, however, that in the second position *dharma* can also refer to the "nature," "quality," or "property" of something, as, for instance, when you hear that the self "has an indestructible nature." You can see that the notion of the self emerges. The term here is usually *ātman.*

Hindus consider that there are three spiritual "disciplines," or *yogas,* by which one can seek to find the right balance between "holding" to what is worth holding to, that is, *dharma,* and "letting go." These three "disciplines," sometimes also called "paths," are *karma,* or "action," by which is meant disinterested action; knowledge; and *bhakti,* or "devotion." These disciplines have to do with seeking liberation either through knowing that one's self, or *ātman,* is identical with the absolute, called *Brahman,* or through devoting oneself to God.

Pāli is the language of Theravāda Buddhism; by name, the "School of the Elders." Most of the terms mentioned have Pāli counterparts. You will find in parentheses the Pāli counterpart of the Sanskrit term on its first occurrence in the book—for example, *dharma (dhamma), nirvāṇa (nibbāna).* Pāli will be cited only when discussing Theravāda materials. All other Buddhist schools use Sanskrit, including the "Great Vehicle" (Mahāyāna), which introduced new teachings around the turn of the millennium.

You can also see that the terminology of caste will be important. Hinduism holds that society should have four castes, or classes: Brahmins are the priests and cognoscenti; Kṣatriyas supply the armed stratum of warriors, from which should come the stock of kings; Vaiśyas are farmers, herders, and tradesmen; and Śūdras are your lowly servants. As you can see, the question will arise as to whether discourse on *dharma*—not only Hindu but Buddhist—is necessarily elitist. In the same vein, even where we find usages in related languages, is it inescapably Sanskritic?

A glossary of frequently used terms can be found at the back of the book.

Two Spiritualities

The important point to begin with is that Buddhists tend to use such common terms differently from Hindus. For instance, the first meaning of *dharma* for Buddhists, one obviously not acknowledged by Hindus, is the Buddha's "teaching." But the two traditions also use such terms as part of a shared and nuanced conversation. I hold that *dharma* is the primary term through which they are having this conversation; to be sure, the conversation is more often than not among themselves, but also, in ways that are not always made explicit, with each other. The best way to understand the concept in its major guises, and among different schools of thought, is to comparatively trace its early evolution in authoritative, mostly "sacred," texts, of which I will concentrate on ten that give the term a spiritual centrality.

Broadly speaking, these two traditions are two incredibly rich and deep spiritualities. To seek to bring their conversations back to life in a series on Asian spiritualities is thus a felicitous challenge to author and reader alike. Yet we had best start on some common ground. I would like to encourage four ways to get into this book.

First, it will be about *dharma in* South Asian spirituality. South Asia takes in India; Sri Lanka, home to Theravāda Buddhism and the formation of the Pāli canon; Nepal, the Buddha's birthplace; and Pakistan and Afghanistan, homes to pre-Islamic traditions of both Hinduism and Buddhism. Buddhism has very different conversations when it interacts with the spiritual traditions of East Asia. Whereas the South Asian conversation was couched in India's analytical spirit, with its methodical and uncompromising quest for a definitive liberation that would master or empty out all traces of illusion, East Asian conversations, beginning in China, with the encounter of Buddhism with Confucianism and Daoism, were couched in more practical terms, with an emphasis on the expression and enactment of enlightenment in this-worldly idioms.

A story about the eastward transmission of the Buddhist *dharma* provides a good example. One of the most repeated stock questions in the anecdotal literature of Chan (or Zen) Buddhism asks, "What is the meaning of Bodhidharma's coming from the west?" "The west" here is India or Central Asia, and the question is about the first Chan patriarch, whose name, in Sanskrit, means "Enlightenment Teaching." The question receives Chinese answers such as, "Ask that post over there!" and "If you find any meaning, you will not save even yourself." One Japanese answer is "The cypress tree in the garden." The question is not only about the enigmatic south Indian monk credited with having brought Chan to China in the late fifth or early sixth century CE, but about the *dharma* he bears in his name, which is often shortened when he is called just "Dharma." To paraphrase, these answers seem to be saying, "Don't look east or west or think about meaning." Enlightened *dharma,* the Buddha's teaching, is right before your eyes. Bodhidharma is said to have made a founding Chan distinction between *dharma* that depends on words and letters and *dharma* that points to the soul of man. You won't find such brevity from anyone representing *dharma* in South Asia.

Second, this book will be about *dharma* as *a* South Asian spirituality. Along with *yoga* and *karma, dharma* is one of a few terms that have come to emblematize Indian spirituality not only in the West but throughout Asia. In our new global context, *yoga* and *karma* are probably the more common of the three terms, and probably also better understood, even in their New Age manifestations. Whatever its complexities, *yoga* is something eminently practical and susceptible to easy visible representation. Whatever its nuances, *karma,* at least insofar as it has to do with reincarnation, is an easily grasped idea, with cross-cultural explanatory power. As in our East Asian anecdote, *dharma* seems to hint at something more multiform and elusive. In the global marketplace of ideas, *dharma,* more than these or any other originally Indic terms, has come to denote South Asian spirituality as a marker of identity, of transplantable values, of Indianness itself, whether at home or abroad. Moreover, "spirituality" seems to have the right tone to bring attention to the way the concept of *dharma* has served to bridge religious and civilizational discourses on South Asia. On the one hand, *dharma,* in one of its many facets, can sometimes be translated as "religion," at least when used by Buddhists and Hindus (Jains do this, too, but seem to have first used the term in a quite different sense, as an ontological category of "motion"). On the other hand, it has also become the term of choice to characterize a distinctive South Asian civilizational worldview. As such, *dharma* has been repeatedly taken up by apologists and critics, "insiders" and "outsiders," practitioners and scholars, historians and philosophers, ethicists and lawyers, and traditionalists, modernists, and postmodernists when they seek to "represent" and "explain" the religious and civilizational values of South Asia.

Third, this book will be about *dharma* as a South Asian spirituality in history. What has not been sufficiently recognized is that *dharma* itself has a history, and its usages are constructs. This is important for thinking about how *dharma* comes to denote South Asian spirituality, for if the chapters of this book can trace its movement toward such a contemporary meaning, it will be through its association with varied South Asian spiritualities of other times. Chapters 2 to 4 will be concerned with the transformations *dharma* underwent from its earliest usages to its adoption by the Buddha and his followers. Here, questions of spirituality will emerge mainly with reference to the early semantics of the term *dharma,* and to the sacrificial ethos, ethical reflections, and meditative practices that came to be associated with it. Chapters 5 to 7 will address the components of Brahmanical spirituality that shape the socio-political institutions of classical Brahmanism or Hinduism. Here, where in some circles *dharma* comes to mean primarily law, we have the good old question of the spirit of the law. But we will also notice that Brahmanical narratives enrich reflection on *dharma* in tales about the justice of kings and the nuanced spiritualities of women. Chapters 8 to 10 will then take up questions raised about the ethics, politics, and interfaith implications of *dharma* in Hindu and Buddhist contexts that address its spiritual meanings directly. Chapter 11 can then ask, what do *dharma*'s earlier spiritualities bring into the twenty-first century?

Fourth, in some of the stories told by both traditions, life is breathed into *dharma* through memorable characters. I have sought energetically to keep their number to a minimum and to introduce them carefully, but there is no getting around the following point. One of the mainstays and potential delights of Indian spirituality is to relax when you meet a new literary character. You can be sure he or she will soon have something fine to tell you.

Classical Dharma *Texts*

In recognizing that *dharma* has a history, a book on the topic must offer a textual chronology, however provisional it may be. The term *dharma* can be found in many South Asian texts, including classical works on statecraft and ritual theory. But in the present work, you will be invited to engage mainly with writings that we can call "*dharma* texts": ones in which *dharma* is *a,* if not *the,* central concept under consideration. From circa 1500 BCE to 300 BCE, from the early hymns of the *Rigveda* through the philosophical speculations of the Upaniṣads, no text is predominantly about *dharma*. For "*dharma* texts," our working chronology will take you into a "post-Vedic" "classical" period. The classical period as a whole can be said to run from the fourth century BCE to the fifth century CE, but our ten "*dharma* texts" can be ascribed to the first six centuries of this period. I use the term "*dharma* texts" to cover both individual texts and text collections, such as those of the Buddha's teachings and the edicts promulgated by the emperor Aśoka. While nine of our ten such *dharma* texts take on some kind of canonical and thus "sacred" status in either Buddhism or Hinduism, the edicts of Aśoka, even though he converted to Buddhism, would have to be called secular. Aśoka was the third emperor of the Mauryan dynasty, which ruled from northeastern India from 325 BCE to 185 BCE. This book treats none of these ten *dharma* texts as pre-Mauryan.

It will help to think of six of these ten texts in two temporal clusters. Since the earliest Buddhist literature probably reflects quite early Mauryan conditions, since Aśoka's *dharma* campaign went on for nearly forty years after his conversion to Buddhism, and since the earliest Hindu *dharma* treatise or *dharmasūtra* may come from such times, it is best to cluster our earliest *dharma* texts together, leaving their relative chronology only suggested by their numbering. It is also best to cluster the two Hindu epics (the *Mahābhārata* and *Rāmāyaṇa*) and *The Laws of Manu*, with their sequence only suggested. During an interval from 185 BCE to 50 BCE, stopgap dynasties, ruled nominally by Brahmins reacting against non-Brahmin movements and foreign incursions, allowed for a resurgence of local and regional Hindu kingdoms. This period has long had its attractions for dating the epics and *The Laws of Manu*, which seem to present intractable inter-referential problems. There is broad agreement that Aśvaghoṣa's *Adventure of the Buddha (Buddhacarita)* was composed in the first or second century CE, when northern India was reunified, to be ruled by clans originally from Central Asia known as the Kushanas, who, like Aśoka, showed an imperial preference for Buddhism. Adding a relative chronology of the four surviving *dharmasūtras*, this book offers the following working timetable:

Cluster A

Early Mauryan period (texts and text-groups 1–3):

1. Early Buddhist texts
2. *Āpastamba Dharmasūtra*
3. Aśokan Edicts

Mid- or Late Mauryan period:

4. *Gautama Dharmasūtra*
5. *Baudhāyana Dharmasūtra*

Cluster B

185–50 BCE (texts 6–8):

6. *Mahābhārata*
7. and 8. *Rāmāyaṇa* and *The Laws of Manu*

Of uncertain date, but probably later than the above:

9. *Vasiṣṭha Dharmasūtra*

Kushana period:

10. Aśvaghoṣa's *Adventure of the Buddha*

Our discussion will begin with Aśoka's edicts (chapter 2), posed as a kind of watershed toward the beginning of the classical period. We then take an excursion back in time through the Vedic canon (chapter 3). Although Vedic texts do not make *dharma* a central concept, they do introduce it. The Vedic canon includes not only the early *Rigveda* hymnal (ca. 1500–1100 BCE) and the later Upaniṣads, but other Vedas and texts, known as Brāhmaṇas, in which *dharma* appears. Tracing *dharma* through the Vedic canon returns us to the classical period. Resuming there with early Buddhist texts (chapter 4), we arrive at the treatises that represent the classical Brahmanical "legal tradition" (chapter 5). Some of these may likewise be from around Aśokan times: the three earliest *dharmasūtras* of *Āpastamba, Gautama,* and *Baudhāyana.* Along with the later one of *Vasiṣṭha,* they will be your entrée to the first great synthesis of the legal tradition, known as *The Laws of Manu,* which will lead us into the great narratives that introduce *dharma* as the key term in envisioning the heroic Hindu or Buddhist life. We thus turn to stories of the kings and queens of two Sanskrit epics, the *Mahābhārata* and *Rāmāyaṇa* (chapters 6 and 7); to the *Bhagavad Gītā,* which concerns the spiritual crisis of the

Mahābhārata's exemplary warrior-prince (chapter 8); and finally, after a wrap-up on *dharma* and divinity in the epics (chapter 9) and our look at *The Adventure of the Buddha* (chapter 10), a glance at *dharma* in the world today.

Since the two epics, *The Laws of Manu* and *The Adventure of the Buddha,* can be called major *dharma* texts by the criteria of size, literary complexity as poems, and interpretative challenges, it is worth briefly summarizing their treatments of *dharma.*

The vast *Mahābhārata,* said to have a hundred thousand verses, features *dharma* in three ways: in didactic sections, in substories listened to by heroes and heroines, and in its main story. The main story concerns a dynastic crisis in which two sets of cousins, the more noble Pāṇḍavas and the more wicked Kauravas, go to war over their divided kingdom, both sides committing dharmic and adharmic acts. *Dharma* is repeatedly said to be "subtle," and the characters are delineated through the dilemmas they face in puzzling their way to righteous solutions. The Pāṇḍavas are helped in this, and ultimately helped to victory, by Kṛṣṇa, who speaks authoritatively on *dharma* throughout, and especially in the *Bhagavad Gītā,* "The Song of the Lord," considered by many to be this epic's centerpiece. Kṛṣṇa is said to be a divine incarnation. (If only one text is read before or in conjunction with this book, it should probably be the Gītā.)

The *Rāmāyaṇa,* of nearly twenty-thousand verses, has much less didactic material and fewer substories for prominent characters to learn from. It focuses on *dharma* primarily through the adventures of King Rāma and his wife Sītā, who are presented as paragons of *dharma*—though not without episodes that raise questions of their meeting its expectations and demands. Rāma exemplifies *dharma* to perfection in all relations with his father and brothers, and that is what motivates him to undertake fourteen years of exile to the forest, where Sītā is abducted by the demon king Rāvaṇa. Like Kṛṣṇa, Rāma is a divine incarnation. But unlike Kṛṣṇa, he thinks he is only human.

The Laws of Manu, 2,675 verses long, features only two named characters and a host of anonymous sages. The sages ask Manu, who is also known as a primal sage and king in both epics, to instruct them in *dharma.* After Manu tells them about the creation of the world up to the emergence of humans and their organization into castes, he then asks his pupil, the sage Bhṛgu, to continue on his behalf and present Manu's teachings, which then proceed from the sources of *dharma* to all variety of implementations.

Finally, *The Adventure of the Buddha* has more than two thousand verses, of which only about the first half survive in Sanskrit, and is the only one of these four works to have been written by a historically identifiable poet. It tells the story of the Buddha's life from his conception, through his great departure from his father's royal city, to his enlightenment, the founding of his order, and his final *nirvāṇa.*

If one wants to get into the spiritual substance of these four major texts, the first answer for a book on *dharma* is to track the way the first three Brahmanical ones depict *dharma* as allegiance to the Veda, which they do with different accents. By looking at the ways the epics and law books reinvigorate Vedic social relations of cordiality, chapter 9 will seek to map out the relation between *dharma* and *bhakti,* or "devotion," across this large textual terrain, and chapter 10 will be about how a Buddhist poet remaps it. While drawing on earlier sources on the Buddha's life, Aśvaghoṣa was familiar with both epics and, like them, cites Manu, and probably his *Laws.* Aśvaghoṣa uses his familiarity with the two epics to critique Brahmanical *dharma* in the name of the Buddhist "true *dharma.*"

Opening Tensions and Basic Questions

The notion of a "true *dharma*" serves notice that you will find tensions running through our ten classical *dharma* texts. From the beginning, Aśoka's written edicts and the Veda will present a striking divide between written and oral texts. In the Brahmanical case, we have both types of texts, but not much is said about *dharma* until we get to the written ones. The earliest aphoristic *dharmasūtras* may draw on oral precursors, but they almost certainly came to be written down early in the classical period. The *Mahābhārata* and the *Rāmāyaṇa* were probably first given extensive written form in the closing centuries before the common era. In the Buddhist case we have only the tradition that the Buddha's oral teachings were committed to memory as the *dharma* (in the sense of the Buddha's teaching) and Vinaya (the Buddha's instructions on monastic life) just after his death, and with this, the claim that they are faithfully preserved as two of the "three baskets" of early Buddhist schools. Our access to the Buddha's oral teachings comes only through these clearly literary texts.

Once *dharma* has become a flourishing literary topic, another divide opens between texts that treat *dharma* primarily as a legal matter, and ones that treat it mainly through narrative. This divide applies not only to the "legal tradition" and the epics, but also to Buddhist literatures. Vinaya rules are broadly legislative; the Buddha's dialogues, *Jātakas* ("birth stories" of his previous lives), and *Avadānas* ("legends") are mainly narrative. The legislative/narrative divide is then bifurcated into a division between texts that emphasize *dharma*'s ambiguity and profundity, and ones that assert or at least attempt to work out its clarity, order, and perfection. Moreover, single texts can be expected to hold these tensions within themselves and cannot be expected to have just one view of *dharma*.

By juxtaposing normative and narrative texts within one concentrated classical period, I hope to open up other intertextual paths and conversations. One finding, however, deserves introductory mention because it came to me as something of a surprise and became part of the plan of this book. While teaching *The Adventure of the Buddha* in a fall 2004 course on South Asian Buddhism, I recognized for the first time that Aśvaghoṣa treats *dharma* not only as a central topic, but as a Buddhist discourse frequently and insistently couched in Brahmanical terms. Moreover, he deploys numerous new Brahmanical usages about *dharma* that cannot be traced to anything earlier than the Brahmanical *dharma* texts of our classical period. This opened the idea that Aśvaghoṣa was not only telling how and why the Buddha searched to discover the "true *dharma*" but was putting *dharma* to use as a term of civil discourse with his Brahmanical counterparts (both people and texts).

This model can raise some engaging questions. To what might such discourse compare in other civilizations? I hope it will be fruitful for readers to further open up this South Asian model, which, to put it most simply, is not only about ethics and law but also about inner wisdom concerning unseen things, to compare it with how similar issues are tackled in other civilizations—for instance, in China, where classical conversations seem to focus mainly on what it means to be human; and in the West, where traditional discourses on family and national values turn so frequently on notions of God's word as law. As I will try to show, *dharma* has been put into service to provide common grounds for talking about both what it means to be human and what God, among other gods, might have to say about it. Granted, when talking across religions and civilizations, it matters what one is talking about. But how one talks about it might matter just as much, or more.

And what of recent and contemporary usages? Mohandas K. Gandhi invoked *dharma* to challenge the British and "Western civilization." And Dr. B.R.Ambedkar, the Mahar (or "scheduled caste" "Untouchable") lawyer who chaired the committee that drafted India's constitution, did the same to challenge Gandhi on matters of caste, converted to Buddhism just before he died, and left a book titled *The Buddha and His Dhamma* (1957). "*Dharma*" remains a live operative model, along with Muslim law, for what is called "traditional law" in contemporary Indian law courts.

But back to our classical period. It turns out that Aśvaghoṣa's usage could be traced back through other Buddhist ones. However, Buddhists were not the only ones to take up *dharma* as a term of civil discourse. The intertextuality of our ten classical *dharma* texts can itself be viewed under this rubric, as can the debates mentioned within them. In narrative texts particularly, women characters make *dharma* a means to promote civil discourse about their status and treatment. But our watershed figure in putting *dharma* to work as civil discourse will be the emperor Aśoka; there is no evidence before Aśoka that *dharma* could be projected as a civilizational or universal value to challenge persons and groups across the spectrum of society to engage in spiritual and ethical reflection. Before we move on to canonical works of sacred literature, Aśoka's rock and pillar edicts allow us to start with *dharma* on the ground.

CHAPTER 2

King Aśoka's *Dhaṃma*

Aśoka's inscriptions were written in an early Prakrit, which includes a variety of regional Sanskrit-related Indo-Aryan languages, including Pāli. In Prakrit our basic term is *dhaṃma*. The edicts are among the first records we have of Indian alphabetic writing. They were apparently no longer readable by the end of the classical period.

Aśoka was not just a king but an emperor, and he used his edicts to broadcast an imperial program. In using the term *dhaṃma*, Aśoka is familiar with its having some specific connotations. For one thing, he is perfectly clear in some inscriptions that he associates it with Buddhism, in its sense of referring to the Buddha's "teaching," which had made him a convert. Aśoka was probably aware that *dhaṃma* carried older Brahmanical implications of royal authority, which we shall trace in chapter 3. We also get some hint of the range of meanings that Aśoka imputed to *dhaṃma* from a trilingual rock inscription where the Prakrit *dhaṃma* is given Greek and Aramaic counterparts. Here, *dhaṃma* is given the Greek translation *eusebia*, "piety, respect for gods, kings, and parents," and the Aramaic translation *qsyt*, "truth." These are the first known attempts to translate "*dharma*" into other languages, supplying terms that would resonate with speakers of these languages in the Kandahar area (in today's Afghanistan) in the northwest of Aśoka's empire. But they cannot necessarily be taken to supply the deepest colorings that *dhaṃma* would have had for Aśoka himself and that he intended for others who knew Prakrit. Clearly, Aśoka felt it was important to set what he had to say about *dhaṃma* in stone and to have officials who could help him proclaim and implement it. The inscriptions record that Aśoka himself went on rural "*dhaṃma*-tours" to bolster his message.

Chronologically, Aśoka's edicts were written between about 260 and 240 BCE and can be traced through that part of his reign (ca.

268–231 BCE). In one famous edict, he records that in his eighth regnal year, he felt remorse over the massive deaths and hardships caused by his conquest of Kalinga (a recalcitrant territory in today's eastern Indian state of Orissa), and now "considers conquest by *dhaṃma* the most important conquest." Two other edicts tell us that he became a Buddhist lay disciple, and that after about a year and a half, circa 258 BCE, following a visit to the Buddhist *saṅgha* (monastic order), which made him more energetic in his efforts, he "set out for enlightenment, inaugurating a *dhaṃma*-tour." The phrase "set out for enlightenment" is surprising and much debated, since Aśoka is never more than a layman and a busy king, to boot, and also since the key term describes nothing less than the Buddha's complete enlightenment. Since no other edict marks Aśoka's progress in such terms, it is best just to acknowledge the Buddhist nature of the spiritual aspiration. This inaugural *dhaṃma*-tour consumed 256 nights and took Aśoka to such places as Bodh-Gaya, scene of the Buddha's enlightenment, and Lumbini, the Buddha's birthplace.

Another rock edict contrasts these "*dhaṃma*-tours" with the "pleasure-tours" of "past kings," who took outings for hunting and "other pastimes." Then, beginning in his twelfth year, with an order that district officers go about teaching *dhaṃma* in five-year circuits, he started to develop a veritable *dhaṃma* bureaucracy. One year later he instituted the office of "*dhaṃma*-overseers," commissioned to work not only among varied sects and the border peoples of the northwest (including the Greeks there at the time) but among soldiers, ascetics, householders, and the poor and aged. Being "assigned everywhere," they served in the capital, "in all the provincial towns, and in the harems of [his] brothers and sisters and other relatives"! Among those charged with inculcating *dhaṃma* were "superintendents of women in the royal household, the inspectors of cattle and pasture lands, and other officials"; others' duties extended to providing medical treatment for men and animals, in addition to rest houses, wells, and shade trees along the roads for them. Finally, his seven pillar edicts all come in a late burst in his twenty-sixth and twenty-seventh regnal years, circa 242–241 BCE. Aśoka brings an almost retrospective tinge to the inscriptions on these highly polished lofty pillars, with deepened reflections on the nature of *dhaṃma,* the control of sin and passion, regulations of feasts and animal slaughter, and means of propagating morality and justice by his officials. The pillar inscriptions suggest that, over the years of his reign, *dhaṃma* had become more and more organized around rules. But at the same time, with what seems to have been a similarly growing spiritual interest, Aśoka came to emphasize that *dhaṃma* is more deeply developed by meditation than by moral prescriptions.

Although there are certainly good reasons to accentuate Aśoka's political and secular motivations, along with his administrative shrewdness in putting a generalized *dhaṃma* to imperial work, we should not doubt his seriousness as a Buddhist. On one pillar edict he condemns schism in the order, among both monks and nuns. In another, he says, "Whatever the Lord Buddha has said is of course well said. But it is proper for me to enumerate the texts which express the true *dhaṃma* and which may make it everlasting." He then names seven such texts (only three of which can be identified with any confidence in early Buddhist literature), and states it to be his desire "that many monks and nuns listen to these texts on *dhaṃma* frequently and meditate on them." We shall see further evidence of Aśoka's familiarity with monastic concerns and idioms—as with the powerful and potentially provocative term "true" or "real" *dhaṃma* or "good law" (*saddhaṃma*), just mentioned. *Saddhaṃma* occurs just this once in the edicts, but clearly in a telling fashion—indeed as the only case in the edicts where *dhaṃma* occurs in a compound as the second member rather than the first. Quite possibly, since this edict is directed to a specifically Buddhist audience, it reflects insider language. In another edict "inscribed to inspire [his] descendants to work for the promotion and to prevent the decline of *dhaṃma*," Aśoka offers the assurance that his "sons, grandsons, and great-grandsons will ever promote the practice of *dhaṃma*." Here, Aśoka would seem to link his imperial will to a Buddhist sense that the "promotion and decline of *dharma*" relates to dynastic time. If so, this would be the first time we meet the notion of the decline of *dharma* in a context that implies a new era.

Regarding the ethical import of his edicts, Aśoka repeatedly enjoins his subjects to be respectful and generous to Brahmins, ascetics, parents, teachers, elders, servants, slaves, the weak, and the poor. Although there are parallels, and no doubt precedents, in the Buddha's canonical sermons, this is the first time we find *dhaṃma intended,* especially officially, as a civil discourse that would cut through and across top-to-bottom social groups.

Aśoka also asserts that *dhaṃma* should be cultivated by all peoples, and by those of varied religious affiliations, whether they are ascetics or Brahmins. These two groups are mentioned frequently in the edicts as jointly deserving of imperial largesse, though when it comes to Aśoka's own patronage, it is usually the Buddhists who are mentioned. Such an intent is also carried to forest peoples and populations on and beyond the imperial borders.

Such a universal *dhaṃma* has legal ramifications. After the Kalinga war, Aśoka reminds his "judicial officers" in this still unpacified country to "try at all times to avoid unjust imprisonment or unjust torture"; when this happens, a prisoner "sometimes dies accidentally, and many other people suffer because of this." On one pillar edict, he tells provincial governors that "impartiality is desirable in legal procedures and in punishments," going on to explain, "I have therefore decreed that henceforth prisoners who have been convicted and sentenced to death shall be granted a respite of three days so that relatives may appeal to the officials for their prisoners' lives; or, if no one makes an appeal, the prisoners may prepare for the other world by distributing gifts or fasting."

This sense of the comprehensive applicability of *dhaṃma* also carries down to minute detail, as can be seen in a linguistic feature of Sanskrit, mentioned in chapter 1, that also applies to Prakrit. *Dhaṃma* occurs in the edicts with significantly high frequency as the first member of compounds, many of which, among them "*dhaṃma*-tours," "*dhaṃma*-gift," and "conquest by *dhaṃma*" or "*dhaṃma*-victory" *(dhaṃma-vijaya),* have been cited. This usage marks a sharp contrast to a prevalent usage in Brahmanical texts, where, as the second term in compounds, *dharma* anchors Hinduism's crisscrossing "laws" or "duties." As we have noted, the edicts' only usage of *dhaṃma* at the end of a compound is the possibly in-house and probably adversarial term *saddhaṃma,* the "true *dharma.*" When Aśoka uses *dhaṃma* in the first position, it is the "qualifying" term that makes everything "dharmic."

Aśoka also brings out the applicability of *dhaṃma* to minute detail in the edicts' critique of useless rites. Aśoka claims that ceremonies performed on the occasions of "sicknesses, marriages of sons and daughters, children's births, and departures on journeys," and especially the "many diverse, trivial, and meaningless ceremonies" performed by women, bear "little fruit" in this world and none in the next. These are probably generalized references to Brahmanical rites, especially of the domestic or household variety. Aśoka also discouraged religious assemblies that do not propagate *dhaṃma.* In contrast, "the *dhaṃma*-ceremony" that "consists in proper treatment of slaves and servants, reverence to teachers, restraint of violence toward living creatures, and liberality to ascetics and Brahmins" does bear fruit in this world and the next. Here, as in a number of edicts, Aśoka addresses a concern that one also finds in the Buddha's early sermons, which is that *dharma* is pertinent, especially for laymen, to happiness in both this and the other world. Fruitful ceremonial can take the form of the "*dhaṃma*-gift" or the reduction or elimination of killing animals, which Aśoka mentions while encouraging new festivals: "But today, thanks to the practice of *dhaṃma* on the part of the Beloved of the Gods, Piyadassi the king, the sound of the drum has become the sound of *dhaṃma,* showing the people displays of heavenly chariots, elephants, balls of fire, and other divine forms." As with the belittling of women's part in domestic rites, Aśoka's emphasis on not killing animals implies a downgrading of Brahmanical animal sacrifices, which privileged certain kinds of Brahmin expertise.

A final area in which the edicts relate *dhaṃma* to varied and minute detail is that of spiritual improvement by meditational self-scrutiny. One rock edict says, "Whatever effort King Piyadassi makes is for the sake of the life hereafter and in order that men may be saved from enslavement. For sin is enslavement. Rich and poor alike find it difficult to do this unless they make great effort and renounce all other aims. It is more difficult for the rich to do this than for the poor." Such effort should take specific forms of self-discipline. On one rock edict warning against unjust imprisonment and torture, Aśoka says, "That is why you must wish to practice impartiality. But it is not practiced with tendencies like envy, anger, cruelty, haste, stubbornness, laziness, and fatigue. One must wish to escape these tendencies. The principle is to avoid inconsistency and haste in the exercise of your functions."

Such an emphasis increases in the late-life pillar edicts, where it concurs with a concern for individual merit and an intensified sense of "sin." One pillar edict says, "It is difficult to achieve happiness, either in this world or the next, except by intense love of *dhaṃma*, intense self-examination, intense obedience, intense fear [of sin], and intense enthusiasm." In another, Aśoka asks, "*Dhaṃma* is good. But what does *dhaṃma* consist of? It consists of few sins and many good deeds, of kindness, liberality, truthfulness, and purity." In another, after remarking that a man is more prone to notice his worthy deeds than his evil ones, Aśoka says, "Such self-scrutiny and insight are difficult. Nonetheless, a man must say to himself, 'Ferocity, cruelty, anger, arrogance and jealousy lead to sin; I must not let myself be ruined by these passions.' He should make a clear distinction among his actions, saying, 'This action is directed to my good in this world and that other to my good in the world to come.'" In his very last pillar edict, which starts off about kings of the past, Aśoka states that advancement in *dhaṃma* comes "by only two means, by moral prescriptions and by meditation." He explains, "Of the two, moral prescriptions are of little consequence, but meditation is of great importance. . . . [I]t is by meditation that people have progressed in *dhaṃma* most." Aśoka's enumerations of faults and virtues for spiritual self-improvement probably reflect what we will see are developments in scholastic Buddhism. In Buddhist scholastic terms, Aśoka would be seeking to clarify how tracking wholesome and unwholesome thoughts and emotions can be cultivated as "mental events" *(dharmas)* by "right effort," "right mindfulness," and the "discrimination of *dharmas*." We shall explore this subject in chapter 4.

What then makes Aśoka a watershed figure? Aśoka is of interest not only to Buddhist history. His two Mauryan predecessors favored other non-Brahmanical ascetic movements, Jainism and Ajīvikism. What makes Aśoka pivotal is that he makes clear through inscriptions that he is favorably disposed toward the ascetic movements, and Buddhism in particular, as increasingly successful and economically viable institutions. Brahmins at large might or might not have ignored the Buddha, but they could not ignore this.

As we shall now see in chapter 3, Vedic Brahmins had done some work relating *dharma* to royal ritual, but they did not envision a king putting the term into his own words, much less supporting a different spiritual tradition, and on a vast imperial scale. Brahmins who preserved areas of Vedic expertise would have found themselves confronted by a campaign that deemed their rites and knowledge imperially useless and implicitly treated them as having the lesser of two spiritualities and unfavored views—whatever they were at this time—of the past, the future, and the legitimate roles of kings. In reply, they would produce texts that featured Brahmanical *dharma* in new post-Vedic genres.

CHAPTER 3

Vedic *Dhárman* and *Dharma*

The *Rigveda* is India's oldest textual source and the fountainhead of Hinduism. It introduces the term *dhárman,* a precursor to *dharma.* Beginning with the *Rigveda* this chapter will explore the earliest meanings of *dhárman* and *dharma* in the larger Veda or full Vedic "canon," taking the discussion down roughly to the time of the Aśokan watershed. The term *dhárman* is far more common and loaded with meanings in the *Rigveda* than the terms *dhárman* and *dharma* are in subsequent Vedic texts, where they seem stripped of their Rigvedic depth and begin, in sparse and intermittent passages, to take on a few of the specialized meanings that will be brought into the classical *dharma* texts of Hinduism.

The form *dhárman* appears to be a Rigvedic coinage. It thus makes its debut as a poetically crafted concept, since the *Rigveda* consists of poetry. *Dhárman* occurs sixty-three times in the *Rigveda*'s 1,028 poems. This is not enough to be considered a governing concept there, but it is found in all the chronological levels of the *Rigveda,* with increasing frequency in late-level hymns. If its Rigvedic meanings maintain an overall consistency, it deserves our attention for two reasons.

First, it raises the question of whether Rigvedic meanings have some staying power in classical meanings of *dharma.* The nature and manner of Vedic continuities is a controversial topic. *Rigveda* prayers or verses require precise utterance rather than understood meaning. Yet it will be the view of this book that important continuities arise from *dharma*'s genesis in poems.

Second, it means that one must be wary of "backreading" classical meanings into Rigvedic usages. Scholarly treatments of *dharma* usually start well after the *Rigveda* or barely pay it lip service by making inadequate summaries and anachronistic translations of the older *dhárman.* Such distortions are important to resolve.

The most common backreading is to see the classical term *dharma* as "replacing" a Rigvedic notion of "cosmic order," and then to backread this understanding into Vedic *dhárman.* The term said to mean "cosmic order" in the *Rigveda* is *ṛta.* Rigvedic *ṛta,* best translated as "truth," is a cosmic order resonant with the "truth" of the Rigvedic hymns and verses. The *Rigveda* poets first discerned it in their inspired compositions, and those who recite their verses ritually can keep this cosmic order functioning. In citing Rigvedic hymns, *ṛta* will appear as "truth." Since *ṛta* no longer means "cosmic order" in classical Hinduism, and *dharma* sort of does, it is convenient to think that *dharma* not only replaced *ṛta* but must always have had some such connotation itself. But it is safe to say that *dhárman* did not mean "cosmic order." Moreover, the ideas of "cosmic order" to which *dharma* becomes attached differ from the Rigvedic "cosmic order" denoted by *ṛta.* Classical usages of "*dharma*" put the term into the service of a *socio*cosmic order that is more ideology than poetry or ritual implementation. The Vedic "cosmic order" is something else.

The other type of backreading, also common but more diverse, is to interpret *dhárman* through lenses of *karma,* "action." It is more diverse because *karma* itself has different meanings and usages, from its earliest sense of "ritual act" to the later sense of a "law of *karma,*" which explains reincarnation as the repercussion of one's acts. While only the first of these meanings has been read directly into Rigvedic usages of *dhárman,* a fusion of the two has also been smuggled into the mix. This is the idea that *dharma* as "duty" and *karma* as "act" imply each other if one acts in accord with "one's own *dharma*" *(svadharma)* in "maintaining the cosmic order." Certain classical texts, most notably the *Bhagavad Gītā,* do equate "one's own *dharma*" with "one's own *karma,*" but that does not justify its importation back into the *Rigveda.* Unlike *dhárman,* both *ṛta* and *karma* are indeed governing concepts in the *Rigveda,* and *karma* remains one through all Indian traditions. But neither of them ever governs the history of *dharma.* This book proceeds from the mantra, or perhaps better, hunch, that *dharma* is never just "action."

I will address two dimensions of *dhárman* that seem to have importance beyond the *Rigveda:* its usage in poetically crafted enigmas, and its ties with kingship. The *Rigveda*'s ten books—composed perhaps between 1500 and 1100 BCE—have older and younger layers (to pursue the topic further, one can refer to the recommended readings). I must ask readers to bear with some moments of obscurity, since that is the nature of Rigvedic poetry and there is no payoff without giving it some play. A basic guideline is that the poets love to play with etymologies. As we saw in chapter 1, *dhárman* derives from the verbal root √*dhṛ*, meaning "to hold" and, beyond that, "to uphold, give foundation to." In most cases the best translation of Rigvedic *dhárman* seems to be "Foundation," which I will capitalize, like Truth, in quoted passages. I will also alert readers to instances where the poets play with variations on the root √*dhṛ*. The poets also like to structure surprise into their poems by creative compositional devices, including framing, that affect the whole hymn.

Dhárman *as Enigma*

Rigvedic poetry simply abounds in enigmatic verses. I will discuss two early examples involving *dhárman.* From the oldest layer of the *Rigveda,* one of the books that brings together the poems of six old Vedic families, comes one of the best illustrations.

Rigveda 5.15 is a hymn to the fire god, Agni. The first verse calls him "Agni the *support* of goods." The fifth (last) verse uses the same term for "support" to describe how the poet imparts strength to Agni so that he may be helped to great wealth. This word for "support" is *dharúṇa,* a derivative of √*dhṛ* like *dhárman.* The poet shapes the hymn's "soundplay" by surrounding *dhárman* with these and other alliterative "supports" derived from √*dhṛ*. Moreover, the poet uses a framing design, familiar from many Rigvedic hymns, of having a poem's first and last verses form a "ring" around the composition. The second verse is the hymn's concentration point regarding *dhárman.* Here, following one of the verbal derivatives of √*dhṛ, dhárman* is surrounded twice, this time close at hand, by the same term for "support," which I continue to italicize:

> In making powerful the sacrifice in the highest heaven, they supported *(√dhṛ)* the Truth, itself a *support,* by means of the Truth / —they who have reached the men that have taken their seat upon the Foundation, upon the *support* of heaven; they who, even though they themselves were born, have reached the unborn.

Two groups, each called "they," have reached heaven. The first refers to ancient poet–ritualists. By making the sacrifice powerful, they became semi-divine ancestors of the poet's family. The second are "men" but appear to be gods, since two things said about the first group are not said about them: The first group reached heaven by sacrifice and were born. In contrast, the apparently "unborn" "men"—who got there first—just sit "upon the Foundation, upon the *support* of heaven."

It does not seem that *dhárman,* mentioned only once, and the "supports" *(dharúṇa)* that surround it are simply interchangeable. *Dhárman* is set off by four usages of *dharúṇa*—two in this verse, and two in the hymn's first and last verses. *Dharúṇa* comes to evoke a fairly ordinary Rigvedic idea of "support" that is sometimes imaged quite concretely—for instance, where the king of the gods, Indra, "expanded the unshakable support that set the atmosphere within the framework of heaven" (*Rigveda* 1.56.5), or where Soma, god of the sacred ritual beverage by that name, is called heaven's "support pillar" (9.2.5; 74.2). The force of our hymn lies in zeroing in on *dhárman* not just as another "support" but as a "Foundation" that is left a little more mysterious than its four surrounding "supports," which look something like flying buttresses. Rather than being interchangeable with these "supports," *dhárman* is the inner "Foundation" of their surrounding rings. We could call it the spiritual kernel of the poem, a Foundation wrought by poets for "making truths powerful" and "reaching" heaven. By the truth of their hymns and rites, the poet's ancestors reached the gods on that Foundation.

Our second illustration also comes from one of the family books. In the first verse of *Rigveda* 3.38, the poet indicates that he reflects like a "fashioner" upon his "inspired thought," and goes on:

> And ask about the forceful generations of poets. Holding *(√dhṛ)* the mind and performing well, they fashioned heaven. / And these are your [Indra's] leadings forth, which grow strong and which are won by thought; therefore they go now upon [that] Foundation.

Here, *dhárman* seems to be the "Foundation" of the older hymns by which the ancient sages "fashioned heaven" by holding *(√dhṛ)* their minds steady and by performing poems or rituals well. Upon this Foundation, new generations of poets can still compose hymns that lead Indra to manifest himself in the Rigvedic here and now. The correlation of early and later generations of poets also describes the early ones while answering a seemingly rhetorical question about them ("And ask about the forceful generations of poets"). We do not know who the poet is addressing, but, whatever the question, the response lies in something he calls upon himself, and probably other poets, to resolve by speaking about a Foundation. The answer would thus be that *dhárman* lies in poetry or its inspired thought.

I would thus propose that with regard to *dhárman* the early *Rigveda* leaves us with two types of deeply wrought enigmas. One, exemplified by our first example, speaks of a Foundation above, with "supports" around and maybe below it. Depending on one's perspective, one could call this type the "highest Foundation" enigma, or the "turtles all the way down" enigma. In the first case, I suggest that readers keep in mind a repeatedly asked and resolutely unresolved question in the *Mahābhārata:* What is the highest *dharma?* And in the second I refer to an oft-cited "Indian story" about an Englishman who asked what was below the turtle who held up the turtle who held up the world and was told, "Ah, Sahib, after that it is turtles all the way down." Either way, although it is couched in circularity, this is a vertical enigma.

In contrast, circularity and reflexivity are the hallmark of the second case, wherein the poet doubles back on his own inspired thought and finds its *dhárman,* or Foundation, in poetry. We could call this type a "sources of *dharma*" enigma, where *dharma*'s source and unfolding is located in the searching yet regulated minds of the learned: the Vedic sages or Ṛṣis. As we shall see, this kind of *dharma* lives on in many surprising places, where epistemic openness continues to thrive.

Early Dhárman *and Kings*

Although *Rigveda* oral poetry required each generation to memorize the hymns of earlier generations, new poets worked from older models by adapting older formulas and themes, including enigmas, to new contexts—among them, changing conceptions of both divine and human kings. Taking the family books together, the god Varuṇa is certainly the main early divine king connected with *dhárman,* whereas human kings *(rājas)* can better be called chieftains. Varuṇa is the foremost celestial sovereign god, sometimes called an "emperor," and is associated with divine "commands." Chieftains are in another league. The family books describe them in two contrasting modes: as leaders in *yoga,* which for now means "harnessing" for a battle march in search of booty; and as leaders during "peaceful settlement." Some passages suggest that a chief could assume both of these leadership roles, but none map his activities with *dhárman.*

On the divine plane, however, peaceful settlement is construed to involve *dhárman,* but war or conquest is not. One early hymn says of Mitra (god of "contracts") and Varuṇa, "By your command, you two are those that give peaceful settlements that endure, assigning places to the people according to your Foundation" (*Rigveda* 5.72.2). This is one of several early verses that speak of *dhárman* in connection with Mitra and/or Varuṇa. One hymn (5.63) is particularly interesting for mentioning their association with *dhárman* twice, and only in its first and last verses:

> Herdsmen of the Truth, you two stand upon your chariot, O you whose Foundations are real, in the furthest heaven.
>
> . . .
>
> In accordance with your Foundation, O Mitra and Varuṇa, who perceive inspired words, you two guard your commands through the craft of a lord. / In accordance with Truth, you rule over the whole living world. You place the sun here in heaven as your shimmering chariot.

The first and last verses frame the hymn by mentioning *dhárman* along with Truth and the solar chariot that the two deities have placed in heaven. But there has also been movement. The first verse begins from the two sovereigns' "real foundations" (*dhármans,* plural) on the now familiar ground of the highest heaven. The last, calling attention to their responsiveness to inspired words, acknowledges their capacities to guard their one Foundation by their commands and to rule the whole living world in accordance with Truth.

Later *Rigveda* books then mark the rise of a more centralized kingship coordinated with the completion of the *Rigveda Collection.* No longer "family books," the newer books initiate widening collection processes that end with Book 10, probably coinciding with the emergence of India's first state, that of the Kurus. Still, however, nothing indicates that Kuru kings are especially concerned with *dhárman.* The only kings associated with this concept remain divine ones, with usages of *dhárman* sometimes figuring in the ways the later books redefine the balance of power between Varuṇa and other gods, notably Indra. In contrast to Mitra and Varuṇa, whose associations are with a transcendent Foundation, Indra, without, as yet, any such association himself, was, with his rowdy warrior band known as the Maruts, becoming "a law unto himself." Here we find him invited to join the ritualists in a ceremony where the celebrants drink *soma,* an exhilarating divine beverage:

> As the lord of his own domain, let Indra journey here for his invigoration—he, the vibrant, who thrusts forward according to his Nature *(dhárman),* / who energetically dominates over all strengths according to his boundless and great bull-likeness.
>
> . . .
>
> Let good things go among us, for I hope for them. Journey here to the *soma*-bearer's stake, which carries his good expectation. / You [Indra] are master. Take your seat here on this sacred grass. Vessels which belong to you are not to be claimed [by another] according to your Foundation *(dhárman).* (*Rigveda* 10.44.1 and 5)

Here *dhárman* is translated initially as "Nature" and could be translated that way the second time as well. This is an important meaning to keep in mind. The poet goes on to laud him as one whose *dhárman* would seem to take after the self-assured manner of a human king. Yet where kingship is concerned explicitly, Indra is still operating upon the *dhárman* of other royal deities who are associated with kingship mainly through Varuṇa.

This brings us to the most famous Rigvedic verse to use the term *dhárman:* often the only one to be brought into discussion of classical understandings of *dharma.* The cosmogonic "Hymn to Puruṣa" (*Puruṣasūkta; Rigveda* 10.90) describes how the gods "divided" Puruṣa, the cosmic "Male" or "Person," to create the cosmos, and speaks of *dhármans* only in its last verse, the sixteenth, whose finality can hardly be accidental: "With the sacrifice the gods sacrificed the sacrifice: these were the first Foundations, / and those, its greatnesses, follow to heaven's vault, where exist the ancient ones who are to be attained, the gods." The paradoxical first line uses three derivatives of the verb "to sacrifice" to convey that Puruṣa's sacrifice initiates the sacrificial process. The translation "Foundations" thus catches the sense in which the ritual is itself a cosmogonic foundation and template for human ritual replication. Rigvedic ritual is still fluid, varied, and not yet systematized. But system is increasing. Verse 9 tells that the "verses, melodies, and sacrificial formulas" were born from Puruṣa. This refers to a differentiation that develops into the three older Vedas. Most momentously, the hymn stratifies the social classes, with the Brahmin coming from Puruṣa's mouth, the nobility from his arms, the Vaiśya from his thighs, and the Śūdra from his feet (verse 12). The hymn probably makes this social structure a charter for the emerging Kuru state, fostering cooperation between the nobility and a newly minted class of Brahmins that now cuts across and unifies the older clans of poet–priests. It also establishes the power of these two classes over the Vaiśya, and implements a further division between the three upper Ārya or "noble" classes and their non-Ārya Śūdra servants. It says nothing direct that would either ground kingship itself in the "first Foundations," or ground the "first Foundations" in kingship. It just mentions the nobility as the "armed" class from which kings would presumably come, and shows its subordination to the Brahmin class. The *Puruṣasūkta* opens a new chapter in the history of *dharma.*

Later Veda

For the earliest post-Rigvedic understandings of *dharma,* we come, after a temporal gap, to a period in which Rigvedic *mantras*—prayer-verses; literally, "instruments of thought"—were sorted out along with other *mantras* for expanding ritual purposes. "Mantra period" projects included the collection of two more "liturgical" Vedas, the *Yajur-* and *Sāma-Vedas.* A fourth, the *Atharva-Veda,* was more concerned with custom. As signaled in the *Puruṣasūkta,* social stratification underlies all Brahmanical texts from now on. A complex liturgical system generated schools of specialists in each Veda. Each school proliferated into "branches" that could bring Brahmanical ritual into new regions wherever branches of the three liturgical Vedas could cooperate. The ritual theologians of the four Vedic schools then continue to lay out the performance and meanings of Vedic sacrifice in prose manuals called Brāhmaṇas. The last Vedic texts to generate innovative, though not numerous, usages of *dharma* are then the Upaniṣads, which round out the Vedic canon.

Coming between the innovative uses in the *Rigveda* and the sudden burst of interest in classical *dharma* texts, later Vedic texts are surprisingly fallow in usages of *dhárman* and *dharma.* Aside from a few scattered instances implying custom and rudimentary legal procedure in royal courts, there is cumulative usage in only two spheres: one, concerning the king, where we can see continued development of Rigvedic themes; the other, a new strain concentrating on assertions of Brahmin privilege. I limit discussion to a few examples of each. Cumulative interest in connecting the king with *dharma* is maintained down to the Brāhmaṇas, and then peters out in the Upaniṣads. Cumulative interest in connecting *dharma* with Brahmins begins in the late Brāhmaṇas and continues in the Upaniṣads.

LATER VEDIC *DHARMA* AND THE KING

Those who did the most to systematize mantra usage in ritual were the Yajurveda priests. Their four extant *Yajurveda Collections* forge new links between the king and *dharma.* According to the main western collection, Varuṇa, Mitra, Indra, and certain other deities are "upholders of *dharma*" who make the new king an upholder of *dharma.* Two great royal rituals are now systematized: the Royal Consecration and the Horse Sacrifice, in which a stallion is released for a year to represent the unlimited sway of the king, for whom it is then sacrificed. In this and the middle collection, after Mitra is invoked as "lord of Truth" and Varuṇa as "lord of *dharma,*" the Royal Consecration calls for the announcement, "This, O Bhāratas, is your king." This designation identifies a new king's people with an early Vedic royal name, Bhārata, that is older than Kuru, and fashions a new unifying conception of royal continuity. Meanwhile, *Yajurveda Collections* systematize the Horse Sacrifice as the exemplary Vedic rite for an ambitious king, and the eastern collection and its *Śatapatha Brāhmaṇa* make it prominent for Kosala and Videha kings.

A few Brāhmaṇa usages continue to associate *dharma* with kingship through Varuṇa. One suggests that *dharma* involves a king's justice in legal disputes (*Śatapatha Brāhmaṇa* 5.3.3.9). In another mention of *dharma,* the focus turns to Indra. In virtually identical passages, once Indra and the king have undergone a "great consecration" and are enthroned, the All-Gods (a generalized divine consensus) announce Indra to the gods while certain "king-makers" present the king to the people:

> Do ye proclaim him, O gods / O people, as overlord and overlordship, as paramount ruler and father of paramount rulers, as self-ruler and self-rule, as sovereign and sovereignty, as supreme lord and supreme lordship, as king and father of kings. The royal power has been born, the Kṣatriya has been born, the suzerain of all creation has been born, the eater of the commoners has been born, the slayer of foes has been born, the guardian of Brahmins has been born, the guardian of *dharma* has been born. (*Aitareya Brāhmaṇa* 8.12, 17)

Theoretically, it is something of an advance on late Rigvedic hymns that begin to focus on Indra rather than Varuṇa. The king now has a whole range of grand titles; he will be a Kṣatriya rooted explicitly in the "royal power"; he slays foes; he devours commoners and guards Brahmins in the name of *dharma.*

LATE VEDIC *DHARMA* AND THE BRAHMIN

Consonant with this assertion of Brahmin primacy, *Śatapatha Brāhmaṇa* 11.5.7 uses a curious metaphor—"cooking the world"—to hail what Brahmins achieve by personal Vedic recitation or "recitation to oneself." Such "personal recitation" becomes a hallmark, if never quite the monopoly (see chapter 5), of the Brahmin class:

> Personal recitation and learning are sources of pleasure for the Brahmin. He acquires presence of mind, becomes independent, and acquires wealth day after day. He sleeps well. He is his own best physician. To him belong mastery of the senses, the power to find joy in a single object, the development of intelligence, fame, and cooking the world. The growing intelligence brings to the Brahmin four *dharmas:* Brahmanical stature, fitting deportment, fame, and cooking the world. The world, as it is being "cooked," gratifies

the Brahmin with four *dharmas*—with veneration, with gifts, with the conditions of not being oppressed, and of not being subject to capital punishment.

By personal recitation a Brahmin self-generates, as it were, four *dharmas* by which the world recognizes him—one of which is that he "cooks the world." And thanks to his having cooked the world, the world gratifies him with four more *dharmas* that amount to class privileges and immunities.

"Cooking the world" by personal Vedic recitation—a truly bottomless resource—is a prose enigma reminiscent of Rigvedic *dhárman.* The cooking metaphor brings out that the ritualist only recooks what has already been cooked by the sun, a form of the fire god Agni. He thereby makes all his offerings, including himself, in a world already cooked. We may correlate such developed and growing intelligence with the *Aitareya Brāhmaṇa* passage just cited, where kings and Indra are "guardians of the Brahmins" and "eaters of the commoners." On the scale of the sun, Brahmins may be cooked, like everyone else, but at least they know how to cook the world so that they are not eaten by kings. Our closest English parallel would be "cooking the books." While poets and Brahmins have been hinting at ways to keep kings from becoming a law unto themselves, some Brahmins have begun to recognize such a potential in their own *dharmas.*

Such treatments of *dharma* continue in the Upaniṣads, which mention *dharma* only where Brahmins concern themselves with matters that do not go explicitly beyond their own class. Thus the early *Chāndogya Upaniṣad* speaks of the "three types of persons whose torso is *dharma*"—"the one who pursues sacrifice, Vedic recitation, and gift-giving"; "the one who is devoted to austerity"; and "the celibate student of the Veda living permanently at his teacher's house" (2.23.1). These three apparently optional and not yet serialized "modes of life" are pertinent mainly to Brahmins.

Such a Brahmin-centered orientation is especially clear in one of the preliminary cosmogonies in the other main early Upaniṣad. In the beginning, *Brahman* was alone and "had not fully developed." First, along with certain ruling gods, it created the "royal power" to which a Brahmin pays homage at a royal consecration (it is as if "Brahmin power" has already been created with the *Brahman*). When *Brahman* still "did not become fully developed," it created the commoners class with various gods; when it still "[had] not become fully developed," it created the servant class with various gods.

> It still did not become fully developed. So it created *dharma*, a form superior to and surpassing itself. And *dharma* is here the Royal Power standing above the Royal Power. Hence there is nothing higher than *dharma*. Therefore, a weaker man makes demands of a stronger man by appealing to *dharma*, just as one does by appealing to a king. Now, *dharma* is nothing but the truth. Therefore, when a man speaks the truth, they say that he speaks *dharma;* and when a man speaks *dharma*, people say that he speaks the truth. They are really the same thing. (*Bṛhadāraṇyaka Upaniṣad* 1.4.14)

Here, for the first time, "law" is an unexceptionable translation of *dharma*. Clearly, it relates to litigation in a king's court. Granted "the weaker man" could betoken anyone who could count on justice in a world of truthful witnesses. But it is especially Brahmins who would be true witnesses for themselves. This passage, and the one on "cooking the world," are from the same school and milieu. In one, the Brahmin grows the intelligence to cook up *dharmas* that favor him; in the other, the pre-cosmic *Brahman* does not fully develop until it has created *dharma* to keep Brahmins on top.

As to the more confidential "secret" teachings for which the Upaniṣads are best known, *dharma* has a few usages that are tangential to expressions of the spiritual oneness of the self *(ātman)* and *Brahman*. Two occur where the *Bṛhadāraṇyaka Upaniṣad* is featuring its famous sage Yājñavalkya. The first passage tells that the self is made of light and the lightless, desire and the desireless, anger and the angerless, *dharma* and non-*dharma*. Since the encompassing self is "made of everything," the list implies an ascendence, with *dharma* and *adharma* encompassing the other pairs. Yājñavalkya then speaks of *karma:*

> What a man turns out to be depends on how he acts and how he conducts himself. By the good, he will turn into something good. By the bad, something bad. And so people say: "A person here consists

> simply of desire." A man resolves in accordance with his desire, acts in accordance with his resolve, and turns out to be in accordance with his action. (*Bṛhadāraṇyaka Upaniṣad* 4.4.5)

"Made of everything" up to and including *dharma* and *adharma,* the self remains unaffected, as the passage goes on to explain: "Now, a man who does not desire—who is freed from desires, whose desires are fulfilled, whose only desire is his self...*Brahman* he is, and to *Brahman* he goes." It is thus explained how *dharma* and its opposite are the highest ground for understanding how karmic retribution works, while the self is something else: indeed, it is the only desire that can be fulfilled. Shortly before this, Yājñavalkya has compared the state "where all the desires are fulfilled, where the Self is the only desire," with a man's embrace of "a woman he loves" (*Bṛhadāraṇyaka Upaniṣad* 4.3.2).

This brings us to Yājñavalkya's love life, though probably the end of it. The second passage using *dharma* appears to be a late and vivid clarification added to one of two versions of Yājñavalkya's famous dialogue with the more philosophical of his two wives (*Bṛhadāraṇyaka Upaniṣad* 4.5). This version calls her "a woman who talks about *Brahman,*" and Yājñavalkya is telling her about the self as he is about to leave her to begin another "mode of life." After a stretch in which he tells her that whatever is held dear, beginning with husband and wife, is dear only out of love or desire for the self, he presents a series of less tangible and more perplexing similes until she finally breaks in:

> "Now, sir, you have utterly confused me! I cannot perceive this at all." He replied. "Look—I haven't said anything confusing. This self, you see, is imperishable; it has an indestructible *dharma.*"

The term *dharma* (actually *dhárman*) here is usually translated as "Nature," and justly so since it follows a long commentarial tradition. It can also be related to Rigvedic usages where *dhárman* can mean "foundational Nature." It is interesting that *dhárman* is used in getting as far as one can to the bottom of the most important things. That is, one could take it that the self "has an indestructible 'Foundation.'" Yājñavalkya has only to explain further that one cannot perceive the perceiver and set off on his way.

Yājñavalkya, a most engaging character, is not only the first Brahmin to speak about karmic retribution. He is the only person in the Upaniṣads to have anything—though, in fact, precious little—to say about *dharma* in the "early" dialogues for which they are famous. It is striking that he never uses the term in his extensive conversations at royal courts, where his hosts and interlocutors include kings. Kings are credited with knowledge of *karma,* and even relate it to the world's sufferings. But no king or Upaniṣadic Kṣatriya gives a thought to *dharma* as a way to further describe their visions of the bigger picture.

Among later Vedic Upaniṣads, the only one to say anything important about *dharma* is the *Kaṭha Upaniṣad,* in its well-known opening dialogue between the boy Naciketas and Death (*Kaṭha Upaniṣad* 1–2). Other than Death, it is again a tale about Brahmins. Naciketas has been sent by his irritated father to Death because he has belittled the bedraggled cows the father passed off as gifts. In Death's house, when Naciketas asks to know whether a man exists after death or not, Death first tells him to ask something else, since "it's a subtle *dharma.*" But when Naciketas demonstrates his worthiness, Death discloses "this subtle matter of *dharma,*" which one learns in the next stanza is "different from *dharma* and *adharma.*" Death's "subtle *dharma*" is thus presented as a spiritual "teaching" or "doctrine," which, again, ultimately refers to the self. Moreover, it is buttressed by two words for "foundation" or "support." First, using an old ritual term, Death tells Naciketas he has been wise to reject the "foundation" of ritual, since by ritual one cannot see "the primeval one who is hard to perceive, wrapped in mystery, hidden in the cave, residing within the impenetrable depth." On the contrary, the "subtle *dharma*" is to be gained by a newer kind of meditative yogic "support" that is now mentioned three times:

> This is the support that's best!
> This is the support supreme!
> And when one knows this support,
> he rejoices in *Brahman*'s world.

This may remind us of the way *dhárman* as a "foundational" enigma was buttressed by more concrete "supports" in the early *Rigveda.*

The *Kaṭha Upaniṣad* is clearly later than early Buddhism. Yet where one meets the term *dharma* in the Upaniṣads, one does well to keep early Buddhism in mind. While the Upaniṣads reflect intensified interest in increasing social stratification, they are largely silent on changing conditions that are challenging it: eastern urbanization, the emergence of large eastern kingdoms and states, and, at some fairly early point, Buddhism itself as well as other heterodoxies. On the other hand, once the eastern provenance of even the early *Bṛhadāraṇyaka Upaniṣad* is recognized, one sees that it extends its Vedic horizons from Afghanistan to Bengal, and that wandering sages travelled extensively exchanging ideas of widening currency.

As with all Upaniṣadic references to *dharma,* kings are only in the background if they are there at all. As to whether Buddhists were in the background, the Upaniṣads are silent. On the face of it, then, an intriguing fact has emerged. Remarkably enough, one could say that the Buddha, reportedly born into a royal family, will be the first Kṣatriya to speak about *dharma.* And he will do so extensively with Brahmins, while also talking often to kings.

CHAPTER 4

Early Buddhism

Three Baskets of *Dharma*

This chapter will investigate Buddhist understandings of *dharma* in the three baskets *(piṭakas)* of the early Buddhist canon, taking them as an intentional organization of three different understandings of *dharma* developed over time. The "three basket" division is not established until about the first century BCE, but it is anticipated in early references to monks who have mastered one or more of three areas of expertise: "those who maintain the Dhamma, the Vinaya, and the Lists of phenomena." These three specializations lie, respectively, behind the "baskets" of the Sūtras (Suttas) or "Discourses," the Vinaya or "Monastic Rule," and the Abhidharma (Abhidhamma) or "Higher Teachings."

Presenting matters around the three baskets brings out the strikingly different ways that the Buddha's *dharma* was developed. Whereas the Sūtras—especially the collection of "Long Discourses"—present the *dharma*'s public face, the other two baskets are addressing in-house audiences. Vinaya defines what monks and nuns should (and should not) do in common. And the Abhidharma refines what those really in the know should know. Yet these two approaches also have their wider public purviews. Vinaya regulates the public interface between Buddhist and non-Buddhist *dharmas* in practice. And Abhidharma stakes out Buddhism's place in the erudite but politically important settings—sometimes including royal courts—of scholastic debate with other Indian philosophies.

Starting with the Sūtras will enable us to keep them in view throughout so as to appreciate how the three baskets bring together overlapping teachings. Coming to the Vinaya last will equip us to take stock of the complexities that distinguish Buddhist and Brahmanical senses of *dharma* before turning to the latter in chapter 5.

Sūtra-Basket Dharma

The Pāli canon provides the most accessible compilation of the Buddha's discourses. While its Sutta Basket includes discourses noteworthy for their basic instructional content, it also includes elegant dialogues famous as narratives. These portray the Buddha in interactive settings where his artful teachings have their maximum impact, thanks to his ethical and philosophical reasoning and stunning similes. We will open this basket onto discourses of this dialogical type and save more-instructional teachings, including the Buddha's famous first sermon, for the next section on Abhidharma. The interactive settings can direct us to the likely historical background that the Suttas reflect in the Buddha's dealings with nobles, Brahmins, householders, ascetics, and those at the low end of the social spectrum.

In the "Discourse with Ambaṭṭha," the Buddha claims that his clan, the Sakyans, are Kṣatriyas who "regard King Okkāka as their ancestor." This would give him royal descent in a tribe reputed to have backed the eastward movement of Vedic culture. The Suttas, however, describe a post-Vedic kind of society. Market towns had emerged, and also contending monarchic and "republican" polities. Urbanization is in full swing, with aggressive metropolitan states. The Buddha can compare discovering the *dhamma* to finding an ancient path to an old and forgotten city.

The "Discourse with Ambaṭṭha" runs the gamut on social issues while foregrounding various challenges that the Buddha puts to proponents of Vedic orthopraxy. It can thus introduce some of the complexities of posing the Buddhist *dhamma* specifically to Brahmins. The Buddha seems to have expected more from his dialogues with Brahmins than he did from those lowest in society. For instance, when he mentions that there are nine "parts" of the *dhamma* and says they are to be examined "with wisdom," he is correcting a "pernicious view" about sex of an errant monk he calls "Ariṭṭha, formerly of the vulture killers" (*Majjhima Nikāya* 22). In mentioning Ariṭṭha's low birth *(jāti)* in the same breath as his "pernicious view," which he does also with "Sāti, son of a fisherman" (*Majjhima Nikāya* 38), the Buddha is practicing a form of *jāti* profiling—that is, he is stereotyping the intellectual deficiencies of disciples from low-caste "births" *(jātis)*.

But while such exchanges are rare, ones with Brahmins are among the most frequent in the Sutta Basket. As we see the Buddha engaging Brahmins on matters of social class, let us keep an open question before us: granting that the Buddha offers new angles on these complex topics, where is the *dhamma* in our text?

The Buddha is touring with some five hundred monks and stays near a Brahmin village. A Brahmin named Pokkharasāti lives there at a populous and well-stocked estate given to him by the king "as a royal gift and with royal powers." Pokkharasāti has heard a "good report" about the Buddha, who he calls Gotama; among other things, he has heard Gotama is "a fully enlightened Buddha" and that he "teaches a *dhamma* that is lovely in its beginning, lovely in its middle, and lovely in its ending." Pokkharasāti sends his pupil Ambaṭṭha to find out about the good report, and to test whether Gotama is a Great Man by seeing if he has the thirty-two physical marks that, "according to the tradition of our mantras," indicate that he would have had the choice of becoming either "a wheel-turning righteous monarch of the law" *(dhammarāja)* or a "fully enlightened buddha." Young Ambaṭṭha is a "student of the Vedas, who knows the mantras" and fully shares his master's knowledge.

Soon invited into the Buddha's dwelling, Ambaṭṭha shows discourtesy by walking and standing rather than sitting like his host. Asked if he would behave like this if he were talking to venerable and learned Brahmins, he says, "No, Reverend Gotama. . . . A Brahmin should walk with a walking Brahmin, . . . sit with a sitting Brahmin. . . . But as for those shaven little ascetics, menials, black scourings from Brahmā's foot, with them it is fitting to speak just as I do with the Reverend Gotama." As commentators on this passage explain and other Sutta passages illustrate, Brahmins held that they were born from Brahmā's mouth, Kṣatriyas from his breast, Vaiśyas from his belly, Śūdras from his legs, and ascetics *(samaṇas)* from the soles of his feet. Since the Rigvedic hymn to Puruṣa describes only four classes, everything, other than the Brahmin who holds place at the mouth, is rearranged (breast rather than arms, belly rather than thighs, legs rather than feet) to make room for the fifth group at rock bottom.

How are we to picture young Ambaṭṭha in this scene? In several discourses, the Buddha dialogues with other pupils of Pokkharasāti, with positive results. Further, this scene is one of several where senior Brahmins turn matters over to a junior Brahmin pupil to match wits with the Buddha, and in one of these, the Buddha gets the young man to change his views on this same insulting slur. These, moreover, are among a still wider set of discourses in which senior Brahmins unwittingly put the Buddha in a position to test the depth of a young Brahmin's Vedic education, which, of course, always comes up short. Although the Buddhist texts are not precise about the status of these young Brahmin men, it would appear that they approximate what Brahmanical *dharma* texts call the "bath-graduate": a young man, typically a Brahmin, who has undergone the sacred bath that marks the completion of his Vedic education, after which he would be expected to remain in a celibate state until marriage and can even continue to be called a "bath-graduate" after marrying. Age-wise, he would be somewhere between a high school graduate and a PhD. In all the discourses just mentioned, the young men's Vedic education is subjected to a Buddhist examination. Ambaṭṭha is the only one of them to affront the Buddha directly. It will be left uncertain whether he ever changes his tune on his insulting words, but it seems he will be left hanging as the exemplary spoiled brat.

The Buddha now tells Ambaṭṭha that his training should have made him more courteous. Hearing himself "being called untrained," Ambaṭṭha angrily insults the Sakyans as "menials" three more times. Asked what the Sakyans have done to Ambaṭṭha that he should so insult them, Ambaṭṭha has a story. Once he went to Kapilavatthu, the Sakyans' capital and the Buddha's natal home in today's Nepal, on some business for Pokkharasāti, and while the Sakyans were "laughing and playing about together" on "the high seats in their meeting hall," no one offered him a seat. The Buddha passes this off as "a trifle," saying, "But Ambaṭṭha, even the quail, that little bird, can talk as she likes in her own nest. Kapilavatthu is the Sakyans' home." Although Ambaṭṭha never denies that the Sakyans are Kṣatriyas, he portrays them as crude ones who "do not pay homage to Brahmins" as menials should.

Saying, "This young man goes too far in abusing the Sakyans," the Buddha tells him not only that "the Sakyans regard King Okkāka as their ancestor," but, turning the tables, that Ambaṭṭha's own

Brahmin clan descends from one of Okkāka's slave girls. The Buddha gets Ambaṭṭha to admit that learned Brahmins have also told him this story of his clan's slave origins. But now, hearing Ambaṭṭha censured by his own companions, the Buddha pulls back. Not wanting these young men to humiliate Ambaṭṭha further, he allows that the slave girl's son "was a mighty sage" who "went to the south country, learned the mantras of the Brahmins there, and then went to Okkāka and asked for his daughter"; when the outraged king readied his bow and arrow, the sage was able to put a spell on the weapons until Okkāka, fearing the Brahmin's "rod of punishment," relented and gave the "mighty sage" his daughter. As if invoking Brahmanical law, the Buddha then takes up two cases of inter-caste marriage and one of banishment from caste to demonstrate, on highly dubious Brahmanical grounds, that Kṣatriyas are higher than Brahmins. Then, in summation, he twice quotes a hallowed verse: "The Khattiya's best among those who value clan; He with knowledge and conduct is best of gods and men." Contrasting features of Brahmanical and Buddhist *dharma,* the saying juxtaposes what is "best" for the Buddha's two current audiences: those who value clan, like Ambaṭṭha; and those who follow the Buddha's teachings on "knowledge and conduct," like the five hundred monks.

For the first time, young Ambaṭṭha is drawn into questioning: "But, Reverend Gotama, what is this conduct, what is this knowledge?" The Buddha says it is not concerned with reputation based on birth and clan or the conceit of giving and taking in marriage; rather, it is declared "from the standpoint of the attainment of unexcelled knowledge-and-conduct" that comes from "abandoning all such things." Ambaṭṭha repeats, "What is this conduct, what is this knowledge?"

> Ambaṭṭha, a Tathāgata arises in this world . . . a fully-enlightened Buddha, endowed with wisdom and conduct, . . . incomparable Trainer of men to be tamed, Teacher of gods and humans. . . . He preaches the *dhamma*. . . . A disciple goes forth and practices the moralities; he guards the sense doors. . . . Thus he develops conduct. He attains various insights and the cessation of the corruptions. . . . And beyond this there is no further development of knowledge and conduct that is higher or more perfect.

The Buddha adds, however, that there are "four paths of failure" along which seekers fail in this pursuit. This grouping seems to sort out ascetics and Brahmins according to their types of hermitages. For instance, the third type who "builds himself a fire-shrine on the outskirts of some village or town and dwells there tending his sacred fires" probably approximates a type of Brahmin frequently mentioned in the discourses: ascetics with matted hair. After hearing of these four in the order of their decreasing austerity, Ambaṭṭha has to admit that he and his teacher not only fall short of the highest standard of "unexcelled knowledge and conduct" but are incapable of undertaking any of the "four paths of failure," down even to the easiest! "And yet," replies the Buddha, "you and your teacher the Brahmin Pokkharasāti utter insulting words about 'these shaven little ascetics, menials, black scrapings of Brahmā's foot' . . . even though you can't even manage the duties of one who has failed. See, Ambaṭṭha, how your teacher has let you down!" We now see that Pokkharasāti had used the same abusive words as Ambaṭṭha. In another discourse, when one of Pokkharasāti's students confirms this, the Buddha lampoons Brahmanical ideas of upper-class purity, saying that Brahmins "are in fact born from vaginas" (*Dīgha Nikāya* 27.4).

The Buddha now depicts the earliest Brahmins somewhat favorably, mentioning most of the great family book sages of the *Rigveda* by name to contrast them with current-day Brahmins of the great halls who, rather curiously, now "collect" mantras. But elsewhere, using the same stock phrasing, he puts the same original Vedic sages at the head of "a procession of the blind" that runs from the "first generation of vain and ignorant Brahmins" down to those with whom he is speaking (*Dīgha Nikāya* 13.15; *Majjhima Nikāya* 95.13; 99.9). Having perhaps said enough here without this added negative twist, the Buddha now gives this dialogue its final turn. Telling Ambaṭṭha that neither he nor his teacher is "a sage or one trained in the way of a sage," he says he will clarify Ambaṭṭha's "doubts and perplexities." He starts to walk with Ambaṭṭha, and, aware that Ambaṭṭha sees all but two of his thirty-two marks, he "effected by his psychic power" for Ambaṭṭha to "see his sheathed genitals, and then, sticking out his tongue, he reached out to lick both ears and both nostrils, and then covered the whole circle of his forehead with his tongue"! Considering his mission accomplished,

Ambaṭṭha asks leave, and returns to Pokkharasāti, whom he finds waiting for him in a park with a number of other Brahmins. First, Ambaṭṭha reports that the Buddha has all thirty-two marks. Then he recounts their conversation, upon which Pokkharasāti exclaims, "Well, you're a fine little scholar," berates him, rues how the Buddha has "brought up more and more things against" the Brahmins, and kicks Ambaṭṭha to the ground.

It is too late in the evening for Pokkharasāti to do what he would like, which is to set out at once to see the Buddha, so he leaves early the next morning by torchlight. Greeted by the Buddha, he exchanges courtesies, sits down, and asks whether the Buddha recalls conversing with his student. Hearing "all that had passed," Pokkharasāti says, "Reverend Gotama, Ambaṭṭha is a young fool. May the reverend Gotama pardon him." The Buddha replies, "Brahmin, may Ambaṭṭha be happy." The Buddha now also sets Pokkharasāti's "mind at rest" as to the thirty-two marks, and Pokkharasāti invites the Buddha and his monks to accept a meal from him that day, which the Buddha accepts by his silence.

In the early morning the Buddha arrives "with his order of monks." Pokkharasāti serves him personally, and the young Brahmin men—Ambaṭṭha is not mentioned, but who knows?—serve the monks. When the Buddha has finished eating, Pokkharasāti takes a low seat to one side, and the Buddha begins a "graduated discourse"—a term describing the Buddha's manner of moving from point to point and never getting ahead of what his listeners can understand.

> And when the Lord knew that Pokkharasāti's mind was ready, pliable, free from the hindrances, joyful and calm, then he preached a sermon on *dhamma* in brief: on suffering, its origin, its cessation, and the path. And just as a clean cloth from which all stains have been removed receives the dye perfectly, so in the Brahmin Pokkharasāti, as he sat there, there arose the pure and spotless *dhamma*-eye, and he knew: "Whatever things have an origin must come to cessation."

Experiencing the *dhamma*-eye can denote attaining the status of a stream-enterer, which puts one who enters the "stream" of the Buddha's teaching irrevocably on the path to *nirvāṇa* so that it can be attained within seven lives. Among the Buddha's landholder Brahmin interlocutors, Pokkharasāti is one of the few to undergo this transformation. The discourse then concludes that, "having seen, attained, and penetrated the *dhamma,*" Pokkharasāti announces that he, his son, wife, ministers, and counsellors will take the three refuges—in the Buddha; the Buddhist monastic community, or *saṅgha;* and the *dhamma.* And he asks the Buddha to accept him "as a lay follower who has taken refuge from this day forth as long as life shall last!" Note that Pokkharasāti commits his family and retainers to this form of conversion, but not his disciples. Yet he may hint at them, too. Henceforth, he says, the Buddha will always be welcome at his estate, and whenever young men and maidens greet him courteously, it "will be for their welfare and happiness for a long time." To which the Buddha replies, "Well said, Brahmin!"

Where then is the *dhamma* in this text? My working premise is that we find it in three places: in the mutual hospitality codes that both sides accept but also put to a test, in the ways that the text moves the exponents of Buddhist and Brahmanical *dharma* from initial incivilities toward a civil and fulfilling discourse, and in the rhetoric of artful spiritual teaching that we have just seen emphasized in closing. These matters would contextualize the Suttas historically, since they must be engaging Brahmanical *dharma* with such persuasive artistry over some particular period. In this Sutta, at least, the Buddha twists the alleged Brahmanical law to Buddhist ends, but he is debating matters that are not codified as Brahmanical *dharma* before the *dharmasūtras:* most notably, mixed social classes, which are not treated systematically in the early *Āpastamba Dharmasūtra,* in addition to marriage law and eligibility for Vedic teaching. But let us work back to this rhetoric by looking first at three ways this Sutta and others juxtapose Buddhist and Brahmanical *dharmas:* in addressing the training of young men, in responding to householders, and in treating relations between Kṣatriyas, kings, and Brahmins.

(1) The training of young men is obviously this Sutta's pivot. It is when Ambaṭṭha hears himself being called "untrained" for his physical discourtesies that he verbally insults the Sakyans and the Buddha, not to mention all the five hundred monks traveling in the Buddha's company. Indeed, we could infer that it is the five hundred who are

well trained, by the evidence that they did not rise to teach young Ambaṭṭha a lesson he deserved. As the Buddha makes clear, whereas neither Ambaṭṭha nor Pokkharasāti is "a sage or one trained in the way of a sage," a Buddha is an "incomparable Trainer of men to be tamed." The Buddha is contrasting Ambaṭṭha's rudenesses with the training of monks and nuns, and particularly the "training rules" by which all monks and nuns govern not only their own communal interactions but their interactions with landholder Brahmins like Pokkharasāti.

(2) We see that the Buddha accepts Pokkharasāti's request to host him with a meal even though the Buddha knows he is behind Ambaṭṭha's big insult. Elsewhere in the Suttas, the Buddha couches his teaching in terms meant for the more ordinary householder, a figure of obvious importance to monks and nuns, who beg for their food. Once, he is asked by a family man from a market town:

> Venerable sir, we are laypeople who enjoy sensual pleasures, dwelling at home in a bed crowded with children, enjoying fine sandalwood, wearing garlands, scents, and unguents, accepting gold and silver. Let the Blessed One teach the *dhamma* to us in a way that will lead to our welfare and happiness both in the present life and in the future life as well. (*Aṅguttara Nikāya* 8.54)

Welfare in the present and future life are two of the three types of benefit that the Buddha's *dhamma* promotes, with the third, unmentioned by this jolly layman, being *nirvāṇa.*

The Buddha replies that four things lead to a householder's welfare and happiness in this life: persistent effort, protection, good friendship, and balanced living. Four others bring him welfare and happiness in the future life: "faith, moral discipline, generosity, and wisdom." Each gets a pithy summary. Persistent effort goes into earning a living; protection refers to "wealth righteously gained"; good friendship is found anywhere "householders or their sons" are "of mature virtue, accomplished in faith, moral discipline, generosity, and wisdom"; and balanced living calls for a balanced budget. The four things under "good friendship"—faith, moral discipline, generosity, and wisdom—are the hinge between the two sets, since they also lead to welfare and happiness in the future life. The Buddha often treats friendship as the first of four "sublime attitudes" that should be cultivated in all circumstances: friendship, compassion, sympathetic joy, and equanimity. He also says, "the entire holy life is good friendship, good companionship, good comradeship" (*Saṃyutta Nikāya* 45.2). But here he links friendship more with the hospitality shown by "good people": the generous family man "dwells at home with a mind devoid of stinginess, . . . delighting in giving and sharing." Ultimately, this program for householders also envisions the third benefit of *nirvāṇa:* the wise family man "possesses the wisdom that sees into the arising and passing away of phenomena, that is noble and penetrative and leads to the complete destruction of suffering."

(3) The *Ambaṭṭha Sutta* mentions several kings in passing, but the Buddha is the only Kṣatriya to appear in person. He mentions two key symbols, the king's *cakra* and the Brahmin's *daṇḍa,* as if in opposition. *Cakra* means "wheel" and *daṇḍa* means "stick" or "rod of punishment." On the one hand, the *cakra,* a symbol for the "wheel-turning monarch," is a reminder that the Buddha could have chosen to be a wheel-turning monarch and just king himself. Elsewhere, the Buddha says a wheel-turning monarch "rules without a rod, without a weapon, by means of the *dhamma*" (*Dīgha Nikāya* 26.1.2; *Majjhima Nikāya* 91.5). Of course, wheel-turning monarchs and just kings are the exception, and the Buddha has his preference for smaller-scale republics, as we have seen in his remark about the little quail. But if there must be those who aspire to empire, they should measure themselves against the highest standard of what governs the *saṅgha:*

> The Blessed One said: "Monks, even a wheel-turning monarch, a just and righteous king, does not govern his realm without a co-regent." When he had spoken, a certain monk addressed the Blessed One thus: "But who, venerable sir, is the co-regent of the wheel-turning monarch, the just and righteous king?" "It is the *dhamma,* the law of righteousness, O monk," replied the Blessed One. (*Aṅguttara Nikāya* 3:14)

Like the wheel-turning king, monks too will be ruled by the *dhamma.* The Buddha makes this corresponding point in the renowned text on his final days: before he dies, he refuses to name a successor to lead the *saṅgha;* his successor will be the *dhamma* (*Dīgha Nikāya* 16.6.1). On the other hand, in the *Ambaṭṭha Sutta* the rod is a pseudo-Brahmin's symbol. As we will see in chapter 5, Brahmanical texts will insist that kings protect Brahmins by applying the rod themselves to those who violate *dharma*, though only lightly if the violator is a Brahmin.

This contrast between the *cakra* and the *daṇḍa* gets us back to the rhetoric of these discourses. For if the *dharma* as teaching lies in the Buddha's artful persuasion, one factor would be that he gives a new, challenging, and critical twist to an old Vedic term that already carries implications of royal authority. As we have seen, the Upaniṣads give us brief glimpses of kings who see things (notably including *karma*) from a wide angle. But those kings are not central speakers in a developed story who put the big picture together for others, for one and all; and when they suggest a vision of the big picture, they do not use the term *dharma*, which, to date, had been coming more and more to define Brahmin privilege. This is precisely the challenge that the *dhamma* poses in discourses where the Buddha's primary interlocutors are Brahmins. For instance, after being asked his opinion on what Brahmins "prescribe," the Buddha replied, "Well, Brahmin, has all the world authorized the Brahmins to prescribe . . . ?" (*Majjhima Nikāya* 96.4, 11). For the first time, *dharma* is presented as a tactic of civil discourse for engaging Brahmins, *among others*, with the wider implications of what has been their own enigmatic and self-promotional term. Especially in the longer Suttas, *dhamma* is for the first time the overarching subject of well-rounded narrative (indeed, of well-framed and well-rounded intersecting narratives). Throughout, it is there to be questioned, tested, and penetrated.

Abhidharma-Basket Dharma

Abhidharma, the "Higher" or "Further Dharma," is the project of those who took such questioning, testing, and penetrating to new heights. Though they fill the Abhidharma Basket with texts said to be the Word of the Buddha, they are clearly later scholastics who expand a plural usage of *dharmas (dhammas)* that has only been hinted at in the Suttas' mention of lists or codes. For this plural usage, the major arcs of meaning can be most fruitfully translated as "mental events," "forces," and "regularities." But "elements," "phenomena," and even "things" can also be useful in making philosophical points.

This *usage* is untraceable to any prior Vedic or Brahmanical plural *meaning* and is an important Buddhist innovation in both usage *and* meaning. Yet varied Buddhist meanings of *dharma* can overlap in given contexts. For instance, "*dharmas* plural" may sometimes gain particular intelligibility as a Buddhist twist on the old Vedic compound meaning of *dharma* as the "nature" or "quality" that something possesses. Its centrality to the Buddha's presentation of the *dhamma* in the Suttas makes it plain that it cannot be passed over lightly, and that it must have spiritual payoff.

DHARMAS PLURAL IN THE SŪTRA BASKET

How is one to contextualize this usage in early Buddhism? The terminology of "*dharmas* plural" comes up in connection with five main Sūtra-Basket concepts: (1) dependent origination, (2) right effort, (3) right mindfulness, (4) discrimination of *dharmas,* and (5) the thirty-seven "*dharmas* on the side of enlightenment," which include "discrimination of *dharmas.*" Each involves ways in which the Buddha breaks down the *dharma* as "teaching" into instructional components, which we could take as an initial practical significance of "*dharmas* plural."

I will not go into the last two topics other than to say the following. "Discrimination of *dharmas,*" which is basically being able to tell one *dharma* from another, makes right effort and right mindfulness increasingly purposeful in the way the Buddha's teaching is presented as a path that leads to *nirvāṇa,* and is particularly developed, as we shall see, in one of the northern Nikāya schools (I avoid the term Hīnayāna for these schools, since it has pejorative connotations). As to the thirty-seven "*dharmas* on the side of enlightenment," they are treated at length in the account of his final days, the *Mahāparinibbāna Sutta* (*Dīgha Nikāya* 16), where he says this set of *dhammas* he has "discovered and proclaimed . . . should be thoroughly learnt by you, practiced, developed, and cultivated, so that this holy life may endure for a long time."

Just as the Buddha offers this summa amid his farewells, it may have some heuristic value to discuss Sutta treatments of the first three contexts for "*dharmas* plural" in relation to the unfolding logic of the teaching of the fully enlightened Buddha as conventionally presented in his life story.

Enlightenment

What is often called the "law of dependent arising" (variously translated) is the Buddha's climactic insight on the morning of his enlightenment and is regarded as tantamount to his *nirvāṇa*. It is instructive to see how his "rediscovery" of this "law" bearing on "*dharmas* plural" comes between incidents where *dharma* in the singular means "teaching." Having learned and rejected one teacher's *dharma* and then another's during his quest for enlightenment, it is only when he gains this insight that he is prepared to teach his *dharma* to others, and at first wishes to impart it to these two former teachers before he realizes they have each passed away. In brief, he is now the Enlightened One, a Buddha, because he has gained insight into the mutual causality of a set of (usually) twelve "causes" or "sources"—as testable "forces" or "regularities" that account especially for rebirth or reincarnation. This, in Buddhist eyes, makes them sufficient to account for the dependent co-arising of all conditioned *dharmas*—a category that in Theravada Buddhism includes all *dhammas* except for the one unconditioned *dhamma* of *nibbāna* (Sarvāstivādins, as we shall see, identify three unconditioned *dharmas*).

The axial importance attributed to this "law" as relating *dharma* as teaching to "*dharmas* plural" can be seen in a succinct statement attributed to Sāriputra, the Buddha's chief disciple on matters of meditation: "He who sees dependent arising sees *dhamma;* he who sees *dhamma* sees dependent arising" (*Majjhima Nikāya* 28.28, 35). Sāriputra does not mention that "*dharmas* plural" are implied in dependent arising. That is left to Sutta commentators, to the Abhidharma, and to the Mahāyāna, for which the ontological status of co-arising conditions eventually comes to be a matter of mutual interest with some Nikāya schools, with sharply contested interpretations. But the terminology of "*dharmas* plural" does have Sutta usages in describing the twelve "causes." Reading from effects back to causes, the first nine explain how old-age-and-death results from birth, and that birth can be traced through grasping and thirst back to the five aggregates—form or body, feelings, perceptions, motivational forces, and consciousness—which, according to the Buddha, are sufficient to account for how the so-called person comes to birth as a composite being without a permanent self. To circumvent a long discussion on this difference between Hindu and Buddhist spiritualities, let us just say that the Buddha's *dharma* offers a path to *nirvāṇa* without positing such an entity. The last three "causes" derive consciousness from motivational forces (including *karma* from previous lives) and ignorance. The total breakdown can thus be analyzed in groupings of *dharmas*. When the Buddha sets this "law" forth to others, his chief purpose is to disclose the conditions that sustain rebirth into *saṃsāra*, so as to be able to show what can be done about it, which he first gets to with our next topic.

Setting the Wheel in Motion

After his enlightenment, the Buddha reflected that it would be a little hard to communicate "this abstruse *dhamma* which goes against the worldly stream, subtle, deep, and difficult to see," and even considered keeping it to himself, until the god Brahmā persuaded him, "There will be those who will understand" (*Majjhima Nikāya* 26.19–20). In Buddhist texts, Brahmā thinks he is the creator—mistakenly, since, as the law of dependent arising can be used to demonstrate, where all causes condition each other there can be no prime mover. In effect, in asking the Buddha to teach it to the world, Brahmā accedes to this truth about himself.

As the Buddha explains in his famous first sermon, the "Discourse on Setting in Motion the Wheel of the *Dhamma*," although he had reached complete and perfect enlightenment, he could not claim "to have awakened to it" until he had "thoroughly purified" his knowledge of the four noble truths to present them in an ordered way. Having reached such clarification, he now teaches how the first three truths are to be known, accomplished, and fully understood, and implies that he does the same for the fourth. The noble truths are those of "sorrow" (quoted earlier as "suffering," and sometimes explained as "unsatisfactoriness"), its "origin," its "cessation," and the "path" to that cessation. The *dhamma* is then set in motion with the first conversion, when one of his five listeners arises with a "dust-free, stainless vision of the *dhamma*" and says, "Whatever is subject to origination is subject to cessation." The utterance is like Pokkharasāti's, but the speaker becomes an *arahant* (Sanskrit *arhat*), "one who is deserving (of reverence)." This is the highest level of attainment, according to

Nikāya schools, and the term for those who attain *nirvāṇa* through the Buddha's teaching.

For what follows, it is useful to mention that the path's eight components are conventionally treated under three headings: wisdom or insight, concerned with right view and right intention; morality, involving right speech, right action, and right livelihood; and concentration, requiring right effort, right mindfulness, and right concentration. Only the wisdom and concentration groups deal directly with "*dharmas* plural." Wisdom calls for "seeing 'things' *(dhammas)* as they are"; concentration involves the effort, mindfulness, and concentration that enable insight.

The most basic way that the Buddha teaches right effort is through "the four right endeavors," which occur in many places in stock phrases:

> A monk . . . endeavors so that bad, unwholesome *dhammas* that have not arisen, do not arise; . . . he endeavors so that bad, unwholesome *dhammas* that have arisen are abandoned; . . . he endeavors so that wholesome *dhammas* that have not arisen, arise; he endeavors so that wholesome *dhammas* that have arisen, are constant, not lost, increase, grow, develop, are complete.

Right effort is thus applied to recognizing *dhammas* under the headings of "wholesome" and "unwholesome" and fostering spiritual progress by abetting or diverting them according to whether they are wholesome or unwholesome and nascent or current. This practice is basic to what follows as right mindfulness and right concentration. Right mindfulness is the most distinctive Buddhist spiritual practice: an attentive and careful but unobsessive watchfulness that provides the mental space where seeing *dhammas* as "wholesome" and "unwholesome" becomes purposeful. And right concentration enables one to enter an initial meditation stage "completely secluded from sense desires and unwholesome *dhammas*" and to remain in "joy and happiness" once one has "perceived the disappearance" of the most pervasive unwholesome *dhammas* known as the five hindrances: sensual desire, ill will, sloth and torpor, worry and flurry, and doubt. In a fashion close to an Abhidharma analysis, one Sutta (*Majjhima Nikāya* 111) has the Buddha speak of the wholesome *dhammas* one experiences with increasing detachment as one attains still higher meditation stages through right concentration.

But in the early Buddhism of the Suttas, the meaning of "*dharmas* plural" comes out most clearly in the practice of right mindfulness. The Buddha says there are four foundations of mindfulness: "A monk dwells watching the body as a body, watching feelings as feelings, watching mind as mind, and watching *dhammas* as *dhammas*." In each case, he is to be "ardent, fully aware, and mindful." Thus, if one is distracted from giving sustained attention to the body as body to watching feelings as feelings, he should be aware that he has moved on to feelings. In this sense the four "foundations" are thus "domains."

The Sutta describes twenty-one exercises: fourteen focus mindfulness on the body, one on feelings, one on thoughts, and five on *dhammas*. Each exercise is followed by a discussion of the insight to be developed as understanding deepens. One singular instance of *dhamma(s)* recurs in all the insight sections, where it is mentioned as a "second" approach. While leaving most occurrences of *dharma(s)* untranslated, I call attention to this one by italicizing its translation as "phenomena." As the monk has dwelt "watching the body per se," "feelings per se," and "thoughts per se," so now:

> Thus he dwells watching *dhammas* per se [in three ways]: first, he dwells watching *dhammas* within himself, or *dhammas* outside of himself, or *dhammas* both inside and outside himself; second, with regard to *dhammas* he dwells watching the *phenomena* of arising, or passing away, or both origination and passing away; third, he sustains the awareness "this is a *dhamma*" insofar as wisdom and recollection allow, and remains detached, not clinging to anything in the world.

This "second" approach probably occurs through all the intervals on insight in anticipation of *dhamma* being the fourth foundation of mindfulness. For the momentum of the Sutta is to break things down from the most solid, the body, to the most insubstantial and evanescent, *dhammas*. Thus, commentaries turn to this Sutta to illustrate that *dhammas* are without essence, lifeless, and empty. Through all these iterations, this second way of watching—no matter what one is watching (from body matters like breathing or corpses, to feelings, thoughts, or *dhammas*)—refers to a way of watching *dhammas* arising and passing away, or in more common terms, watching "phenomena" in their "rise and fall." In the five exercises that come under the fourth foundation of watching *dhammas* as *dhammas*, all this is practiced with regard to the five hindrances, five aggregates, and six sense fields (which include mind, and being aware of the mind as the sense base for *dhammas* as "thoughts" or "ideas"), a group that includes the "discrimination of *dhammas*," and the four noble truths. Closing on the four noble truths is climactic. Here the practitioner is reassured that since detached mindful attentiveness cannot be accompanied by grasping, grasping ceases—like anything else that arises.

DHARMAS AND ABHIDHARMAS

With the topic of "discrimination of *dharmas*," we must now shift to more philosophical matters that separate the subdivisions of Buddhism—in both Nikāya schools and in the Mahāyāna. The Sarvāstivādins, the main northern Nikaya school, make "discrimination of *dharmas*" a linchpin of their *dharma* theory. In defining *abhidharma* as liberating "insight" or "wisdom" attained by "discrimination of *dharmas*," their abhidharma even offers a new "controlling faculty of insight" beyond the six sense faculties. A new claim is made that one can discriminate *dharmas* each according to its "intrinsic nature," while doing so is compared to the work of a jeweler, or to selection of the right flowers.

Much effort goes into new taxonomies. With the Sarvāstivādin Abhidharma and commentarial discussions, we meet not only the classical *dharma* theory among the Nikāya schools, but the handling of this topic that was most directly critiqued by the Mahāyāna. A Mahāyāna view of the perfection of wisdom rejects discrimination of *dharmas* for its ideal practitioner, the *bodhisattva* ("one whose nature is enlightenment"). Around the turn of the millennium, the Mahāyāna claimed that such beings were superior to *arhats* because their superior wisdom into the emptiness of all *dharmas* entailed compassion for all beings: "A bodhisattva should therefore be trained in non-attachment to all *dharmas*, and in their unreality—in the sense that he does not construct or discriminate them" (*Mahāprajñāpāramitā Sūtra*, 1:1.3.13).

What do such Abhidharma discussions amount to in everyday language? I will consider a few topics for which the Sarvāstivādin Abhidharma is famous in order to underline their differences principally with the Theravādins. Sarvāstivādins, who can be thought of as everyone else's foil, are by name "Those Who Say All *(Dharmas)* Exist" or "Pan-Realists." They are most readily distinguished for a view of time in which *dharmas* have real existence not only in the present but in the past and future. Yet they get most idiosyncratic about *dharmas* themselves in their taxonomies, and in three concepts about them: "intrinsic nature," one of fourteen "dissociated forces" called "possession," and space as one of three "unconditioned *dharmas.*"

Sarvāstivādin Dharma *Ontology*

In "watching *dhammas* as *dhammas,*" all schools viewed them as "mental events." But while the Pāli Abhidhamma left the ontological nature of *dharmas* largely implied, the Sarvāstivādins made "what they are" central. Intensifying the preoccupation with "lists" or "codes," the Sarvāstivādins worked up "matrices of matrices" to offer an abstract web that could account for all the possible conditions and characteristics that *dharmas* could exhibit.

The most representative Sarvāstivādin grouping lists seventy-five *dharmas* in a "fivefold taxonomy." Therein, one finds eleven *dharmas* of material form, one of thought, forty-six thought-concomitant *dharmas* (wholesome ones, such as faith; unwholesome ones, such as anger; and other related *dharmas* that accompany thought), and fourteen "dissociated forces" (*dharmas* that are neither physical nor mental). This fourth category was completely novel and includes some *dharmas* meant to account for events occurring within this doctrinal matrix. Beyond these seventy-two conditioned *dharmas,* there are also, as mentioned earlier, three unconditioned *dharmas.* These seventy-five *dharmas* are considered to be irreducible "primary existents" by the fact that each has its "own" *(sva-)* "intrinsic nature" *(bhāva).* They are thereby distinguished from secondary "conceptual existents" like a table or a dog, which are real unities for pragmatic purposes only, can be broken down, and are considered to be "empty" of "intrinsic nature." Mahāyānists have their most basic disagreement here. For them, *all dharmas* are empty and "lack intrinsic nature."

Svabhāva

Svabhāva is a key term. Using the verbal root √*dhṛ*, Sarvāstivādins, in their Abhidharma commentaries, define *dharmas* both etymologically and via *svabhāva* as "holding" or "upholding" their "intrinsic natures." Being utterly impersonal, what Sarvāstivādin *dharmas* "do" is simply "hold their intrinsic natures." Amid the flux of "conceptual existents" the scholastic codifier–meditator can rely on them as irreducible "holds" precisely because each such *dharma* holds "its own." If one were watching faith or anger rise and fall, one could put a wholesome hold on the one and let the other go. In everyday English, it would be, in the first case, something like saying "hold that thought" and reducing it to "let that mental event take hold,"and in the second case, something like saying "let it go." Sanskrit etymologies from √*dhṛ* are interesting in light of usages where *dharma*, at the end of possessive compounds, means "nature" or "quality." Such usages also link *dharma* with its own etymology, suggesting that the Sarvāstivādin usage correlates with this grammatical implication.

Theravāda Abhidhamma commentaries take this possessive compound meaning differently, as "the natural condition of something," but also use the Pāli term *sabhāva*, equivalent to Sanskrit *svabhāva*, to explain its meaning. Again, one could say that the possessive compound usage and the *sabhāva* meaning overlap. But Pāli *sabhāva* should not be translated as "intrinsic" or "inherent nature." Rather, it is meant to explain that *dhammas* are called "particular natures" or "qualities" because they "hold" or "maintain" themselves in relation to causal conditions. But whether or not *dharmas* are "ontological irreducibles" or just "co-emergent or correlative conditions," they have the similar quality and function of being "holds."

Prāpti

One of the Sarvāstivādins' seventy-five *dharmas* that functions most clearly as a kind of "hold" is *prāpti*, "possession" or "ownership"—one of the fourteen "dissociated forces" *(dharmas)* that are neither physical nor mental. Although it has been compared with other "pseudoselves" adopted by various schools to explain facets of the personal continuum without a permanent personal substratum or "soul," it is an ingenious Sarvāstivādin doctrine that provoked intense debate. Like all other conditioned *dharmas, prāpti* itself is impermanent. A series of *prāptis* explains how a bad intention keeps having a new "possession" to make the bad intention "one's own." In effect, everyone lives almost inescapably in an "ownership society"—and is bound to stay in it by their own *karma,* as in "You do it, you own it." For unenlightened persons, *prāptis* are "own-its" in series. The advice, "Don't own it," is thus good Buddhist advice, and also ontologically on target, since no matter what your school, it is never "really" yours to begin with or to end with. How then do Sarvāstivādins envision getting to an end without ownership? Fortunately, for an enlightened person, there is also a *dharma* called "non-possession" *(aprāpti)* that keeps negative taints from recurring. It accounts for how the ownership series can lose its hold. No other schools held both of these *dharmas.* One Nikāya school with an intensified emphasis on the "momentariness" of *dharmas,* the Sautrāntikas, rejected them as "unnecessary" and "absurd"—a way of connecting the dots by adding missing ones. The main Mahāyāna Abhidharma tradition, the Yogācāra, kept the Sarvāstivādin fivefold taxonomy and added ten *dharmas* in the "dissociated forces" category; but, while keeping *prāpti,* they abandoned *aprāpti!* Theravādins were probably outside this debate.

Space and Object-Support Conditions

If *prāpti* is meant to explain how certain things *(dharmas)* hold course, how do all things hold course with respect to each other? Here we come to space as one of the Sarvāstivādins' three unconditioned *dharmas,* along with *nirvāṇa* and another type of "cessation" that we need not go into.

In Sarvāstivādin terms, unconditioned *dharmas* are permanent rather than impermanent. They do not arise, pass away, or undergo modification; are unaffected by any cause or multiple causes or conditions; and do nothing that brings about a direct effect. Here, if one asks what they "do," it is helpful to speak of "function": how *dharmas* "function" both specifically and in general, and how the universe "functions," given *dharmas.* The distinctive function of space is "not obstructing." Commentaries prove it exists by *reductio*-type inferential arguments, and exemplify it by the way space functions to provide a place for light, perception, consciousness of material forms, and so forth. The argument positions this Buddhist view over and against most forms of Brahmanical scholastic thought, which have what may be called "ontologies of substance" that view space or "ether" in a continuum of unfolding substance that conveys sound rather than light. Yet as an "ontology of openness" developed around lists and categories, the Sarvāstivādin view has affinities with one of the scholastic Brahmanical philosophies known as Vaiśeṣika, "Particularism." And both may recall the Vedic "ontology of openness" that opens spaces for light, worlds, movement, and phenomena. Tracing thought phenomena in this manner is reminiscent of some Rigvedic enigmas. The Sarvāstivādin emphasis, however, is less cosmological than practical. It describes the mental space that makes it possible to deal with immediate stimuli.

Vinaya-Basket Dharma

Not everybody, of course, wants to be a metadharmician. We now meet the "maintainers of the Vinaya" who specialized in the monastic discipline. Vinaya regulates the *saṅgha* both in monastic matters and in interactions with society at large, which in India meant interacting with Brahmanical *dharma.* As hermeneuts of both types of human interactions, "maintainers of the Vinaya" are "experts in law."

Obviously, the name "Vinaya" for a category of the Buddha's teachings is early. But one must distinguish between Vinaya texts and the early monastic code, since the code itself is a Sūtra (Sutta) that stands outside the Vinaya Basket. Perhaps its periodic recitation gave it such separate status, but it may also have been a prior text around which portions of Vinaya composition nucleated. The two main portions of the Vinaya-Basket proper, the *Sūtra Vibhaṅga (Sutta Vibhaṅga)* and *Skandhaka (Khandhaka),* treat individual and communal rules, respectively.

THE MONASTIC CODE

Vinaya differences lie behind the formation of each of the Nikāya schools. To cooperate in reciting the rules *(dhammas, dharmas),* a group of monks would have to share the same code. Each fortnight the group would ratify the code as a formulary of rules that it was consensually committed to recite, with everyone accepting the discipline stipulated for any admitted infraction. Nuns did the same. If as few as four monks disagreed with others over the rules, they could form their own *saṅgha* with a revised code; and this could eventually be perpetuated in a "school" or "sect" with its own ceremony of higher ordination. Six Nikāya schools have left extant Vinayas: one of them the Theravāda in Pāli, and all the others in either Chinese or Tibetan translations from original Sanskrit compositions, only fragments of which survive.

Since commitment to the communal recitation of the code is fundamental, it is worth outlining the eight basic rule categories shared by all six Nikāya schools. I list them in the conventional order of their recitation, which moves from the most severe to the most incidental and procedural, pausing over rules 1 and 2 in the first category for their paramount significance.

1. Four rules whose infraction requires expulsion from the *saṅgha:* sexual intercourse, theft, murder, and flaunting spiritual attainments.

The Theravāda is the only school to make the rule "He cannot have sex" an absolute condition for staying in the monastic community. In the Theravāda Vinaya, sex is most basically defined as "that which is not the true *dharma*" and called "village *dhamma*" and "vile *dhamma*." The Buddha devises a rule that defines penetration, and thus expulsion, by the "length of the fruit of a sesame plant." As the first rule recited at every ceremonial recitation of the code, it calls on each monk, right at the beginning, to search his memory, confess to anything that might qualify, and if conscience allows, to renew a commitment that stands as an index to the monastic law in its entirety. Rule 1 is "the one work," "one instruction," "equal training." And although it applies first and undoubtedly foremost to celibacy, and, since men were admitted to the order before women, above all to not having sex with women, and, with this, to the ideal of leaving home for a life of homelessness free from passions, the "case law" on this rule surely spills over into the imaginary. The Buddha is said to have applied it to monks who had sex with corpses, dolls, visible and invisible species, and all conceivable bodily orifices.

Rule 2, prohibiting theft, is then the one rule that sees a monk punished by a king: "I prescribe, O monks, that you obey kings." In contrast to the totally monastic character of rule 1, rule 2 establishes the principle that monks are accountable to the political and social world around them and to the king's law, whatever his religion.

The other six categories are then as follows:

2. Thirteen offenses calling for a probationary period of temporary exclusion from the order. These deal with sexual transgressions, dwelling places, schisms, and wayward monks.
3. Two offenses where a monk is accused on the testimony of a trustworthy female lay follower, whose word, as sole witness to a sexual impropriety, can be evaluated to assess whether it is a category 1, 2, or 5 offense.
4. Thirty offenses requiring expiation and forfeiture after confession. These pertain to monastic paraphernalia, medicines, gold, and silver. This is the first class to diverge much in the way the rules are numbered in various Vinayas.
5. Ninety to ninety-two offenses, numbered variously by school, requiring expiation or penance. These govern lying, food and drink, accepting food from lay households, conduct with nuns and other women, and so on.
6. Four offenses requiring confession, all concerned with taking food in forbidden situations.
7. Training rules for daily monastic conduct and manners, calling for no sanction or punishment. This most disparate grouping, both in order and total number, includes numerous guidelines for "going amongst the houses" and eating decorously.
8. Seven rules providing procedures for resolving disputes over offenses, including means of reaching verdicts, such as majority vote by tickets; appeals; criteria for assessing insanity; smoothing things out with other monks and, where an offense is "connected with householders," with the laity; and a requirement that a verdict may not be carried out without the confessing monk's acknowledgment.

A few overall points must suffice. Nuns' codes have one less category (the third) and considerably more rules in most other categories. Category 3 is interesting not only for its lack of a reverse gender perspective but for its affirmation that laywomen can be legal witnesses.

Category 7 leaves Vinaya casuists considerable opening to adapt rules to local cultural variations. Meanwhile, category 8 shows considerable litigious experience.

I have mentioned the casuistic nature of these rules to suggest that the Vinaya's implementation of *dharma* as "rule" could have had implications for the way *dharma* as law was developed in South Asia. I broach this matter with a closing illustration that may also bear on the genesis of the Vinaya.

VINAYA AND SMALL-SCALE EARLY REPUBLICS

Small-scale "republican" tribal states proliferated during the early phase of urbanization in northeast India, where their histories are reflected in narratives about the Buddha. Their currency raises the question of whether the consensual nature of Vinaya reflects internal laws and polities, such as those of the Śākyans from whom the Buddha is said to have come and of whom he could speak with nostalgia, as when he compares their conduct to a little quail at ease in her nest. Such polities were endangered during the Buddha's lifetime by the ambitions of rising monarchical states and were also headed for tension with the ways that Brahmanical law had begun to theorize royal power in the context of social-class hierarchy.

We see the first of these oppositions, and probably also a glimmer of the second, in a famous passage that begins the long account of the Buddha's last days. One of those ill-fated "republics" is in the way of the expansionist king of the rising power of Magadha, who has by now killed his father to get the throne. The king tells his Brahmin chief minister to go tell the Buddha, "King Ajātasattu wants to attack the Vajjīs. He said, 'I will annihilate these splendid and powerful Vajjīs, destroy them, bring them to utter ruin.'" The king orders the Brahmin to listen carefully and report what the Buddha says. Upon hearing this parricide king's precise words, the Buddha avoids replying directly. Instead he asks his beloved disciple and cousin, Ānanda, seven times what he has heard about the Vajjīs with regard to seven aspects of their laws and conduct; and after each answer, the Buddha replies that so long as the Vajjīs continue that behavior, "one can expect them to prosper, not to decline." Finally, he tells the minister that he once taught the Vajjīs these very seven things himself. Here we see the Buddha as a virtual (though only partial) law-giver to the Vajjīs, while we can assume that the king is getting his main advice from this Brahmin, who now, as his sly response shows, tells the Buddha he sees that the king will "not be able to conquer the Vajjīs, at least not [simply] in warfare, without deceit and [fomenting] internal dissension."

Once the minister leaves with "a lot to do," the Buddha assembles all the monks dwelling in the capital to commend seven analogous things that will lead them to prosperity. The passage thus establishes parallels between the seven aspects of the laws and conduct of the Vajjīs and the Vinaya code for monks, with both said to have the Buddha's authority behind them:

> (1) Just as the Vajjīs were told they should "continue to meet together in assembly frequently," so should monks; (2) both should assemble and conduct their affairs harmoniously; (3) just as the Vajjīs were not to "establish [any laws] which are not already established" or "rescind any established [law]," and should "proceed in accordance with the traditional way of the Vajjīs," monks should "not establish [any monastic rules] which are not already established" or "rescind any which are [already] established," and should "proceed in accordance with Training Rules as they have been established"; (4) both should venerate and heed their elders; (5) just as the Vajjīs should not "carry off forcibly women and girls of good family to have as their wives," monks should "not fall under the sway of the [kind of] desire which leads to rebirth, when it arises"; (6) just as the Vajjīs should venerate and maintain their shrines both inside and outside the city, monks should "look to [secluded] forest dwellings"; and (7) just as the Vajjīs should guard, shelter, and protect their *arahants,* welcoming future ones and maintaining comfortably those now in their territory, monks should keep their mindfulness "so that congenial companions in the celibate life" might be welcomed to their monastery in the future and maintained comfortably there now.

Set at the beginning of the Buddha's final journey, the passage seeks to secure the Vinaya's future while anticipating the imminent passing of the laws of the Vajjīs, which, no matter how excellent they may be as commended by the Buddha, are unable to protect the Vajjīs, who are soon to be overwhelmed by a monarchic order coaxed by Brahmins.

Parallels between Vinaya and "republican" polities bear not only on the genetic question of the origins of Vinaya, but on consensual features in early Indian law. Guilds, commercially linked with urbanization, may also have had consensual legal charters. In the case of Vinaya, however, comparisons with secular or Brahmanical law must acknowledge that, as Vinaya requires celibacy, it cannot be law for a whole society. In fact, the Buddha recommends only seven things to the Vajjīs, not a total legal charter. Clearly the two sets of seven come to focus not on the transient value of the first set for the Vajjīs but on the more enduring importance of the second set for the *saṅgha*. We can see in them some of the things that make Vinaya jurisprudence distinctive. The Buddha begins with clear references to the monastic code. In the first three directives he addresses rules concerning schism, admonishes against adding or rescinding rules, and singles out the training rules for careful maintenance. The last four directives then begin with strong reminders of rule 1, celibacy. It is suggestive that the desire mentioned is compared to marriage by abduction, which Brahmanical law will deem a low form of marriage unsuitable for Brahmins. Respect for seniority and emphasis on both forest and monastic residence then bring the whole to focus on the hospitable comfort of *arahants* and the pursuit of meditation among congenial companions in the celibate life. Yet, although Vinaya law is distinctive, it remains a royal road into the complexities of both Buddhist and Brahmanical *dharma*.

CHAPTER 5

Classical Brahmanical *Dharma*

We now turn to the post-Vedic texts in which Brahmanical *dharma* blossomed: the *dharmasūtras, Manu,* and the two Sanskrit epics. These texts open up the concept of *dharma* for what will come to be called Hinduism. If Indians recall the epics for their manner of relating *dharma* to what is familiar in everyday lives, they tend to cite *Manu,* often enough polemically, for its proverbial authority on particulars of traditional law. This chapter will foreground the legal meaning of *dharma* by often translating it as "law."

Since the *dharmasūtras* and *Manu* are named after authorities on law, we can refer to their titles in italics as a shorthand (e.g., *Manu*), and to their reputed spokesmen by citing their names without italics (e.g., Manu, Āpastamba). To probe *Manu*'s relation to the *dharmasūtras,* one must differentiate Sūtras from Śāstras. *Sūtra* means "thread," and Sūtras are short pithy aphorisms, typically in prose, which, in their sequence, call for a guru's explanation of the thread that connects them. Two of the oldest *dharmasūtras, Āpastamba* and *Baudhāyana,* come at the end of longer texts, where they follow earlier discussions of Vedic solemn and domestic ritual. This makes them continuations of aphorisms on Vedic ritual and implies that the spiritual thread of what they have to say about *dharma* is transmitted within a Vedic school. The two other surviving *dharmasūtras, Gautama* and *Vasiṣṭha,* are more independent works named after ancient Vedic sages and have only tenuous associations with Vedic schools. *Śāstras,* from a root meaning "to instruct," are more straightforward "manuals" or "treatises," and are typically composed in verse. *Manu,* as an independent "treatise" of this kind, is entirely in verse, and goes one better than the *dharmasūtras* in claiming the first man, Manu, as its authority on law. *Manu* does not name other textual or sagely authorities on *dharma.* But it clearly builds on what the earlier *dharmasūtras,* particularly

Gautama, have said about it, and uses the term *dharmaśāstra* in a way that covers both *dharmasūtra* and *dharmaśāstra.*

While introducing *dharmaśāstra,* this chapter will also begin to introduce the epics around the figures of their great kings and queens—Rāma and Sītā of the *Rāmāyaṇa;* Yudhiṣṭhira and Draupadī of the *Mahābhārata*—whose stands for *dharma* we shall study more closely in chapters 6 and 7. But herein we will center discussion on *Manu*'s relation to the *dharmasūtras,* since with this "legal tradition" we get down to the social and customary thicket of it. We may think of chapter 5 as a sociological interlude. And since we must, to a certain extent, relish this thicket, it may be useful to remember how Brer Rabbit got Brers Fox and Bear to throw him into a briar patch so that he could devise his escape from them. *Dharmaśāstra* is the sociological thicket of Brahmanical *dharma,* and the spirituality of Hindu *dharma* must be traced through its "thorns," which is what *Manu* itself, from its elitist and totalitarian perspective, calls reprobates it wants its king to summarily eradicate.

The "Five Great Sacrifices"

Let us start with a group of piety practices that sets the tone and spirit of Brahmanical hospitality: the prescription of a novel cluster of routines for householders of the three upper classes, called "twice-born" because their access to Vedic ritual gave them a spiritual second birth. This set of rites, developed in the early *dharmasūtras,* after first being mentioned in discussions of domestic ritual, called for the daily practice of "five great sacrifices": (1) a food offering on the ground or in the air to beings (e.g., crows), (2) food hospitality to guests, (3) some wood as a fire offering to the gods, (4) a water offering to ancestors, and (5) personal Vedic recitation or "recitation to oneself" as the offering to *Brahman,* the world-source or absolute as embodied in holy Vedic utterance. We may recall that personal recitation, which we met in chapter 3, was a Brahmin's main means of "cooking the world" and think of it now as the spiritual unifier of all five offerings, since *Brahman* is the spiritual All, and the other four are also done with Vedic utterances or overtones. Using a term that described "great" and complex Vedic ceremonies for these five simple rites, it was claimed that their daily performance was enough to assure Ārya status and to secure the spiritual rewards of a pious life. In the late Vedic period, when the formulations on domestic ritual were composed, the home life enhanced by these practices was that of the village, as the Brahmanical system was still poorly adapted to the growth of market towns and cities then underway in eastern regions. The *dharmasūtras,* for which the "five great sacrifices" exemplified Brahmanical *dharma,* remained centered on this village ideal despite the further gains of urbanization and state centralization that went on, especially in the east, during the centuries of their likely composition.

We can see the rise to prominence of this new emphasis on domestic spirituality in the attention it received in Buddhist sources, which, as we saw in chapter 4, honor the pious lay householder who pursues the reward of heaven even if he falls short of pursuing *nirvāṇa.* Several Pāli Suttas offer intriguing treatments of the "five great sacrifices" as practiced by both landholder and ascetic Brahmins. There, the Buddha contrasts what we may call the five *little* "great sacrifices" described so far, which he basically endorses as piety practices wholesome for lay Brahmin converts, with five *big* "great sacrifices," referring to solemn Vedic rites with animal victims, which he condemns, implying that the *little* "great sacrifices" supposedly reformed them. Moreover, the Buddha seems to introduce, as a further and still more acceptable modification of both types of "great sacrifices," a grouping of "five things *(dhammas)* that Brahmins prescribe for the performance of merit, for accomplishing the wholesome": truthfulness, austerities, purity in sexual life, erudition, and charity—each term having a thoroughly Vedic pedigree. The Buddha favors this set by recommending an additional sixth *dhamma,* "the motive of compassion," and goes on to interpret them in relation to the four "sublime attitudes" (see chapter 4) of friendliness, compassion, sympathetic joy, and equanimity that, he now says, form "the path to the company of Brahmā." His conclusion, that what they really are is "equipment of the mind," is said to have thrilled a great landholder Brahmin who was a colleague of Ambaṭṭha's teacher Pokkharasāti (*Majjhima Nikāya* 99).

Dharmaśāstra finds a different route to unifying these matters. Leaving the *big* "great sacrifices" to the older Vedic schools as matters of solemn ritual, it fosters the *little* ones as markers of householder spirituality. In a lengthy discussion of these rites, Manu introduces them by the "inevitable violence" of "the householder's five slaughter-houses": the fireplace, grindstone, broom, mortar and pestle, and water pot, which the great sages designed the five "great sacrifices" to expiate. Manu, too, thus makes the five little "great sacrifices" conducive to nonviolence *(ahiṃsā)*. Although Manu substitutes teaching for personal Vedic recitation as the offering to *Brahman* or the Veda, he also encourages the latter, and goes on to say that the five can be performed by interior meditative means: by the sense organs, speech, breath, or knowledge. *Manu* thus spiritualizes these practices as the Buddha did. If it is still unclear that the five great sacrifices are to be performed in market towns and cities, Manu makes their significance cosmic: "He should apply himself here daily to his personal Vedic recitation and to making offerings to gods; for by applying himself to making offerings to gods, he upholds this world, both the mobile and the immobile" (3.75). The set of five offerings supports five worlds: those of animal "beings," human guests, gods, ancestors, and Brahmā or *Brahman*.

Innovations of Manu

While there are continuities such as these from the *dharmasūtras* to *Manu*, *Manu* is also innovative, beginning with the introduction of a fourth "source" of *dharma* beyond the three mentioned by the *dharmasūtras*; greater attention to the king and the king's part in statecraft and legal procedure; and philosophical and lyrical moments (which could also be called poetic). We shall come to the king shortly, and will have to let *Manu*'s lyrical side emerge from some of what we quote. But the first matter is important in showing how all these texts take up post-Vedic considerations in spelling out the authority behind prescriptions on *dharma*. The four *dharmasūtras* each enumerate only three sources of *dharma*, which can be summarized as Veda, custom, and tradition. *Manu*, however, adds "what is pleasing to oneself" (2.6). It is debated whether this fourth source spiritualizes *dharma* as a kind of personal conscience or is merely a provision for deciding legal matters where the other three criteria leave matters unresolved.

Among other innovations in *Manu*, a fourth, mentioned in chapter 1, is a frame story that introduces Manu as an exalted promulgator of laws who addresses a celestial audience eager to receive his instructions. A fifth innovation is that it is composed entirely in verse, which *Manu* carries out in a meter that is typical also of the epics. The frame story clearly offers a new way for a treatise on *dharma* to formulate authorship and textual authority. And so does composition in verse. However modest Manu may be in claiming nothing for being a poet, it will be profitable to recognize him as one, and profitable as well to keep him close to the epics not only by their common verse composition but as their near contemporary.

A sixth innovation—*Manu*'s flirtations with narrative, especially regarding the king—is evident in the frame story and the poetry. To get to the king, we begin with the categories that *Manu* and indeed all our classical *dharma* texts dilated upon: the four castes or classes and the four patterns, orders, or stages of life.

Social Classes, Life-Patterns, and the King

If one were to seek to inculcate a body of behavioral norms, roles, and rules that should inspire each person's social life in all its transactions across the spectrum of social classes and likewise each person's individual life and spiritual development through all life's existential options or stages, and further to cover not only individuals in every social class but every "intermediary" or "mixed" caste (those supposedly conceived through one or another form of ancestral miscegenation), one might come up with something like the theory of "Class and Life-stage *Dharma*," which textbooks on Hinduism are prone to attribute to *Manu*. Since the social classes, class mixture, and the life-stages each have their own calculus, which becomes virtually infinite when the three are interrelated, we will be exploring some of their facets elsewhere in this book. This section will begin by making a few limiting points.

Regarding the four classes and the mixed classes, *Manu* is adamant on one limiting point: there is no fifth class. Manu takes this stand while introducing mixed classes to open a discussion of "Laws for Times of Adversity":

> Devoted to their own jobs, the three twice-born classes should study the Veda; but it is the Brahmin who should teach them, not the other two—that is the firm principle. The Brahmin must know

> the means of livelihood of all according to rule, and he should teach them to others and follow them himself. Because of his distinctive qualities, the eminence of his origin, his holding (√*dhṛ*) of restrictive practices, and the distinctive nature of his sacrament, the Brahmin is the lord of all the classes. Three classes—Brahmin, Kṣatriya, and Vaiśya—are twice-born; the fourth, Śūdra, has a single birth. There is no fifth. (10.1–4)

This blast reinforces the explanatory power of the theory of mixed classes, which explains the origins of all "subcastes," tribal groups, barbarians, and outcastes as the outcome of mixed-caste unions resulting from dereliction in *dharma*. Even while Manu works out this calculus to new and advanced degrees mainly with regard to communities of the northern plains, he extends the principle to "subcastes" from the north and south and to outsiders such as the Greeks.

As to the four life-stages, one finds an equally fluid situation likewise brought under constraining norms. The four *āśramas* begin more as "life-patterns" than "life-stages." The *dharmasūtras* give them varied names and sequences, and, sometimes disapproving of them, treat them as four different lifelong choices to be made before marriage. *Manu* then promotes the "classical system" in which the four begin with a celibate student stage followed by the stages of householder; forest dweller or anchorite, who may still dwell with his wife; and full renunciant. *Manu* thus staggers the four through a man's lifetime and seeks energetically to suppress the pro-choice position. Meanwhile, the *Mahābhārata* airs both systems, keeping them under debate. And the *Rāmāyaṇa* mentions life-stages explicitly in only one verse, where the exiled Rāma hears that he should return home and rule rather than remain in the forest, since the householder life is superior (*Rāmāyaṇa* 2.98.58). All these texts agree that the householder life is the best, mentioning such reasons as its being the only one prescribed in the Vedas, its supporting *all four* life-patterns, and its being the only one to enable socially responsible human reproduction. The householder who makes the five "great sacrifices" exemplifies Vedic spirituality.

Coming now to the crediting of "Class and Life-stage *Dharma*" to *Manu*, the text never actually mentions it; nor, for that matter, does its first main successor, the *Yājñavalkya Smṛti*. The term seems to have emerged among commentators on these texts, who name it as one of the five or six *dharma* topics they cover: (1) injunctions based on class alone; (2) injunctions concerned directly with life-stage behaviors; (3) rules concerned with their points of intersection; (4) virtues or duties appropriate to personal qualities, such as a king's duty to protect subjects; (5) occasional duties, such as expiation for doing something forbidden; and (6) universally held *dharmas* or virtues such as non-violence and truth. Such an abstract suggests that, prior to the joint consideration of "Class and Life-stage *Dharma*" as topic three, class-*dharma* and life-stage *dharma* each had separate status. This is borne out for the former in the opening question the sages ask Manu, which is only about the classes, including mixed classes: "Please, Lord, tell us precisely and in the proper order the Laws of all the social classes as well as those born in between" (*Manu* 1.2). Life-stage is likewise introduced separately, as we shall see. How *Manu* gets to mentioning the two together might thus be significant.

The verse where *Manu* first joins class and life-stage is revealing. Class *(varṇa)* is a topic from *Manu*'s very beginning, and remains so virtually throughout. But "life-stage" *(āśrama)* emerges only intermittently until it is taken up as the main topic of chapter 6—the only chapter in which class is *not* mentioned. Their first joint mention comes early in chapter 7, the first of *Manu*'s three "innovative" chapters on "the laws pertaining to kings": "The king was created as the protector of people belonging to all classes and life-stages who, according to their rank, are devoted to the law specific to each of them." Clearly, *Manu* introduces the joint topic of "class and life-stage" as belonging to his expanded coverage of the king. In emphatically mentioning "the law specific to each of them," *Manu* is mentioning the concept of *svadharma:* a notion that will "henceforth" entail consideration—indeed, calibration—of the countless ways that class and life-stage would intersect *in a kingdom.*

Manu's seventh chapter in fact begins with a celebrated section on the creation of the king that ends with the verse just cited, for the next verse marks the transition to a new topic, which we will turn to shortly; that is, how a king should spend his day. *Manu* gets to that by telling how Brahmā created the king by "extracting eternal particles" from eight deities associated with the cardinal and intermediate directions;

in his grace and anger, the king is also respectively the Lotus goddess of prosperity, and Death. The passage has often raised the question of whether *Manu* holds the king to be divine, which Manu admits to in a qualified way: "it is a great deity who stands here in human form."

This creation of the king builds up to *Manu*'s first joint mention of class and life-stage by entailing both of them in a most intense passage about the birth also of Daṇḍa, Punishment personified. Daṇḍa is "created" or "issued" just like the king, and possibly before him, which would make Punishment the king's older brother:

> For his [the king's] sake, the Lord formerly created Punishment, his son—the law and protector of all beings—made from the energy of *brahman.* It is the fear of him that makes all beings, both the mobile and the immobile, accede to being used, and they do not deviate from the laws proper to them. The king should administer him appropriately on men who behave improperly, after examining truthfully the place and the time, as well as their power and learning. The king is (in reality) the Man, Punishment; he is the leader; he is the ruler; tradition tells us, he stands as the surety for the law with respect to the four life-stages. Punishment disciplines all the subjects. Punishment alone protects them, and Punishment watches over them as they sleep—Punishment is the law, the wise declare. . . . If the king fails to administer Punishment tirelessly on those who ought to be punished, the stronger would grill the weak like fish on a spit; . . . no one would have any right of ownership; and everything would turn topsy-turvy. . . . All the classes would become corrupted, all the boundaries would be breached; there would be revolt of all the people as a result of blunders committed with respect to Punishment. Wherever Punishment, dark-hued and red-eyed, prowls about as the slayer of evil-doers, there the subjects do not go astray. . . . For Punishment is immense energy, and it cannot be wielded by those with uncultivated selves. It assuredly slays a king who deviates from the law, along with his relatives; then [it] oppresses the fort, the realm, and the mobile and immobile world, as well as the sages and gods dwelling in mid-space.

One can now see that in building up to the verse cited above that pulls class and life-stage together, *Manu* would have Punishment correct two problem areas in seemingly different ways, or at least with what appear to be different motivations.

First, those who deviate from the four life-stages are to be punished after their power and learning is determined. I take the notion of deviants to imply "infidels"—above all Buddhists—having mendicant practices that fall outside the life-stages and lack the right Vedic learning, but also perhaps having some royal backing.

Second, irrespective of learning but with power hanging in the balance, those who breach the boundaries of the four classes from below should be punished lest they give rise to revolt or tumult among the lower classes. Where *Manu* speaks of Punishment protecting the weak in the context of the right of ownership, it is clear that the weak to be protected are primarily Brahmins, whom *Manu* (like all our classical *dharma* texts) systematically exempts from all but the mildest punishments. *Manu* is unparalleled in classical Brahmanical *dharma* texts in the way it puts revolution, and suppressing it, so openly in the air. *Manu*'s Punishment, watching us red-eyed even in our sleep, is something like George Orwell's Big Brother—a point that might bear further consideration as regards the epics whose two kings, Rāma and Yudhiṣṭhira, are elder brothers of a more humanly appealing type whose word is nonetheless law—even, and indeed especially, when it is harsh in its outcome (see chapter 6).

This brings us to *Manu*'s flirtations with narrative regarding the king himself. Two are most prominent: the construction of a fortified capital, and the description of a king's day, along with what he should think during its passing.

We have met *Manu*'s first mention of the royal fort in the passage that describes how unused Punishment boomerangs from the fort and kingdom up to the gods and sages. Soon after this, *Manu* speaks of starting up a fort (which the king could presumably conquer or build). Only after securing a fort "in a region that is dry, abounding in grain, populated mainly by Āryas, healthy, beautiful, with submissive neighbors," and having made nothing more than a "house" for himself, this start-up king should marry and appoint a chaplain and other trusted Brahmin officials. These guidelines have *Mahābhārata* parallels. King Yudhiṣṭhira and his brothers select a similarly salubrious region for their new capital and new bride—though they would not have had "submissive neighbors," since rival cousins ruled the kingdom's other half. This is not to say that *Manu* draws on the *Mahābhārata,* or vice versa. Yet *Manu* knows epic idioms. For instance, why should *Manu*'s king, who has no particular location for his capital, be urged to deploy soldiers "from the lands of the Kurus, Matsyas, Pāñcālas, and Śūrasenas" on his front lines when he goes to battle (7.193)? These are all lands central to the *Mahābhārata* war.

As to the king's ideal day, *Gautama* had applied this theme to the "bath-graduate," who should carry out his daily round pursuing *dharma,* wealth *(artha),* and pleasure *(kāma),* with *dharma* foremost among them. It is the only *dharmasūtra* to mention these three values together, not to mention ranking them as daily pursuits (9.46–49). *Manu* now makes the triple set a consideration of the king's day:

> When a king administers Punishment properly, he flourishes with respect to the triple set.
>
> At midday or midnight, when he is not tired or worn out, he should think on these matters either in consultation with his counselors or alone—on law, wealth, and pleasure, and on how they may be acquired all together when they are in mutual opposition. (7.27; 151–152)

One may wonder that *Manu* should transfer a theme from the bath-graduate to the king. But the *Gautama Dharmasūtra* already brings these two figures together:

> [The bath-graduate] should approach the king for the sake of livelihood, but not anyone else except gods, elders, and law-abiding people. He should try to live in a place well supplied with firewood, water, fodder, [sacred] Kuśa grass, and garland material, served by many roads, inhabited mainly by Āryas, full of energetic people, and ruled by a law-abiding man. (9.63–65)

Manu, however, goes beyond any such practical rationale for bringing the bath-graduate and the king together. Making one surprising twist, he treats them both in the same way as characters whom he addresses by usages of a verbal root meaning "to think." This allows Manu to tell kings and bath-graduates—and them alone—not only what they should do but what they "should *think.*"

Manu's fourth chapter on the bath-graduate clusters these usages in something of a sequence. First, the bath-graduate "should wake up at the Brahmā hour and should think on law and wealth"; next, where the question of suspending Vedic recitation has come up, he is told of untoward circumstances where "he should not think of it even in his mind"; and the very last instruction to the bath-graduate, who has just been told how to retire peacefully and leave everything to his son, tells him:

> Living alone in a secluded place, he should think always on what is beneficial to himself; for by reflecting alone, he attains supreme bliss.

As the last of these three points makes clear, *Manu*'s bath-graduate is no longer just a young man who has finished his Vedic study at the home of a guru, bathed, and returned to his parental home, optimally to marry. He has stayed home as the ideal householder until ready to retire, having produced a son. Manu rounds off his classical prescription that the life-stages be taken up in sequence and without choice by giving the bath-graduate lifelong status. His purifying bath is made good for a lifetime.

As to *Manu*'s king, he is told what he should think five times, first in a section on warfare in two epigrammatic verses that are all but identical with two verses found in the *Mahabhārata*'s postwar instructions to King Yudhiṣṭhira on "*Dharma* for Times of Distress" (*Mahābhārata* 12.138.24–25):

> He must not let the enemy discover any weakness of his, but discover any weakness of the enemy; he should hide his limbs like a tortoise and conceal his own weak points. He should think over his affairs like a heron, dart off like a rabbit, snatch like a wolf, and attack like a lion.

Herons supposedly think a lot while they stand still waiting to pounce on a fish. Second, already noted, once the king's day is underway and he can find some time for it, either at noon or at midnight, "he should think" with his counsellors or alone over the complexities of the triple set. He gets similar advice on how to strategize regarding the "circle of neighboring kings," and how, after his afternoon meal, "he should relax in his private quarters with his women, and after relaxing, once again he should think at the proper time about his affairs." It is a day-long round of near-constant vigilance. Within the legal tradition, it is thus one of *Manu*'s "new fictions" that kings "should think" about *dharma.* With this crypto-narrative device, Manu gets his teachings not only under the king's skin but into his head.

It should be no surprise to find this usage in the *Mahābhārata,* or to discover that its main appearance there is in instructions to King Yudhiṣṭhira, as in the line about the heron (Yudhiṣṭhira chooses to call himself "Heron" for the year he must spend in disguise). In both texts, everything the king "should think" is a *dharma*-topic, though of course Yudhiṣṭhira has more than a day to think about it. In the *Mahābhārata* this usage is a character-building device and a means to instill the king with appropriate spiritual virtues, which we shall see him draw on in chapter 6. *Manu,* on the other hand, uses it to give narrative form to a nameless, silent, and neutral king who has no character at all and who would get his virtues only secondhand. Just before turning to the law of kings, Manu summarizes his wisdom on virtues by formulating the *dharma* of ten virtuous qualities that pertain to Brahmins in all four life-stages: "resolve, forbearance, self-control, refraining from theft, performing purifications, mastering the organs, understanding, learning, truthfulness, and suppressing anger" (6.91–97). The epics will make these qualities inherent to the royal life.

Manu's king thus has some narrative and ethical potential, but only by default. He is a king through whom *Manu* can fashion a model that could apply to all kings, little and grand. No matter how we date the *Mahābhārata* relative to *Manu,* we should not fail to appreciate the latter's originality here. *Manu* projects a fairly grand monarch in the divine infusions that go into the original king's creation, and in this hint at monarchy on a hereditary and potentially dynastic scale: "A king, though a mere child, must never be treated with disrespect, thinking he is just a human being" (7.8). *Manu* also says the king is, or makes, the age (9.301–302). But for the most part, his king keeps a "small-scale" profile. *Manu* positions him with start-up capital, not even married before he establishes himself as a king, on an insecure throne. Much as with the bath-graduate, marriage is among the first orders of business, and with that, including

Pleasure in his balancing of the triple set. To enable these portrayals and give direction to their intersecting paths, *Manu* adds a chief trait for each: for the bath-graduate, a lifelong title to twice-born purity that comes from his initiatory bath; and for the king, a ruling that he can wield the rod of punishment with "statutory purity" or "instant purification," leaving him unaffected by the impurity of bloodshed. Says *Manu:* "The taint of impurity does not affect kings, those undertaking observances, and those engaged in sacrificial sessions; for they are seated on the seat of Indra and are ever one with *brahman*" (5.93). So that the king can exercise the violence necessary to the *dharma* of kings, he is given a purity even more sweeping than the Brahmin's. I would suggest that this ascription of lifelong purity to both the bath-graduate and the king allows us to identify the limiting feature by which *Manu* makes them both role models for "dharmic thinking."

Both the *Mahābhārata* and *Manu* also want their start-up kings not to be upstarts, but this calls for them at least to be Kṣatriyas. Yet all our Brahmanical *dharma* texts would know a "real world" in which "real Vedic" Kṣatriya kings had, for centuries, already been hard to find. In effect, with only minimal help from the *dharmasūtras,* the two epics and *Manu* had to reinvent the Vedic Kṣatriya king if he was to have more than local importance. Whereas the *Gautama Dharmasūtra* urges that the bath-graduate live in a kingdom "inhabited mainly by Āryas, full of energetic people, and ruled by a law-abiding man" (9.65), *Manu* warns his bath-graduate not to "live in a kingdom ruled by a Śūdra, teeming with lawbreaking people, overrun by people belonging to heretical ascetic sects, or swamped by low-born people" (4.61). Nor should his bath-graduate accept gifts from a king who "follows a wrong śāstra" (4.87)—probably referring to heterodox scriptures.

Manu's orchestration of a rapport between the bath-graduate and the king plays on a theme that was crucial to the way Brahmanical culture distinguished itself from the heterodoxies, that is, with the still-wider rapport between the Brahmin and the king. For classical Brahmanical authors, such a mode of self-distinction was both a necessity and a matter of choice as to how to go about theorizing *dharma* and personalizing it through stories. It was necessary in that the heterodoxies did not concede superiority to the Brahmin, and it was a matter of choice where it came to making the king so pivotal, and not only the king but the urgency of his being a Kṣatriya with Vedic credentials. The heterodoxies had no qualms about non-Kṣatriya kings and had nothing at stake in tracing that class back to the Veda.

CHAPTER 6

Two *Dharma* Biographies?

Rāma and Yudhiṣṭhira

The question mark in this chapter's title looks ahead to chapter 10. There I will argue that our last classical *dharma* text, the *Buddhacarita* or "Adventure of the Buddha," offers a critical reading of both the *Mahābhārata* and the *Rāmāyaṇa*. As mentioned in chapter 1, where all three works were briefly summarized, Aśvaghoṣa, the *Buddhacarita*'s poet, was familiar with both epics. He portrays the Buddha as finding many ways to speak of *dharma*, but one of the most important is that he uses the *Mahābhārata*'s term *mokṣadharma*, "laws of salvation," for the pursuit of *nirvāṇa*. In brief, when the Buddha-to-be says "there is no such thing as a wrong time for *dharma*," meaning the quest for *nirvāṇa* (*Buddhacarita* 6.21), both Rāma and Yudhiṣṭhira fail to realize this, according to Aśvaghoṣa, because they are caught up in the particulars of Brahmanical *dharma*.

A preliminary picture of Rāma and Yudhiṣṭhira's *dharma* biographies can be given in outline in relation to the similar ways their royal lives are structured through each epic's organization into "books." I present a template shared by both epics that will be fleshed out further in chapter 7, when we focus on the two epics' queens. Capitalized words identify themes the books share in common. In each epic,

- Book 1 begins with Frame Stories that make the poets characters in their own poems and tell how the poem is composed and transmitted. A Dynastic History leads to a set of brothers as the lead male characters. These are Rāma and his three brothers in the *Rāmāyaṇa*. In the *Mahābhārata*, it is the Pāṇḍava heroes (the five sons of Pāṇḍu), of whom one needs to remember the three eldest—Yudhiṣṭhira, Bhīma, and Arjuna—and recall that their mother, Kuntī, secretly bore another son before she was married;

that son is Karṇa, who sides with the Pāṇḍavas' paternal cousins and rivals, the hundred Kauravas led by Duryodhana. Rāma marries Sītā. All five Pāṇḍavas marry Draupadī.

- Book 2 then describes a pivotal Court Intrigue resulting in exile. In the *Rāmāyaṇa* it unfolds around a rivalry between two co-wives of Rāma's father; Rāma, Sītā, and one brother, Lakṣmaṇa, depart, while another brother, Bharata, remains in the capital to rule in Rāma's stead. In the *Mahābhārata* it culminates in a dice match; the Pāṇḍavas and Draupadī depart, while King Duryodhana takes over their half of the kingdom.
- Book 3 then tells of Forest Exiles: fourteen years for Rāma and company; twelve for the Pāṇḍavas and Draupadī. The exiled kings receive Instructive Guidance from Great Sages, and there are attempts to abduct their wives—in the *Rāmāyaṇa* a successful abduction of Sītā by the demon Rāvaṇa. After Monstrous Encounters (in Yudhiṣṭhira's case with his father Dharma disguised as a murderous goblin), the heroes return to society (in Rāma's case a society of monkeys).
- Book 4 is about Inversions. Rāma gets involved with the upside-down world of the monkeys' capital, in which the royal monkey brothers play out a reverse image of Rāma's own story of exile, wife-abduction, and fraternal rivalry for the throne. The Pāṇḍavas assume topsy-turvy disguises in the kingdom of "Fish"—Yudhiṣṭhira under the name "Heron," an eater of fish.
- Book 5 is about "Efforts" made in Preparation for War—by all the monkeys and Rāma in the *Rāmāyaṇa*, and by both sides in the *Mahābhārata*. A Divine Messenger—Rāma's devoted monkey Hanumān in one epic, Kṛṣṇa in the other—goes into the Enemy Camp, where he Reveals an Overpowering Nature while upstaging Attempts to Hold Him Captive.
- *Rāmāyaṇa* 6 and *Mahābhārata* 6–11 are War Books.
- *Rāmāyaṇa* 7 and *Mahābhārata* 12–18 provide the Denouements and return to the frames. Here the two kings' *dharma* biographies are handled very differently. Once their main exploits are over, Rāma becomes the primary listener to his own adventure, whereas Yudhiṣṭhira goes on learning more and more about being a Dharma King.

As the differences show, the common blueprint belongs mainly to Books 1–5, which means that one text must have established it. In drawing such a conclusion, one must bear in mind that the comparison is complicated by Yudhiṣṭhira's relation in the *Mahābhārata* to Kṛṣṇa, the avatar or incarnation of the principal deity Viṣṇu. In the *Rāmāyaṇa,* Rāma is likewise Viṣṇu incarnate. That is one source of his perfection and truth, however unbeknownst it may be to him. Whereas Kṛṣṇa knows and indeed occasionally confirms his divinity, Rāma must consider himself human until he has killed Rāvaṇa because Rāvaṇa can be killed only by a man. Uncomfortable though it has always been to modern readers, one of the implications of Rāma's not knowing that he is really divine until Brahmā tells him so twice is that he must have a split personality. His *dharma* biography as a human is ruptured at these two points, both of which occur after he has killed Rāvaṇa and submitted Sītā to ordeals because he or others doubted that she would have been chaste with Rāvaṇa. Even after Sītā leaves the world forever rather than submit to the second ordeal, Rāma's human life is depicted as going on without ostensible reflection on his divinity. Yudhiṣṭhira, on the other hand, must puzzle his way to truths in relation to a divinity whose advice is not only subtle but shady and often withheld from him, and who often, I dare say, simply cannot be believed. In this regard, each epic works out what I will call a politics of *bhakti,* or "devotion": in the *Rāmāyaṇa* through a master–servant dialectic centered on exaltation of a divine king all should serve, obviously including monkeys; in the *Mahābhārata,* a politics of friendship where Kṛṣṇa is ultimately "a friend alike to friend and foe." Kṛṣṇa is particularly the spiritual friend of Draupadī and of Arjuna, who hears the *Bhagavad Gītā* or "Song of the Lord" from Kṛṣṇa and gets much more advice from him than Yudhiṣṭhira does. We shall look further into *bhakti* and its bearing on *dharma* in our remaining chapters. In this one, while considering *dharma* as the legal and ethical tangle through which the two epics' kings find their way through moral and spiritual dilemmas, we will be getting to know Sītā and Draupadī for chapter 7 and Arjuna for chapter 8.

This chapter will concentrate on Rāma and Yudhiṣṭhira's parts in killings in the two scenes where the morality of their doing so comes most into question: Rāma's killing the monkey king Vālin from ambush, and

Yudhiṣṭhira's lying to enable the killing of the Brahmin Droṇa. In this I confess a bias. I find Rāma's self-exoneration unconvincing, whereas Yudhiṣṭhira has a complex defense that is waiting to be made.

There is a tradition of comparing these two episodes. An early comparison is interpolated into the *Mahābhārata* itself in the aftermath of Yudhiṣṭhira's lie and Droṇa's death. There Arjuna tells Yudhiṣṭhira, "As with Rāma in the killing of Vālin, so in bringing about the fall of Droṇa the ill fame will stay long in this triple world" (*Mahābhārata* 7.1375* lines 1–2). Such an interpolation suggests that a tradition of focusing on the episodes together emerged after the two epics had come to be widely seen as complementary. But the point is not to make a direct comparison between these asymmetrical scenes: one a martial act with an arrow shot to kill a monkey king, the other a verbal act of lying to abet killing a Brahmin; one done before the *Rāmāyaṇa* war, the other during the *Mahābhārata* war. Rather it is to see how these two *dharma* biographies (to the extent that they are such) are constructed with such famous sins made so prominent in the telling.

I must be brief with Rāma, and save comparison for the end. Rāma befriends the younger of the two royal monkey-brothers, Sugrīva, an exiled king like himself, who wants to kill his older brother Vālin, from whose standpoint Sugrīva had come to the throne only as a usurper. Without questioning either brother, Rāma hears Sugrīva's dubious stories about how Vālin recovered his throne from him and forced him into exile. Rāma then tells Sugrīva to challenge Vālin to single combat, and shoots Vālin from ambush. Against the dying Vālin's complaints that Rāma bears the banner of *dharma* unrighteously, Rāma has only dubious replies, even though the text and its commentators certainly honor them. Among them are: Rāma acts as the proxy of his younger brother, King Bharata, in that princes go about the world guarding *dharma;* Vālin is only a monkey and cannot understand *dharma,* yet deserves the rod of punishment for the sin of taking his brother's wife; Rāma had promised Sugrīva that he would kill Vālin and his truth is unexceptionable—indeed, he has already promised it; "Men seeking meat shoot animals that are attentive or inattentive or even facing the other way, and there is nothing wrong with this"; and finally, kings should not be harmed or censured as "they are gods in human form going about on earth" (*Rāmāyaṇa* 4.17–18). We do not know whether it is Rāma's divine or human side that is speaking, and neither does he. And perhaps that uncertainty leaves him less subject to criticism. My impression is that this grab bag of arguments, which are strict to the extreme in their rationalizations of "punishment" in the name of *dharma,* are implicitly left open to further questioning by listeners and readers who are not monkeys.

That Rāma can invoke his truthfulness in the killing of Vālin even in support of an ethically dubious and self-serving promise is testimony to his reputation for this virtue, on which his exemplification of *dharma* unquestionably stands. Rāma's *dharma* biography revolves around upholding not only his own truth but his father's. In the *Rāmāyaṇa,* no virtue is higher. It is a different matter in the *Mahābhārata,* which resists universalizing any virtue and always has a contextual answer when someone asks, What is the highest *dharma?* There are, however, three leading answers to this question: non-cruelty, truth, and nonviolence. The story of Droṇa's killing brings each into play. The ambiguities call on us to get to know a few new epic characters, beginning with Karṇa.

Truth and Other Virtues: Where Good Men Are Hard to Find

Ever since the dice match set its contestants on a collision course toward war, Yudhiṣṭhira has been obsessed by Karṇa, who is fighting against the Pāṇḍavas for their Kaurava foes, and is their best hope of killing Arjuna. As war approaches, Yudhiṣṭhira conspires to have Karṇa's fighting undermined. Yet unbeknownst to him, even though it is made known to Karṇa by both Kṛṣṇa and Kuntī before the war, Karṇa is the Pāṇḍavas' elder brother. Kuntī bore him while she was still an unmarried girl and abandoned him at birth, to be raised in a low-caste carpenter family.

Karṇa has been called a tragic hero. As Kṛṣṇa puts it—with terrible irony—after Karṇa's death: "He who announced Draupadī won by dice" was "the vilest of good men" (*Mahābhārata* 8.69.17). This term is used consistently for Karṇa and for no one else. Yudhiṣṭhira is never called a "good man," although before the dice match he was naive enough to chide his opponent about the deceitfulness of gambling and say, "the vow of a good man" is to undertake "honest, uncrooked war" (2.53.6–8). Nor is Arjuna ever called one. Indeed, when Arjuna is about to kill Karṇa, Karṇa says to him, "Having seen this wheel of mine swallowed by fate, Arjuna, abandon the intention practiced by a lowly man" (8.66.61)—the very opposite of a "good man." Karṇa aspires to be a "good man" by showing "non-cruelty" even to the mother who abandoned him (5.149.19), and is said to have been one because he was always extraordinarily "giving" (8.68.44). These are exemplary royal virtues, but Karṇa seems to be singled out because he is good without the benefit of high social station. That the *Mahābhārata* invests such energy in an exemplary good man of low station means that there may be others of his kind whose mistreatment and killing might trouble the conscience of a fairly good king.

Two low-status characters of this type figure in the episode that precedes the death of Droṇa. One, killed just before it, is Bhīma's son Ghaṭotkaca, whom he sired with a forest demoness before he married Draupadī. The other is a lowly "tribal" named Ekalavya. Neither is ever called a "good man," but both exhibit extraordinary loyalty and generosity, like Karṇa.

The sub-book before "The Death of Droṇa" recounts a terrifying night battle (*Mahābhārata* 7.129–154). Bhīma's son's demonic powers grow so great at night that Duryodhana presses Karṇa to kill him by using up a one-use weapon he was saving for Arjuna—all of which Kṛṣṇa has a hand in engineering. Kṛṣṇa tells Arjuna he will now be able to kill Karṇa, and adds that several other foes, including Ekalavya, "were one after another all slain by diverse means for your sake by me." Kṛṣṇa says he killed these foes because, had they sided with Duryodhana, he could have conquered the earth:

> For your sake the tribal's son, whose prowess was true, who was incapable of being baffled, was deprived of his thumb by Droṇa, assuming the position of his preceptor, by an act of guile. . . . With his thumb, Ekalavya was incapable of being vanquished. . . . For your sake he was slain by me at the van of battle.

Kṛṣṇa thus reminds Arjuna of Droṇa's guile and cruelty in getting this young tribal to give Droṇa his thumb as something done for Arjuna's sake, as was killing Ghaṭotkaca. Ekalavya's disablement was really prompted by Arjuna, who, in his youthful training in arms, felt threatened that Ekalavya would replace him as Droṇa's best disciple. This reminiscence complicates any view of Droṇa and Arjuna's motivations in the Droṇa-killing episode.

Kṛṣṇa also adds that Ghaṭotkaca hated Brahmins and that Kṛṣṇa would have killed him too if no one else did for the sake of upholding *dharma*. Kṛṣṇa is making all this up about Bhīma's son's *adharma* and hatred of Brahmins. When the Pāṇḍavas were in exile and Bhīma called on him to carry Draupadī on his back to fly her over a mountain, his *dharma* was underscored and he even carried the Pāṇḍavas' attending Brahmins on his back along with her (3.144–145)!

Here I begin to make two arguments. First, Yudhiṣṭhira's complicity in the death of Droṇa has not been sufficiently understood because no one has taken account of this interim sequence. Second, his part in killing Droṇa now begins to be intertwined with his desire to kill Karṇa because Arjuna seems dilatory in fighting either of them.

To move ahead, however, I must say a few words in advance on the *Bhagavad Gītā*. First, it is inappropriate to think that Kṛṣṇa's advice should always be squared with what he says there to Arjuna. Kṛṣṇa is quite capable of talking out of different sides of his mouth to different people. What he has to say to Arjuna in the *Gītā* is for a particular time and place, and is neither his once-and-for-all pronouncement to Arjuna nor his one-cut-for all-sizes message to everyone else in the *Mahābhārata*. Thus, second, even if one grants that Arjuna gets Kṛṣṇa's most carefully considered spiritual teachings in the *Gītā*, those teachings do not let Arjuna off the hook for his actions and especially his inactions in battle. Many think Arjuna deserves a free pass for having heard the *Gītā* and continued to act on it to the minimal extent that he always heeds the battle advice of Kṛṣṇa, his divine charioteer. But as we shall see, once Droṇa is killed, Arjuna will admit to *in*action out of the desire *for* fruits, the very inverse of one of Kṛṣṇa's main *Gītā* teachings. Yudhiṣṭhira, on the other hand, is usually left to his own resources in the *Mahābhārata* war, except when he is fortunate enough to hear from Kṛṣṇa or from that other unimpeachable authority, his special prompter, Vyāsa: the *Mahābhārata*'s author. Vyāsa now makes just such an appearance before Yudhiṣṭhira in the dead of night right at the hinge between the two episodes.

Yudhiṣṭhira has just questioned Kṛṣṇa and Arjuna's delay in fighting Droṇa and Karṇa, and protested their failure to protect Ghaṭotkaca, whose death he laments. He then sets off to fight Karṇa to avenge Ghaṭotkaca. Since Yudhiṣṭhira has no chance of success in this, Kṛṣṇa tells Arjuna they had better watch him, which they do at a distance. Vyāsa sees Yudhiṣṭhira speeding toward Karṇa and tells him some, but not all, of what Kṛṣṇa has *not* told him: by good luck Arjuna is still alive; by good luck Ghaṭotkaca was slain, indeed on your behalf as well:

> "In five days the Earth will be yours! And always, O tiger among men, just keep thinking about *dharma!* Highly pleased, Pāṇḍava, let yourself resort to non-cruelty, austerity, generosity, forbearance, and truth. Where *dharma* is there is victory." Having so spoken to the Pāṇḍava, Vyāsa disappeared right there.

Non-cruelty is the first virtue mentioned, truth the last. Coming from the author, I believe we are within reason to take this as a set of virtues concerned with what one philosopher calls "the values of truth," and see it as a framework for Yudhiṣṭhira's actions in killing Droṇa, which now becomes the focus of the fighting.

What can we learn about non-cruelty, and how Yudhiṣṭhira comes by this ethical value? The *Mahābhārata* relates it to a primary context in the family, and since it tells a story about kings, it is saying something distinctive about the *dharma* of kings. For a king, non-cruelty is a family value in the largest spiritual sense, one that honors the bonds that connect humans and animals, the living and the dead, and ultimately, all forms of life through the spiritual presence that permeates all beings. When Yudhiṣṭhira's father Dharma, disguised as a monstrous goblin, asks Yudhiṣṭhira what is the "highest *dharma,*" Yudhiṣṭhira chooses "non-cruelty," and Dharma endorses this choice after revealing his paternal identity. It is a "creature-feeling" that extends "across the great divides": of those of high and low standing, as in Yudhiṣṭhira's feeling for his brother Bhīma's lowly son Ghaṭotkaca.

As with Kṛṣṇa's reminding Arjuna of the lowly tribal Ekalavya, then, I take Vyāsa's words about "non-cruelty" to hang over Droṇa's killing. If Arjuna has listened to Kṛṣṇa, he might want to spare his benefactor Droṇa. If Yudhiṣṭhira has listened to the author, he might find grounds to kill Droṇa by putting non-cruelty before truth.

The battle over Droṇa now begins with the resumption of the night fighting. Droṇa opposes the Pāñcālas, Draupadī's people. Through her marriage, they are the Pāṇḍavas' closest allies. Their leading fighters are Draupadī's twin brother and her aged father. The father and Droṇa have feuded since they were young men.

Kṛṣṇa now tells Arjuna to position himself to fight Droṇa and Karṇa. Bhīma seconds this, calling Arjuna "Bībhatsu": a name of his that can mean the Repugnant One, "the one who is averse to something," which can be suggestive when Arjuna is averse to fighting Droṇa and Karṇa. Bhīma says that if Arjuna dawdles, it would be a non-cruelty and an untruth:

> O Arjuna, Arjuna Bībhatsu, listen to my word truly. . . . If at this time you do not strive to win the good, . . . you will do a non-cruelty. Pay with vigor the debt you owe to truth, prosperity, *dharma,* and fame.

Bhīma's call for Arjuna to override non-cruelty in the name of truth is a reminder and reversal of Vyāsa's words to Yudhiṣṭhira. Yudhiṣṭhira should heed five virtues with non-cruelty first; Arjuna should dismiss non-cruelty and heed four other values headed by the truth of his martial vows. If Arjuna is disposed toward non-cruelty now, it can only be toward Droṇa. And Bhīma is saying that this is a cruelty towards their mother and brothers, not to mention the Pāñcālas, that would amount to a lie should he continue in it. Here we see a deeper level of Arjuna's complicity with Droṇa over the disabling of Ekalavya. Droṇa had Ekalavya cut off his thumb not only so that Arjuna would be Droṇa's best disciple but so that Arjuna would help Droṇa avenge himself against Draupadī's father.

Still at night, Droṇa, avoiding Arjuna, starts mowing down the Pāñcālas, killing their aged king. When the sun rises, Draupadī's brother swears he will avenge his father by killing Droṇa today. Yudhiṣṭhira rallies his forces, but all are fearful that Arjuna lacks commitment to fight Droṇa.

Kṛṣṇa now makes a pitch to have someone lie. In effect, he is screening Arjuna from the charge of not pitching in. Arjuna does not approve Kṛṣṇa's counsel, but the rest approve, Yudhiṣṭhira with difficulty, whereupon Bhīma goes off and kills an elephant with the same name as Droṇa's son, Aśvatthāman. One would think others would know what Bhīma does, but apparently they do not! Bhīma kills the elephant, it seems, to give himself an excuse to tell Droṇa that "Aśvatthāman" is dead. Bhīma then says to Droṇa, apparently without others in earshot, and "with some bashfulness," "Aśvatthāman has been slain."

Droṇa does not believe Bhīma and returns to killing Pāñcālas. Seeing Droṇa acting "for the non-existence of the Kṣatriyas," the Seven Sages and various other heavenly beings, desirous of leading Droṇa to the world of Brahmā, now say he is acting contrary to *dharma;* such highly cruel *karma* does not befit a Brahmin enjoined by the *dharma* of truth. He should lay down his weapons. Droṇa becomes downcast and asks Yudhiṣṭhira whether his son is "not slain or slain," as he had hoped for truth from Yudhiṣṭhira since he was a boy. Not mincing words, he puts Yudhiṣṭhira on the spot not only to tell the truth and to tell it now, but *to say that Bhīma is not a liar.*

Knowledgeable listeners could now recall a scene where Bhīma upheld Yudhiṣṭhira's truth even when it was most doubtful. At the climax of the gambling match, when Draupadī asked whether Yudhiṣṭhira had bet himself before he bet her, which she knew he had, Yudhiṣṭhira kept silent. When Duryodhana called for his answer, Bhīma, showing deference to his elder brother, a "guru," said that as the "lord" and "owner" of all the Pāṇḍavas' merits and austerities, Yudhiṣṭhira was within rights to wager Draupadī even after he had wagered himself. Arjuna, however, suggested that Yudhiṣṭhira would no longer have been master of anyone once he had bet and lost himself (2.60–63). Now, facing Droṇa's question, Yudhiṣṭhira is once again well aware of the demands of truth, but this time silence is not an option. But if he listens to the author and puts non-cruelty before truth, he does have the choice of the lesser of two cruelties. It is better to slay Droṇa than to make Bhīma a liar. Each side of this equation must be weighed. Droṇa is on a terrible rampage killing Pāñcālas, and is doing so with a somewhat illicit weapon. Meanwhile, Bhīma is not only Yudhiṣṭhira's most loyal brother; *he has just lost his son.*

Kṛṣna now tells Yudhiṣṭhira "truly" that if Droṇa fights for half a day Yudhiṣṭhira's army will be annihilated:

> Save us, honored one, from Droṇa. Falsehood would be better than truth. By telling an untruth for saving a life, one is not touched by sin.

Kṛṣṇa may not be too credible when he says that Droṇa can now do in half a day what he had put off for fourteen, but his subordination of truth to saving life is consistent with other passages in the *Mahābhārata,* and can be squared here with Yudhiṣṭhira's chosen value of non-cruelty. Yudhiṣṭhira does not act directly on Kṛṣṇa's prompting but only after Bhīma fills in what *he* has done. As soon as Bhīma heard the means, he killed an elephant named Aśvatthāman: "I then went to Droṇa and told him, 'Aśvatthāman has been slain, Brahmin! So stop fighting'" (102). We get the impression that this is news to both Kṛṣṇa and Yudhiṣṭhira. Kṛṣṇa is still asking, ostensibly, that Yudhiṣṭhira tell a straight lie, even if it is "with difficulty." It is what Bhīma has done that gives Yudhiṣṭhira the added urgency to do it "with difficulty" *now.* While Bhīma is simply telling the truth as to what he did, he encumbers Yudhiṣṭhira with a further complication: What to say about the elephant! Bhīma tells how Droṇa didn't believe him and presses Yudhiṣṭhira to tell him the same:

> As you are desirous of victory, accept the words of Govinda. . . . In this world of men you are reputed to be truthful.

At the words of Bhīma and Kṛṣṇa and because of "destiny," "sinking in fear of untruth but addicted to victory," Yudhiṣṭhira indistinctly said "elephant" when he pronounced "killed" (he does not mention Aśvatthāman by name), and his chariot touched the ground. Droṇa now hears this disagreeable word repeated by Bhīma, who tells him that Brahmins should stick to their own jobs rather than engage in fighting; reminds him that as a man learned in *Brahman,* he should know that "nonviolence *(ahiṃsā)* to all creatures" is the highest *dharma;* and says he should not doubt Yudhiṣṭhira's word. Becoming dejected, Droṇa restrains his celestial weapons, and Draupadī's brother beheads him.

There now follows a closing sub-book on recriminations and further fighting (7.166–173). Arjuna, even after charging Yudhiṣṭhira with the unrighteous killing of Droṇa, admits "Droṇa was neglected by me even though he was being killed because of my desire for the kingdom." Aśvatthāman, who had been elsewhere during his father's beheading, calls Yudhiṣṭhira a "flag-waver of *dharma*" or hypocrite; this "'Dharma king' made the teacher surrender his weapons by fraud." Later, he says Yudhiṣṭhira resorted "to the garb of *dharma*." On the other hand, Draupadī's brother says Yudhiṣṭhira did *not* lie: "Calling himself a Brahmin, Droṇa summoned an illusion *(māyā)* of an unendurable kind, and by an illusion has he today been killed, Arjuna, what is improper in this?" To kill such a warmongering Brahmin is nothing but *dharma:* "The eldest Pāṇḍava is not untruthful! I am not lawbreaking, Arjuna. The sinner slain was a disciple-hater!" The charge of disciple-hater could remind Arjuna of how Droṇa treated Ekalavya. Meanwhile, it begins to look like Draupadī's brother appreciates Yudhiṣṭhira's linguistic improvisation as something that would fit Vyāsa's advice to put non-cruelty before truth. Fully cognizant of the moral difficulty in following through on the advice of the master illusionist Kṛṣṇa, Yudhiṣṭhira upheld the truth of Bhīma and arrested the unendurable slaughter of the Pāñcālas.

The *Mahābhārata*'s three "highest *dharmas*" have now all been under review. Non-cruelty remains the ideal for a king, even trumping truth. Nonviolence is mentioned when Bhīma wants Droṇa to lay down his weapons and reminds him that he should consider it "the highest *dharma*"—for Brahmins. But in the same context, the Seven Sages had told Droṇa that a Brahmin should be responsive to the *dharma* of truth. The *Mahābhārata* puts its most decisive twist on *ahiṃsā* into the mouth of a virtuous meat salesman, whose assessment is related to Yudhiṣṭhira in the forest:

> Surely what was said by those astonished men of old was, "Nonviolence!" Who in this world does not harm living beings? Having given it much consideration, no one in the world does nonviolence. Even ascetics devoted to nonviolence surely do violence, although by their effort it may be lessened. (3.199.28–29)

At best *ahiṃsā* is a noble ideal that can be implemented only selectively, as when a Brahmin may be urged to relinquish his weapons. Vyāsa could not have recommended it to Yudhiṣṭhira in the heat of battle as he did non-cruelty. Yet truth should override non-cruelty for the pure Kṣatriya Arjuna where non-cruelty allows him to evade battle out of "repugnance" to fight his guru.

The tensions between these values continue to unfold as each of the three oldest Pāṇḍavas has his final say about Droṇa's killing. Having listened to Arjuna denounce him and Bhīma defend him, Yudhiṣṭhira speaks for the first time since muttering "elephant." Seeing his fighters listless, in despairing words that brim with stinging rebukes for what he has had to hear particularly from Arjuna, and also with seeming sarcasm for Kṛṣṇa who has likewise said nothing since he urged Yudhiṣṭhira to lie, he tells his remaining Pāñcāla allies and Kṛṣṇa's kinsmen they may as well go home and flee the fighting:

> *Dharma*-souled Kṛṣṇa will also make himself safe. He is competent to instruct the world, what more himself! . . . Let the desire of this Bībhatsu [Arjuna] succeed quickly with regard to me. The preceptor of fine conduct has been felled by me in battle, . . . who did supreme high goodheartedness to us—(now that Droṇa is) slain, for his sake I will die with my kinsmen.

Yudhiṣṭhira accepts fault in bringing about the death of this guru, but paints his "goodheartedness" to the Pāṇḍavas, which Arjuna has kept touting, as a fraud. All the while pointedly saying that the current impasse is in some way an outcome of Arjuna's desire, he recalls matters that would sting Arjuna most, including Droṇa's part in killing one of Arjuna's sons.

Finally, dueling with Aśvatthāman, Arjuna insults him despite their "great respect and affection for each other." Asked about this, the narrator explains that Arjuna was

> pierced to the vitals by Yudhiṣṭhira's words, and when an inner breaking was produced, having been reminded of that grief, lord, Bībhatsu's wrath arose from that grief as had never been before. Therefore, he addressed Droṇa's son unworthily, coarsely, disagreeably, the preceptor's son who was worthy of honor, harshly like a lowly man.

Arjuna is brought to behave as a "lowly man," just as he will two days later, at least according to Karṇa, when he shoots Karṇa from advantage.

Rāma and Yudhiṣṭhira: Some Comparative Points

Karṇa's charge that Arjuna would be a "lowly man" in shooting him at a disadvantage might suggest that we should be comparing the sins of Rāma and Arjuna rather than those of Rāma and Yudhiṣṭhira. The killings of Vālin and Karṇa are certainly an iconic and structural pair. Both are deemed lowly when shot at a disadvantage. The opponents in each case have the same divine parents, but crisscrossed: Arjuna and Vālin are sons of Indra; Karṇa and Sugrīva are sons of the Sun god. An incarnation of Viṣṇu in each case provides the justifications. Whatever else that comparison might lead us to by itself, it is illuminating for the mirror it holds up to the comparison of Rāma with Yudhiṣṭhira.

One thing it tells us is that both epics take pains not to portray either king as a lowly man. Another is that the reasons for sensing affinities between these acts of Rāma and Yudhiṣṭhira lie not in the acts themselves but in the language used in accusing them. A third is that unlike either Yudhiṣṭhira or Arjuna, only Rāma feels called upon to defend himself. Fourth, only Yudhiṣṭhira admits guilt, that is, admits himself accountable as a sinner. To do something with difficulty is to do so having considered the consequences and been willing to suffer them. Whether the word "elephant" came out impulsively because of an inner inclination to truth, or because he improvised an illusion of truth that satisfied some verbal scruple, he can be said to have recognized the difficulty and put non-cruelty before truth, as the author had told him to do.

Rāma, of course, does not put non-cruelty above truth or have his words ever challenged. He also gets away with numerous cruelties unchallenged, unless it is by Sītā and the *Rāmāyaṇa* poet Vālmīki (see chapter 7), or vainly by Vālin; and he is never called upon to weigh truth against these cruelties. It just trumps them. We hear about him as he hears about himself, only from Vālmīki. With Yudhiṣṭhira, his cruelties and non-cruelties are for all to weigh, including himself. If extenuating circumstances should lighten Yudhiṣṭhira's sentence, the loss of his chariot's air cushion and a brief agonizing look at Hell before he finally reaches Heaven at life's end seem just about right. I assume that these are effects of an "author function." Though recent historical comparisons leave a bit to be desired, we might compare

Yudhiṣṭhira's elephantine lie and subsequent punishment with Bill Clinton's "I did not have sex with that woman, Monica Lewinsky" dodge, whereas Rāma gets off with instant legislation about a monkey similar to the decision U.S. courts worked out to exempt Chiquita Banana executives who subcontracted paramilitaries to kill union leaders in Colombia—or, more to the point, the run of retroactive decisions that the imperial Bush presidency obtained to abet corporate and private immunities to international law.

With Yudhiṣṭhira we have a rare kind of man in the Indian epics. The prevailing idea, which Rāma and Arjuna—or better, Rāma, Arjuna, and Kṛṣṇa—exemplify to the hilt, is that the knowing Self knows itself not to be accountable for staining acts. The compound "of stainless acts," reserved for men, is used mainly for these three characters, and for Rāma in both epics. What is striking about Yudhiṣṭhira is that even though he hears of this no-fault clause in stories told to him while he is in the forest, when it comes to thinking through matters in terms of *dharma,* as is his wont, he seems to have no use for it. Yudhiṣṭhira's *dharma* biography comes from within. Unlike Rāma's, and like the Buddha's, it is one of moral and spiritual reflection.

CHAPTER 7

Two *Dharma* Biographies?

Sītā and Draupadī

Turning to women and *dharma*, we continue to explore the relationship between narrative and norm. Brahmanical norms for women are set forth broadly through the concept of *strīdharma*, "law(s) for women" or "women's *dharma*." In many of our classical texts, these norms come with some version of an adage that *Manu* 5.147–148 elaborates as follows:

> Even in their own homes, a female—whether she is a child, a young woman, or an old lady—should never carry out any task independently. As a child, she must remain under her father's control; as a young woman, under her husband's; and when her husband is dead, under her sons'.

Such a norm will have narrative subversions.

Narrative Openings of Women's Dharma

A heroine of one of the *Mahābhārata*'s famous substories gives testimony in court when she demands that a king attest that he is the father of their son (*Mahābhārata* 1.67–68). The pair had met when the king was out hunting and found Śakuntalā alone in a forest hermitage. She had been conceived by a man of princely pedigree and a celestial nymph, left there at birth, and raised by Brahmin hermits as a foundling. The king cites *Manu Svāyambhuva* on the eight types of marriage in the same order as *Manu*, and praises the Love marriage mode, seeking to seduce her. She agrees on condition that her son be his heir, and soon he goes on his merry way. Some six years later, she demands that he acknowledge his paternity of the boy she has with her:

> Your heart knows the truth of it! Good sir, alas, you yourself are the witness to your truth and your lie. He who knows himself to be one

> way and pretends it is another is a thief who robs his own self—what evil is beyond him? You think "I am alone," but don't you know the ancient Muni who dwells in the heart? Him who knows your evil deeds? It is before him that you speak your lie! A man who has done wrong thinks, "Nobody knows me." But the gods know him, and his inner soul. Sun and Moon, Wind, Fire, Heaven, Earth, and Water, the heart and Yama, Day and Night, both Twilights, and Dharma know a man's conduct.

A Muni is a sage, but especially a silent sage—this one in the heart. In court, the inner witness in the heart is also the sage and god Yama, god of karmic justice as king of the dead in his heavenly court. A good conscience in court saves one's merits both in this world and the next.

Manu provides a similar speech by which a judge (who could be a king) should admonish court witnesses to be truthful. The judge should say:

> Whatever good deeds you have done since birth, dear man, all that will go to the dogs, if you testify dishonestly. "I am all alone"—should you think like that about yourself, good man; there dwells always in your heart this Muni, who observes your good and evil deeds. This god, Yama Vaivasvata, dwells in your heart. (*Manu* 8.90–91)

This speech resonates with a recurrent notion in *Manu* that a spiritual inner witness is the "friend" or "escort" that accompanies a man to the afterworld.

Manu says nothing about women's testimony here. Yet even as the epics expand women's worlds, *Manu* still leaves the tiniest room for such narratives to breathe. Although it is problematic, *Manu* says just before this,

> When there is no one else, even a woman, a child, an old man, a pupil, a relative, a slave, or a servant may give testimony.

Manu quickly contradicts himself, as if wanting to take this back, saying women may never be appointed as witnesses, "even if they are many and honest, because the female mind is unsteady." But the possibility of women giving testimony could recall Śakuntalā, whose day in court foreshadows Draupadī's. On "Law Concerning Husband and Wife," *Manu* 9.1 begins, "For a husband and wife who stay on the path pointed out by the law, I shall declare the eternal laws for both when they are together and when they are apart." Such a verse could launch an epic.

Sītā and Draupadī

There are two planes on which the Sanskrit epics unfold what *dharma* holds for their heroines' spirituality. On the one hand, both agree with *Manu* that women find, or should find, their first spirituality in the home, and above all in the context of marriage. Normatively put, and restated countless times, the ideal woman is a "faithful wife" or, more literally, "one whose vow is to her husband"; and her husband is a god. Sītā and Draupadī, who embody this ideal far more than ordinary women, that is, as queens and cultural icons, never tire of speaking up for it. But something more is going on with them that we would not expect to find in a "law book." Their spiritual life comes to be intertwined with *bhakti,* "devotion"—and devotion not only to one's husband but to God. Later vernacular *bhakti* traditions are well known for making the woman's voice a vehicle for strong devotional sentiments, but this is already happening in the epics. Sītā would be bringing her two types of spirituality together in her devotion to one figure: her husband Rāma, whom neither he nor she can *really* know to be god, at least on the scale of his being the incarnation of Viṣṇu. Draupadī, on the other hand, can keep her two types of spirituality separate: her five husbands are gods of one kind, as husbands; her special friend Kṛṣṇa is something else.

We began to meet Sītā and Draupadī in introducing the two epics as *dharma* biographies of their kingly husbands. Yet these heroines have powerful *dharma* biographies of their own that are much more than complements to those of their husbands. This comes across clearly if we reconsider the two epics' common archetypal structure from their perspective.

- Book 1. Draupadī is not prominent in the *Mahābhārata*'s frame story, but Sītā is in the *Rāmāyaṇa*'s. The *Rāmāyaṇa* uses the term "adventure" several times to describe itself in its short preamble

(*Rāmāyaṇa* 1.1–4). First, Brahmā enjoins the poet–author Vālmīki to "compose the whole adventure of Rāma." Once it is implied that Vālmīki has done so, the second usage calls "the whole *Rāmāyaṇa* poem the great adventure of Sītā!" The complete poem will thus be about both adventures intertwined. Then, at the end of the preamble, where Rāma launches the poem's recital, he says: "Moreover, it is said that the profound adventure . . . is highly beneficial even for me. Listen to it." The "profound adventure" is their double one, and eventually one will learn why it will be "beneficial" for Rāma to hear the poem sung. The first books go on to tell of the two princesses' births: Sītā from a furrow, from which she takes her name; Draupadī from an earthen altar shaped like a woman's torso. After Draupadī chooses Arjuna at her Self-choice ceremony, all five Pāṇḍavas marry her, and each has one son with her. Rāma marries Sītā after a somewhat similar ceremony, with as yet no issue.

- Book 2. The pivotal Court Intrigue unfolds a plot to deprive the heroines' husbands of kingship, and results in their accompanying them into exile. Each new queen first finds her voice, raising questions of *dharma*. In Sītā's case, the Intrigue revolves around the rivalries between the wives of her father-in-law. The wronged party is not her but Rāma. Sītā uses some sharp words to convince Rāma to bring her to the Forest. They begin some early forest life, but only so long as the Court Intrigue remains unresolved. Sītā still has no children.

In the *Mahābhārata* the wronged party is Draupadī, staked, lost, and enslaved by Yudhiṣṭhira's gambling (2.60–63). Draupadī's first spokesman in court is an usher who Duryodhana, the "winner" of all Yudhiṣṭhira's losses, had sent to bring her from the women's quarters. Using her wits, and knowing the *procedural* answer from what the usher has told her, Draupadī had told the usher to ask in the court what Yudhiṣṭhira had lost first, "yourself or me?" Duryodhana senses that he can catch Yudhiṣṭhira in a lie, and sends the usher back to bring Draupadī into the hall, menstruating and in a single garment, to ask the question herself. Dragged unwillingly, she recalls the words of the All-Ordainer, that "in this world *dharma* is alone supreme," and says he will protect and "dispose peace." She challenges her change in legal status from queen to slave by invoking the eternal *dharma:*

> From of old, we have heard, they do not bring virtuous *(dharmya)* women into the hall. This ancient eternal *dharma* is lost among the Kauravas. How can I, wife of the Pāṇḍavas . . . and friend of Vāsudeva [Kṛṣṇa] enter the hall of kings? Is the wife of Dharmarāja whose birth matches his a slave or not a slave?

Once her question is raised, it unfolds into a profound legal and spiritual riddle. Does a king own his wife like other property? What is a "self" that one can wager it, or another's after one has bet and lost one's own? It is addressed sixteen times from various angles while Yudhiṣṭhira keeps silent. As a strictly legal matter, no answer is forthcoming. As the aged Bhīṣma, the family's main legal expert, says twice, the question is "subtle." Rather surprisingly, "the people" have a presence in this royal court, and "cry out" for a resolution. Yet some kind of justice is done. The attempt to disrobe Draupadī is thwarted, as explained in varied interpolations by her prayer to Kṛṣṇa. Or, in what seems to be another early interpolation, a "concealed" *dharma* or Dharma repeatedly covers her with unending saris. Duryodhana's father, the blind witness to the proceedings and their only plausible judge as the nominal king of this court, also brings a certain resolution by giving Draupadī boons. Whether Yudhiṣṭhira was free to wager her or not, she chooses his freedom. The two sides then play dice again over the stake of twelve years of Forest Exile and a year incognito. When Yudhiṣṭhira loses again, Draupadī accompanies the Pāṇḍavas into the woods, leaving their boys with Kṛṣṇa's people.

- Book 3. Unencumbered by children, the exiles undergo Forest Trials and receive Instructive Guidance from Great Sages. Toward the beginning of these books, each heroine sounds words of concern: Draupadī wishes to prod Yudhiṣṭhira to action; Sītā tells Rāma, in light of his determination to leave a peaceful hermitage because of his fondness for hunting, that in the next forest they go to he should be wary of committing wanton violence with his bow and arrows (*Rāmāyaṇa* 3.6–8). Compared to the Pāṇḍavas and Draupadī, it is not obvious that Rāma often listens to Sītā on matters of *dharma*, but this may be an exception. Yet Sītā still pulls back from her words of caution, saying she has uttered this only from a woman's frivolity, and after all, what does she know about *dharma?* Rāma seems to be listening, but his love of hunting soon comes to the fore. When Sītā sends him after a golden deer, saying she would prefer to have it as a pet than as a hide, Rāma is intent only on killing it (3.41–42). Hearing the deer's death cries, Sītā sends Lakṣmaṇa to see if Rāma is all right. And it is while she is left alone that Rāvaṇa abducts her. Of course the deer was a demon in disguise, but still, what if Rāma had gone to the trouble of trying to capture it? Insofar as Sītā's abduction by Rāvaṇa provides the provocation that makes the Great War inevitable, it is the counterpart to the outrage against Draupadī in *Mahābhārata* Book 2. Draupadī also undergoes a Forest abduction, but briefly, and when her husbands recover her, they all sit down to hear a version of Rāma and Sītā's story.

- Book 4. To pass their thirteenth year incognito, Draupadī and the Pāṇḍavas assume topsy-turvy disguises in the kingdom of "Fish," where a general, brother of the queen, is killed while attempting a tryst with her. While Rāma gets involved with the topsy-turvy world of the monkeys, Sītā begins to endure Rāvaṇa's captivity in Laṅkā (Sri Lanka), where he rules as king.
- Book 5. As War-Preparation Efforts proceed, the Divine Messengers who go into the Enemy Camp—Kṛṣṇa and Hanumān—have in each case a special role regarding the heroine. In the *Mahābhārata,* Kṛṣṇa's motivations include his special friendship with Draupadī and her demands for revenge over her violations following the dicing. In the *Rāmāyaṇa,* just as Sītā contemplates committing suicide and giving way to despair, Hanumān, Rāma's loyal and divine monkey, who has leapt to Laṅkā to see if Sītā is there, finds and recognizes her, consoles her, and takes her message back to Rāma, calling for him to rescue her and kill Rāvaṇa. Encouraged, Sītā maintains her vigorous defiance of Rāvaṇa.

- Book 6 in the *Rāmāyaṇa* and Books 6–11 and the first part of Book 12 in the *Mahābhārata* then deal with the epics' Great Wars and their immediate aftermaths. Draupadī figures in a few war episodes, but more often her mistreatment at the dice match is recalled as a motivation for War. The *Rāmāyaṇa* shifts its more bicameral attention to Sītā in captivity several times during the War. In the immediate aftermaths, Draupadī and Sītā's treatments are starkly different. Draupadī, having endured the slaughter of her five sons and a curse to barrenness at the War's end, remains a respected member of the Pāṇḍavas' inner family circle as they discuss what to do after the War's devastation. At Yudhiṣṭhira's coronation, she seems to be jointly enthroned with him. Before Rāma takes Sītā back to the capital, he first repudiates her for having been alone all this time with Rāvaṇa, and is willing to reunite with her only after she submits to an ordeal by fire.
- In the Unravellings and returns to the Frames of *Rāmāyaṇa* 7 and the rest of the *Mahābhārata*, like most other characters, each heroine dies, but in circumstances that could not be more contrastive. Draupadī remains a party to all her husbands' doings, including ritual ones, until she is the first to die, offering no final word, on their final journey into the high Himalayas. Sītā on the other hand gets banished by Rāma due to the persistence of rumors about her time with Rāvaṇa, and, even though she is finally pregnant, is led by one of Rāma's brothers to Vālmīki's hermitage. She is thus excluded from Rāma's ritual duties. Bearing twin sons during her banishment, she eventually refuses to reunite with Rāma during a second ordeal, at which her memorable final words are, "If I have thought with my mind of none other than Rāma, let the goddess Earth give me an opening" (*Rāmāyaṇa* 7.88.10)—upon which the Earth, her mother, opens to entomb her as evidence of her chastity. Around these events, Rāma becomes the primary listener as the twins recount their parents' adventure, the *Rāmāyaṇa*. Here we come back to Rāma's words in the Frame that listening to this "profound adventure" might be "beneficial" even for him. The singers turn out to be his sons and heirs.

Yet despite these contrastive closures, the last living picture of each heroine has something remarkable in common: a recognition of her freedom. Although Draupadī has no final word, Yudhiṣṭhira explains her fall as the result of her great partiality for Arjuna (*Mahābhārata* 17.2.6), the only man she chose. Sītā's last words assert the freedom of a devoted wife to decide when she has had enough. Of such heroines, it is hard to maintain that women can never be "independent."

Now insofar as the two epics share a common skein, it clearly unfolds from the men's adventures. The two female leads get more staggered attention at different points and with more contrasting accents. Sītā is more prominent in the Frame than is Draupadī. Draupadī has children early; Sītā very late. The defining outrage against Draupadī occurs in Book 2, against Sītā in Book 3. From the end of war to the ends of their lives, the differences increase.

We have, however, posited that their *dharma* biographies introduce two exemplary strands of women's spirituality. To explore this, I concentrate on passages where their voices are strongest—not only in what their words recall but in what they anticipate in the fuller narratives. I choose episodes where the heroine's very embodiment of the cultural ideal of the faithful wife is first strained to the limit. Given the parallels and asymmetries that we have outlined, we may first mark out what the two episodes have in common. Each marks the point where the heroine first speaks out after she has suffered the deepest outrage she experiences as a devoted wife and queen. And in each case, she addresses her kingly husband. The first difference is that whereas Draupadī addresses Yudhiṣṭhira in person, Sītā, who has been abducted, speaks to a Rāma who is not there.

SĪTĀ IN CAPTIVITY

Rāvaṇa has given Sītā two months to live and left her in a grove guarded by demonesses, threatening that if she does not come to love him they will prepare her for his breakfast or eat her themselves. Yet Hanumān has found her. While he hides in a tree, deciding how best to speak to her, she makes three speeches, ostensibly to herself (*Rāmāyaṇa* 5.23–26). Going beyond *Manu,* here is a woman thinking for herself.

One can see Sītā's deepening despair through her exclamations and interjections. She makes five appeals using words whose overlapping range can be translated "oh" or "alas," plus three "curses," one in each brooding: first, cursing the human state; second, cursing herself as "ignoble and unchaste" to have survived even a moment without Rāma; and then cursing life itself, which she would abandon had she poison or a weapon to do so. In the first speech, she calls out by name to Rāma, Lakṣmaṇa, and their two mothers. The other four outcries all occur in her third speech, which she begins, "Alas, virtuous folk in the world have a popular saying that there is no such thing as an untimely death. Alas, it must be true if I, who lack all merit, have managed to survive even for a moment under such abuse." Next, she says, "Alas, the two months allotted me . . . will soon elapse," and again calls on the four mothers plus her own mother as well. Finally, she saves her last call for Rāma only, and with rather clear *bhakti* overtones—"Alas, you benefactor and beloved of the living world!"—from which point she launches her closing apostrophe to him.

Let us listen to Sītā where she addresses Rāma directly, even though he is not there. Be it noted that while translators, quite sensibly, have wanted to keep Sītā talking on a human and wifely plane, it has meant undertranslating certain loaded words: most notably the impossible-to-translate *ātman,* "self" or "soul," but also words that I will translate with reference to gratitude, pity, compassion, lordship, power, abandonment, seeing, and belovedness so as to bring out *bhakti* overtones. Some translators, inclined toward *bhakti* excisions, have cut Sīta short, removing the end of the second speech and all of the third. But the devotional overtones have direction, and run throughout. I am not saying this is the "right" way to translate these passages, just that we may trace a devotional thread that is intertwined with the ruptured domestic thread of Sītā and Rāma's marriage, and also her thoughts on Rāma simply as a human king.

As Sītā's first speech opens, she recalls a popular maxim quoted by learned persons on how death comes only at its appointed time, and grieves that hers will come now separated from Rāma, whom she then dwells on until this train of thought ends:

> This pitiable woman, whose merit must be small, like a woman without a lord must surely perish. . . . Unable to see my husband and come under the demon women's power, I am collapsing under my

> grief. . . . How fortunate are those who are able to see my lord—his eyes like the inner petals of a lotus—who walks with the valorous gait of a lion and is yet grateful, a speaker of what is beloved. Separated from Rāma who knows himself, there is no way that I can survive. . . . What kind of sin did I commit in a former body that I obtain such cruel and terrible suffering? Engulfed by this great grief, I want to abandon life. . . . A curse on this human state! A curse on being under another's power. Although I wish to, I cannot end my life.

Sītā imagines the good fortune of others who might *see* Rāma, without yet saying who they might be. She builds up a shaky image of him. She thinks he "knows himself," but he cannot really know his divine nature until he has killed Rāvaṇa. She grieves at being under "another's power," which in *Manu* defines lack of freedom. Ostensibly, she is held captive by the demonesses and Rāvaṇa. But she intimates that she is under some still higher power: her own *karma?* The power of a lord who should be grateful, who should know himself? As her own imaginings continue, Rāma will not be so perfect.

In her second and longest speech, Sītā "broods" further on her captivity under the "demon women's power," and ends on the theme of being under "Rāvaṇa's power." Here, she first centers her attention on Rāma, wondering why he does not come for her:

> Rāghava is renowned, wise, grateful, and compassionate. Therefore I think it must be the exhaustion of my good fortune that has made this man of good conduct uncompassionate. For why has he who singlehandedly annihilated fourteen thousand demons . . . not come for me? . . . Surely my husband is capable of killing [Rāvaṇa] in battle. Why then has Rāma . . . not come for me? Granted, it is difficult to assault Laṅkā, which is situated in the middle of the ocean. Still, there is nothing in the world that can stop the flight of Rāghava's arrows. Why has Rāma, so firm in his valor, not come to rescue his cherished wife, who is carried off by a demon? I think [he] must not know that I am here.

Her key verse here is the first one, bringing Rāma's compassion into question around the thought that he might become uncompassionate now that she has been abducted—as he will in fact be when he imposes her two ordeals on her. But then, when was God's compassion something one could secure just by loving him? Sītā then multiplies these anxieties in this second speech's closing:

> How, in my great suffering, shall I do without him—without seeing my beloved Rāma, the corners of his eyes blood red? . . . Rāma must not know that I am alive. . . . Surely [Rāma] has gone—out of grief for me—from here to the world of the gods, having abandoned his body on earth. Fortunate are the gods, Gandharvas, Siddhas, and supreme Ṛṣis who can now see Rāma, my lotus-eyed lord. Or perhaps this wise royal Ṛṣi Rāma who loves *dharma* and who is the Supreme Self *(Paramātman)* has no use for me as his wife. There would be love for the one that is seen; there is no affection on the part of one who does not see. Ingrates destroy; Rāma will not destroy. Is it that I am completely devoid of qualities, or is it just the exhaustion of my good fortune, that I, Sītā, should be without Rāma, who is deserving of the best? . . . Or perhaps the two brothers, best of men, have laid down their weapons and are wandering in the forest as forest dwellers, subsisting on roots and fruits. Or perhaps Rāvaṇa . . . has slain [them] . . . by means of some trick. At such a time as this I can wish only to die. . . . Fortunate, indeed, are those great-souled, great-fortuned Munis who are revered for their truth, their selves conquered, for whom there is neither beloved nor unbeloved. Homage to those great-souled ones who detach themselves from both! Abandoned here by my beloved Rāma who knows himself, and fallen under the power of the wicked Rāvaṇa, I shall end my life.

The passage is a spiritual treasure trove. While imagining that Rāma may have gone to heaven out of grief for her, or that he and Lakṣmaṇa have relinquished their weapons and become forest wanderers, or that Rāvaṇa could have killed them by some trick, she broods on the "fortunate" celestial supreme Ṛṣis or great-souled Munis in tellingly contrastive terms. First she imagines them greeting Rāma in heaven, "fortunate" that they "can now *see* Rāma, my lotus-eyed lord." But then she brings them down to the circumstances of her despair: the Munis' good fortune is that they are "revered for their truth" and have transcended the categories of the beloved and unbeloved. According to commentators, she is saying that they transcend *saṃsāra.* Sītā cannot aspire to this kind of detachment. Moreover, in the midst of all this, she has had the disturbing yet also penetrating thought that "perhaps this wise royal Ṛṣi Rāma who loves *dharma* and is the Supreme Self has no use for me as his wife." One commentarial view is that, as the Supreme Self, he does not require a wife to assist him in practicing *dharma*. Sītā brings her thoughts on this disjunction to some complex and subtle questions. If, as a Brahmanical philosophy of "Reflection" (Mīmāṃsā) on ritual maintains, the fruits of *dharma* can often be unseen, what of Rāma and Sītā's love when she is unseen? Sītā imagines Rāma as a potential ingrate, who, to the extent that he does "know himself," would "love *dharma*" more than her. She reassures herself, perhaps wishfully, that Rāma "will not destroy," yet asks whether her own "qualities" *(guṇas)* are such as to have left her now without him. Indeed, Rāma will not involve Sītā in his ritual duties after the war. Her wifely *dharma* will be cast aside because he feels he must acknowledge the public's doubts about her time with Rāvaṇa.

Between the second and third speeches a good demoness describes a dream that augurs well for Sītā. In enumerating the auspicious tidings, she says, "I saw that lotus-eyed woman rise from her husband's lap to stroke the sun and moon with her hands"; and, while identifying other good omens that show Sītā will soon hear welcome news, she says, "This lady *(devī)* does not deserve to suffer, and she is the one I saw standing in the sky."

Sītā does not hear the good demoness describe her dream, and her third speech now shifts to a more complicated doubled meter, intensifying her lonely soliloquy until even she senses the favorable omens that presage the presence of Hanumān. She closes,

> Surely if Rāma, the lord of the world, does not come, the demon king will soon dismember me. . . . Then it will be for me just as it would be for a thief, imprisoned and condemned to death for a crime against the crown, on the morning of his execution. Oh Rāma! Oh Lakṣmaṇa! Oh Sumitrā! O mother of Rāma and my own genetrix as well! I, this luckless woman, will perish like a ship foundering in a storm at sea. [Rāma and Lakṣmaṇa] must have been killed on my account through the strength of that creature in the form of a deer. . . . It must have been Time itself in the guise of a

> deer who deluded hapless me at that time when, fool that I am, I sent away my husband . . . and Lakṣmaṇa as well. Alas, Rāma of the long arms, true to your vows! Alas, you whose face rivals the full moon! Alas, you benefactor and beloved of the living world! You do not realize that I am to be slain by demons. My taking you for my sole divinity, my long suffering, my sleeping on the ground, and my rigorous adherence to *dharma*—this devotion to my husband has been fruitless, like the favors men do for ingrates. Surely this *dharma* adventure of mine has been vain and my exclusive devotion to my husband useless. For, pale and emaciated, I cannot see you; I am cut off from you without hope for our reunion. Once you have carried out your father's orders to the letter and have returned from the forest with your vow accomplished, you will, I think, make love with wide-eyed women, carefree, your purpose accomplished. But as for hapless me, Rāma, after having loved you so long, given you all my heart—to my own undoing—and practiced my vows and penances in vain, I shall abandon my accursed life.

Those who *see* Rāma, always potentially a *bhakti* idiom, are no longer the celestial denizens but wide-eyed lovers. We see how Sītā keeps *dharma* and *bhakti* at play along with all the strands of her predicament before finally letting them unravel in her version of a wife's worst-case imaginings, well in tune with Rāma's overriding concern for his father's truth, if not when imagining his infidelities. Sītā also deepens the implications of her first invocation of Rāma, Lakṣmaṇa, and their mothers, this time mentioning all four again but adding "and my own mother." For this, she uses an appropriately different term for "mother" that means "begetter" or "genetrix," hinting that she is speaking of her mother the Earth, to whom she will finally appeal at her last ordeal when she will really end her life. But for now, as she determines to hang herself from her ponytail, her thoughts turn more fondly to Rāma as she too becomes aware of the good omens and takes hold of the branch of a great flowering tree.

DRAUPADĪ IN EXILE

When Draupadī first speaks out after the dice match, she has her husbands with her (*Mahābhārata* 3.28–35). It is their first conversation in exile. Draupadī berates Yudhiṣṭhira for his lack of kingly authority and manly wrath and tells him a story to chide him for exalting patience and forbearance. Though he soon claims that he felt manly wrath when the Kauravas were cheating at the dice match, making this a novel and weak excuse for not stopping the game, he begins by defending patience in the name of overcoming ordinary anger. Hearing this mild self-defense, with her exasperation mounting, Draupadī exclaims, "Glory be to the Placer and the Ordainer who have befuddled you!" Who are the Placer and the Ordainer—beyond being two old Vedic abstract deities and, in the epics, a pair of epithets used for a variety of gods? Clearly, she is talking about a divinity or two, though, as with Sītā, it is not obvious that her words have devotional implications.

Setting out their differences, Draupadī and Yudhiṣṭhira repeatedly use the philosophically potent term *buddhi* with nuances that range from "intellect" or "mind" to "spiritual attitude." She first remarks on his listless turn:

> By my mind, you would abandon Bhīma and Arjuna, the twin sons of Mādrī, and myself before you would forsake *dharma.* When a king is a protector of *dharma, dharma* guards as it is guarded—so I have heard from the Āryas. Never straying, your intellect always pursues *dharma,* tiger among men, as one's constant shadow pursues a man.

Draupadī is not praising Yudhiṣṭhira with her simile that he pursues *dharma* like a shadow. She has been hearing about it endlessly and is saying that his mind follows it as if "on autopilot." In this, Yudhiṣṭhira is different from Rāma, who Sītā must worry about more for his strictly adhering to *dharma* than for his shadowing it. But both register that their husbands' allegiance to *dharma* can leave them unprotected. Also worth noting is Draupadī's "so I have heard from the Āryas," since she goes to a little trouble to explain how she comes to have heard such elevated talk. She will conclude her part in this dialogue by explaining that once, while she was doing errands and sitting on her father's lap, she overheard a learned Brahmin who had come to her father's house and spoken to her brothers on subjects that had first been propounded by Bṛhaspati, the divine chaplain of the gods. As with Sītā's citation of various maxims, this vignette offers a glimpse of a female's eavesdropping position. Note, however, that whereas Sītā cites *paṇḍits*, Draupadī is described as a *paṇḍitā* or "lady pundit" herself in the build-up to this exchange.

Draupadī refers her account to an "ancient tradition" about how the Placer is behind everything: "As wooden puppets are assembled, so are these creatures, king; he makes the body and limbs move." Yudhiṣṭhira rises to her challenge by linking her with "those of slow mind." But soon he wants to change her mind in a reasoned debate, one in which he must be willing to weigh her charge that his mind was overtaken by the "spiritual attitude of gambling." He is thus intellectually engaged when Draupadī moves on to challenge him to "exertion" by arguing that "it is the spirit to act that is extolled"—from which she goes on to speak of the fatalist as of very bad intellect and the believer in chance as one whose spiritual attitude disposes him to just getting by. Eventually she builds to her last word on the subject: she wants Yudhiṣṭhira to be "resolute on his own with his intellect in front," rather than trailing him like a shadow. At the heart of what they are debating is the nature of *karma* with regard to what Yudhiṣṭhira calls the "fruits of *dharma*"—a topic on which he appears to share a view that the spiritual fruits of ritual action are "unseen." Since he charges her with "heresy," their differences thus amount to contending spiritualities. I limit discussion to what I believe are two levels to Draupadī's alleged heresy, and, to the extent that this heresy would appear to be about a divinity (or two) that neither speaker decisively names, to the question of whom they would appear to be talking about.

The first level comes out in Draupadī's "puppet speech." It is about the Placer: "As wooden puppets are assembled, so are these creatures, king; he makes the body and limbs move." There would be a certain experiential quality to Draupadī's heretical disposition on this point, since one of her birth-given names, Pāñcālī, not only means a woman from Pañcāla but evokes a word for "marionette." Carrying this idea along with several "string" similes ("like a pearl strung on a string," among them), and remarking that creatures can be pushed along by the Lord to heaven or hell, she builds up to this:

> So all beings come under the Placer's sway. Adjoined to noble or again wicked acts, the Lord, penetrating beings, moves them, and

he is not perceived. This body they call the "field" is the Placer's mere instrument by which the Lord causes action that has good or bad fruit. Behold this magical prowess as it is done by a Lord who kills beings with beings, having bewildered [them] with his own magic. . . . Having made a disguise, Yudhiṣṭhira, the god Bhagavān, the Self-Existent Great Grandfather, hurts creatures with creatures. Joining them together and disjoining them, doing as he will, the Lord Bhagavān plays with beings like a child with playthings. The Placer does not act toward beings like a father or mother. He seems to act out of fury. He is like another person.

Let us note that even after Yudhiṣṭhira has mentioned heresy, Draupadī does not change her tune that the body is an instrument by which the Placer, now as the Great Lord, makes powerless beings move along enjoined to this or that task.

Of the two dimensions of heresy, Yudhiṣṭhira seems least interested in this one, probably getting to it only toward the end of his response, when he reminds Draupadī of her birth, ostensibly to illustrate the principle that acts bear fruit:

So it is in you: recall your birth, Kṛṣṇā, as it is heard. . . . This is a sufficient analogy, sweet smiling woman. [Knowing that] "[o]f action, there is fruit," the wise man is content with even a little. . . . Fruition of both meritorious and wicked acts and their origin and disappearance are mysteries of the gods, beautiful woman. Nobody knows them, these creatures *are* bewildered about them. They are guarded by the gods; surely the gods' magic is hidden.

Draupadī's birth from an earthen altar is frequently cited as something known to the principal epic characters. In advancing an outlook typical of the Mīmāṃsā school of "Reflection" on ritual, Yudhiṣṭhira can remind her of her birth not only as one of the "mysteries of the gods" but as a ritual still bearing "unseen fruit." Granting that beings are bewildered, but not the puppets of a divine puppeteer, he rather suggests that they make up a bewildered audience to a divine plan. If he is bothered by the theology of the puppeteer heresy, it is not much. Rather, he concludes with a ringing endorsement not only of the ontology of acts but of *dharma* and of everything the Placer does:

> Resolving that "Everything is," set free your heretical heart! Do not revile the Placer, the Lord of the beings. Learn of him, bow to him. Let not your mind be like this. It is by the supreme deity's grace that a devoted *(bhakta)* mortal attains immortality—do not censure him in any way.

The puppeteer heresy is thus more Draupadī's problem than Yudhiṣṭhira's.

But it is the other way around with her second heresy, which gets to the core of Yudhiṣṭhira's self-understanding. Virtually the first thing he says in response is, "My mind is beholden to *dharma* by its own nature *(svabhāvā),* Kṛṣṇā." We have seen the second heresy taking shape in their conversation about the fruition of *karma.* What exercises Yudhiṣṭhira is what Draupadī says last, condemning the Placer before asking a question with two possible conclusions:

> Duryodhana transgresses the noble treatises and is cruel, greedy, and disrespectful of *dharma.* Having given him prosperity, what fruit does the Placer eat? If *karma* done pursues its doer and not another, then surely the Lord is stained by the wicked *karma* he has done. Or if the wicked *karma* done does not pursue its doer, then mere power is the cause here, and I grieve for weak people.

It is true that one would not want to translate the idiom "eats the fruit" every time it is used with *karma* as "the fruit of one's acts." But Draupadī is definitely being literal, for even after Yudhiṣṭhira has mentioned heresy, she comes back to this image with unmistakable clarity in her only other reference to both the Placer and the Ordainer since she opened this topic saying "Glory be" to them. Having first mentioned the example of babies suckling their mother's breast to show that all beings obtain livelihood from what they do, she says:

> All beings know exertion, Bhārata, and visibly, having the world as witness, they eat the fruit of their *karmas.* I see that creatures live off their own total effort—even the Placer and the Ordainer, as does this crane in the water.

We can detect a Materialist bent in Draupadī here, for in philosophical terms she is an empiricist, stating that "visible evidence" or "perception" *(pratyakṣa)* is her standard for knowledge. Nor would she be contradicting herself by mentioning deities, since Indian materialism does not require atheism. Moreover, Draupadī may also be echoing the Jain notion that one is stained by one's *karma,* which, unlike Brahmanical notions, involves a *material* concept of *karma.* She has stood her ground against Yudhiṣṭhira's claim that "having the world as witness" is for the fool who pleasures his senses and is confused about everything else, and she has not given in to his interpretation of *karma*'s fruition through hidden divine forces. Not only does she want effort. She wants to *see* results!

Such materialism would be heresy enough, and that is what appears to bother Yudhiṣṭhira when he defends his innate bent toward *dharma* and turns the conversation from one about the unseen fruits of action to one about the unseen spiritual "fruits of *dharma.*" He defends the Placer and *dharma* together for establishing the "Ṛṣis' standard" *(pramāṇam),* without which "the universe would sink into darkness without foundation." He has been speaking like a good theist in seeing divinity behind the spiritual fruits of *dharma.* But in rising to such a defense of *dharma,* which is also an expedient self-defense, Yudhiṣṭhira is again indirect at best in addressing Draupadī's heresy. No doubt he wants to assure her that since his acts flow from his innate bent toward *dharma,* they would not stain *him.* But Draupadī has been talking of a stain on the Placer. Who is he—at least for now, to these two speakers?

In mentioning mainly the Placer, Draupadī and Yudhiṣṭhira seem to be talking about the creator Brahmā, at least in using some of his epithets. But she also uses the names Bhagavān, Īśvara, and Maheśvara, which have wider and more devotional ambience. It has been suggested that when the Placer and the Ordainer are named in situations of misfortune, it is as if the speakers are reluctant to blame their personally chosen grace-bestowing highest deity by name. In such a world two characters could be talking about the same or different deities in a way that each might or might not understand. Draupadī's story about the Placer comes from Bṛhaspati, who, as the chaplain of the Vedic gods, gets a reputation for having composed a Materialist *Sūtra!* There are also Jain and Buddhist texts that mock the idea of a creator god. The *Mahābhārata* does not openly cite heterodox texts (real or imaginary), but here it seems to do so covertly, under a Vedic cover and in a woman's voice! Draupadī is particularly out of sorts at this point, and openly fed up with Yudhiṣṭhira. But she would also have reasons to be fed up with a divine plan that has put her through her ordeal at the dicing and now "placed" her in the forest where she, being a woman, is the most discomfited of all those beginning their years of exile. If she would have a complaint about the Placer, then what about a friend who leaves things to some unnamed agency to rescue her with unending saris, or who left it to a "concealed" *dharma?*

It could thus be that Yudhiṣṭhira is heading Draupadī off, implicitly, from speaking ill of her friend Kṛṣṇa, that grand illusionist who will tell Arjuna in the *Bhagavad Gītā,* "The Lord of all beings resides in the region of the heart, Arjuna, making all beings reel, mounted to a device by his power of illusion" (*Bhagavad Gītā* 18.61). Yudhiṣṭhira could have reasons to hear Draupadī's words that way. When she was summoned to the gambling hall, menstruating and in a single garment, he heard her say,

> So now the All-Ordainer disposes, touching both who are touched, the wise and the fool. He said, "In this world *dharma* is alone supreme." Protecting, he will dispose peace. (*Mahābhārata* 2.60.13)

Her words are the epic's single mention of the All-Ordainer, who seems to cover both the Placer and the Ordainer, and to leave open the possibility that she is talking about Kṛṣṇa.

In fact, there are vivid echoes between Draupadī's "heresy" and Kṛṣṇa's words with his other special friend Arjuna in the *Bhagavad Gītā.* Like Draupadī, who protests the point, Arjuna hears that he should consider himself a "mere instrument" (*Bhagavad Gītā* 11.33) of a god on whom everything is "strung like heaps of pearls on a string" (7.7). Indeed, she says things that would rather defy the *Gītā.* Whereas Draupadī says, "The Placer does not act toward beings like a father or mother. He seems to act out of fury. He is like another person," Kṛṣṇa says, "I am the father of this universe, the mother, the Placer, the grandfather" (9.17). When Draupadī asks, "What fruit does the Placer eat?" that might either stain him or leave people powerless before mere power, Kṛṣṇa says that he eats whatever is offered to him with devotion *(bhakti)*—"a leaf, a flower, a fruit, or water"—so as to free devotees from the good or bad fruits of binding *karma* (9.26–28), while Arjuna sees him with crushed heads stuck between his teeth (11.27). Kṛṣṇa would not confirm Draupadī's supposition that "the Lord is stained by the wicked *karma* he has done," since he says, "Acts do not stain me; I have no yearning for the fruits of acts. Whoever comprehends me thus is not bound by acts" (4.14).

Bhakti allows for numerous arguments with God. Sītā's and Draupadī's arguments certainly differ, but there are also similarities. Intellectually, both put a twist on the visible evidence that, if God is as supreme as he is reputed to be, he would appear to have put each heroine's *dharma* on trial with a certain transcendent aloofness. But the emotional tone differs. Sītā in captivity, more than Draupadī in exile, anticipates the convention of having a woman's voice express the emotional side of *bhakti.* As we turn next to the *Bhagavad Gītā,* we cannot contrast Draupadī's spirituality as emotional with Arjuna's as intellectual. If anything, it is more the other way around. Unlike her beloved Arjuna, the exemplary man of action, the learned lady is a philosopher.

CHAPTER 8

Dharma in the *Bhagavad Gītā*

The *Bhagavad Gītā* makes a number of philosophical points, and no one would deny that it also deserves a reputation as a text about *dharma*. Yet it really says only a few things about *dharma* per se. Most of its prominent references to *dharma* occur in what I will call an informal ring structure: not a formal ring of the type appreciated by folklorists, where a text exhibits a self-conscious geometry of units and themes converging on a central nugget, but one that allows the *Gītā* to be also about other things to which *dharma* is kept pertinent through deepening reminders of its relevance. There may be yet a further ring that is off-center or deferred. We shall examine what these patterns tell us about *dharma* as these rings close in on the text's grand spiritual teachings.

Dharma *Rings in the* Bhagavad Gītā

Let us peel away the outer layers. We return to terms that we have been meeting increasingly. I render them mainly as I have done there, leaving *svadharma* to speak for itself and translating *svabhāva* and *svakarma* as "inherent nature" and "own jobs," respectively.

> Ring 1: a. In the *Gītā*'s very first words, Dhṛtarāṣṭra asks Sañjaya what happened "on the field of *dharma*, the Kuru field" (*Bhagavad Gītā* 1.1), between "my sons," the Kauravas, and their foes.
>
> b. As the *Gītā* ends, Sañjaya tells Dhṛtarāṣṭra that the last thing Kṛṣṇa told Arjuna, before asking him if he understood, was that theirs was a "righteous dialogue"—that is, it was *dharmya*, about *dharma*—and that whoever learns it will offer it up as a sacrifice of knowledge to Kṛṣṇa, and whoever listens to it will be released to blessed worlds. (18.70–72)

To grasp this first ring one must know that the *Gītā*'s Kṛṣṇa–Arjuna dialogue is framed by a dialogue between Dhṛtarāṣṭra, blind father of the doomed Kauravas, and the bard Sañjaya. Thanks to a recent gift of the "divine eye" from the epic's putative author Vyāsa, Sañjaya can report the entire war as an account of what the blind old king—and all other audiences—would otherwise be missing. The *Gītā* ends with Sañjaya telling Dhṛtarāṣṭra that its supreme secret comes to them by "Vyāsa's grace" (18.75).

In fact, this framing dialogue makes *dharma* the *Gītā*'s very first word, while the last mention of *dharma*, by Kṛṣṇa, confirms the "righteous" nature of the whole exchange. Arjuna then replies that he will stand firm and do as Kṛṣṇa bids with his confusion gone and his memory restored (18.73), after which Sañjaya again speaks from the frame to wrap things up (74–78). These opening and closing usages are more subtle than they look.

The opening has several reverberations. The reference to a "field of *dharma*" recalls that the rules of fair fighting were agreed upon earlier that day, when both sides "established the *dharmas* (laws, rules of engagement) of battle" (*Mahābhārata* 6.1.26–33). Most of these rules will be broken on this very field, and not infrequently at the advice of Kṛṣṇa. That this *dharma*-field is "the field of Kuru" also recalls an ancestor of the Kuru line, Kuru, who "made Kurukṣetra meritorious by his austerities" (1.89.44). During the war narrative, we learn that King Kuru did such severe austerities at Kurukṣetra that Indra granted that both ascetics and warriors who died there in battle would go straight to heaven cleansed of their wicked acts by its very dust (9.52.13–18). These uses converge when the aged legal expert of the family, Bhīṣma, is about to give his lengthy *dharma* oration after the war. As Kṛṣṇa and the Pāṇḍavas come to the spot where Bhīṣma lies on his hero's bed of arrows, Kurukṣetra is called "the field of the whole of the law" (12.53.23), expanding on the first words of the *Gītā* and projecting them toward some kind of completion in the *dharma* instructions of Bhīṣma, which the war's survivors are arriving to hear before he dies and goes to heaven. Further, the opening "field" references resonate with what Kṛṣṇa has to say within the *Gītā* about the "field-knower." In the *Gītā*'s philosophical context, the "field" of "Nature" is not only the body and mind but the world of cosmic evolutes made up of three ever-entangling "qualities" known as goodness *(sattva)*, passion *(rajas)*, and darkness *(tamas)*, which the "knowing" or "witnessing" self can level from its transcendent standpoint. This brings out another sense of the "field of *dharma*" as a field where seeds of merit *(dharma)* and demerit *(adharma)* are sown and their fruits reaped.

The *Gītā*'s usage of "field-knower" can be illumined by a sub-tale, found earlier in the epic (1.81–88), where another ancestor of the Kuru line, more ancient than Kuru, serves as a kind of Upaniṣadic guide to the afterworld during an interval after he has been bounced out of heaven for a prideful utterance and is headed for hell. Rather exceptionally, he is able to steer himself along the path of his fall, and heads for some smoke he sees rising from a hallowed forest. He is aware that where there's smoke like this, there's a Vedic sacrifice, and thus people who are "good." The smoke turns out to be rising from a sacrifice being performed by his four grandsons, the first of whom is introduced as "a protector of the rules of the true *dharma*." When the four realize who he is and see him hanging in midair, they think he might know something about the "laws" of the "field" of retribution. So they each address him, "You are, I think, a knower of the field of this *dharma*." Their usage suggests that "this *dharma*" would have the sense of a "doctrine," "law," or "teaching" that the fallen one might impart to them, much as with Yama's *dharma* in the *Kaṭha Upaniṣad* (see chapter 3), and, of course, like the Buddha's *dharma*. The story uses the phrase "knowledge of the field . . . of *dharma*" with reference to its "doctrine" of retribution, which turns out to concern a notion of "merit" by which the man's grandsons can transfer their own merits to him to reverse his downward course and enable all five of them to ascend to heaven together. From this we can extrapolate that where Kṛṣṇa concludes the dialogue with Arjuna saying that it "has to do with *dharma*," his portion of that dialogue could also be taken as his "teaching." There is one place in the *Gītā* where he uses *dharma* in that way. As Kṛṣna prepares Arjuna to see his cosmic divine form, he bills the revelation as a "royal wisdom, royal mystery, and ultimate purifier" that is "lawful" or "about *dharma*" *(dharmya)*, and says, "Men who lack faith in this *dharma*, enemy-burner, having failed to reach me, return to the runaround of deaths" (9.2–3). But for the most part, Kṛṣṇa's teaching is presented not as a single *dharma* but as a variety of "disciplines" or *yogas.*

When Kṛṣna says at the far side of Ring 1 that his dialogue with Arjuna has been "righteous" or "about *dharma,*" it is striking in another way, too. Sañjaya also qualifies "this dialogue" twice as "wondrous" and once as "hair-raising" or "enrapturing" (18.74, 76). And Kṛṣṇa speaks of it indirectly as *dharmya* toward the *Gītā*'s middle:

> But those who revere this righteous *(dharmya)* elixir as it has been uttered, having faith [in it?] and intent on me, these devotees are exceedingly dear to me. (12.20)

For this one "wondrous" dialogue to be a "righteous elixir" means that it can be spiritually fulfilling to those who have knowledge, faith, and devotion.

To summarize, Ring 1 first mentions *dharma* in a way that resonates with geo-dynastic, political, soteriological, ethical, and philosophical ideas, and closes with a confirmation that *dharma* has been what the whole Kṛṣṇa–Arjuna dialogue has been about. When the *Gītā* mentions the Kuru field as a *dharma* field in its very first words and closes on its being "about *dharma,*" it encircles Kṛṣṇa's argument for "just *(dharmya)* war" (see Ring 3), placing its dialogue in an especially politicized "field of merit" that gives warriors slain there a ticket to heaven and probably still evokes what is left of the prestige of the Vedic "Kuru state." The compound *Kuru-dharma,* "law of the Kurus," has six usages in the *Mahābhārata,* the most interesting being where the Kauravas are said to have breached the "limit of the Kuru *dharma*" (2.60.33) during the disrobing of Draupadī. *Manu* also hallows the place of "the Kurus" as a holy site (8.91) that would lie within his heartland of *dharma* in north-central India (2.17–24). And surprisingly, even Buddhist commentaries acknowledge the region as one of purity suitable for the special *dharma* teachings that the Buddha is alleged to have imparted there.

> Ring 2: a. The *Gītā*'s principal dialogue first makes *dharma* a focus when Arjuna relates his despondency over fighting kinsmen to his angst about "clan" or "family *dharma,*" "the *dharma* of social class by birth," and "class-mixture," and his fear of hell. (1.40–44)

b. Kṛṣṇa brings these matters to resolution near the end when he tells Arjuna he should abandon all *dharmas* since Kṛṣṇa will release him from every sin. (18.66)

Arjuna explains his famous despondency, which brought him to lay down his weapons, as arising from the "the taint caused by destruction of the clan" (1.38–39). But the heart of it is his horror of class-mixture that is really miscegenation: if he kills his relatives, *adharma* will result for his clan and social class because the women of the clan will become corrupt and engage in mixed unions. If that occurs, the ancestors will go to hell because no one will perform their rites, and he will go to hell for enabling it (40–44). There have been attempts to widen the scope of "Arjuna's dilemma." One is to interpret it as an aversion, however fleeting, to war and killing. But the word for what makes Arjuna despondent, by which he is twice said to be "possessed" (1.28; 2.1), means "pity" before "compassion," and is the first thing he asks to be clarified, admitting that he is "afflicted by the taint" of it (2.7). A paragon warrior, Arjuna is pitying those he has been trained to kill. Another is to consider it as a conflict of duties within the framework of the "law of class and life-stage." Along with being a Kṣatriya, Arjuna is married, and has been imagined to be pinioning his domestic duties over and against an inclination toward renunciation and nonviolence. Cited in this regard is a verse in which he says it would be "better to enjoy almsfood" than "enjoyments smeared with blood" (2.5). But Arjuna remains focused entirely on the clan and class issues of killing his elders. Never, like Yudhiṣṭhira, does he consider the beggar option a real one. Indeed, the *Gītā* never mentions "life-stage" considerations at all.

We may thus say that when Kṛṣṇa tells Arjuna at the far side of Ring 2 that he should abandon all *dharmas,* which may refer as well to *adharmas,* he is referring above all to those that have reduced Arjuna to this temporary inaction and pity. Though the verse uses the root √*muc,* "to release," when Kṛṣṇa says "I will free you from all sins," he is not talking about *mokṣa* as final liberation. As Ring 3 now makes evident, for Kṛṣṇa to release Arjuna from every sin will still hold him to doing his Kṣatriya duties, but in a new spirit of abandoning the desire for fruits or results.

Ring 3: a. Kṛṣṇa gets Arjuna to concentrate his multiple *dharma* anxieties on just one matter: Kṣatriya *svadharma.* When Arjuna says his inherent nature *(svabhāva)* is afflicted by the taint of what comes from pity and asks Kṛṣṇa to relieve his confusion about *dharma* (2.7), Kṛṣṇa answers that a Kṣatriya can find nothing better than a "lawful" or "just war" in which "either you are killed and go to heaven" or you "win and enjoy the earth" (2.31–37). Kṛṣṇa then rounds off the point with two adages: first, a little *dharma* goes a long way (2.40); and second, doing "one's *svadharma*" is better than doing another's (3.55) because "the best" is the man who acts disinterestedly for the "holding together of the world," just as Kṛṣṇa does himself (3.19–26).

b. This round of topics is brought to resolution, still near the end, when Kṛṣṇa explains *svadharma* in terms of each class's "own jobs" and inherent natures (18.41–47).

Ring 3 concerns the special spirituality of a warrior. That, and not a king, is what Arjuna truly is. Modeled on the warrior, each social class will work for the "holding together of the world" by doing its *svadharma* in the "own jobs" that are inherent to them.

The correspondences between the near and far sides of Ring 3 are the clearest we encounter, as is the movement toward closure. The central passage on the near side reads:

> Look to your *svadharma* and do not waver, for a Kṣatriya can find nothing better than a lawful war. It is an open door to heaven, happily happened upon; and blessed are the warriors, Pārtha, who find a war like that! Or suppose you will not engage in this lawful war: then you give up your *svadharma* and honor and incur sin. (2.31–33)

The idea of "lawful" or "just" *(dharmya)* war is challenging. It cannot refer to the compact both sides make to fight fairly, which Kṛṣṇa himself will ignore. But it would have behind it the justice of the Pāṇḍavas' cause, and, coming from Kṛṣṇa, the fact that he was the last to make efforts to negotiate a peaceful settlement. In legally representing the Pāṇḍava cause, however, Kṛṣṇa was speaking primarily for Yudhiṣṭhira, the Dharma King. Here he is speaking to Arjuna, for whom he has reduced what is "lawful" entirely to Kṣatriya *dharma*—indeed, to Kṣatriya *svadharma,* which promises heaven for those who die in battle. Although *Manu* also says that slain warriors go to heaven (7.89), it is worth mentioning the Buddha's nonconcurrence on this point. When pressed by martial types of "headmen" who are clearly dubious about such guarantees, he revealed with great reluctance that a soldier who dies in battle does not go to heaven but to the "battle-slain hell," since he dies with "his mind already low, depraved" and "misdirected" toward killing others (*Saṃyutta Nikāya, Gāmaṇisaṃyutta* 3–5). Yet Buddhism influenced another usage that could point to a deeper sense. This is the idea broached by Aśoka after the terrible Kalinga war that henceforth he would consider "conquest by *dhaṃma* the most important conquest" (see chapter 2). The real "just war" would be the one fought within. Gandhi brought out this interpretation of Arjuna's true battle in the *Bhagavad Gītā,* and with it the idea that *svadharma* means something like "conscience."

On the far side of Ring 3, Kṛṣṇa is not encouraging of such an interpretation. Backed up by his final words on the three qualities of matter, he returns to the topic of *svadharma* after explaining the proper functioning of the four classes:

> The jobs of Brahmins, Kṣatriyas, Vaiśyas, and Śūdras, enemy-burner, are distinguished according to the qualities that spring from their inherent nature. Tranquility, restraint, austerity, purity, patience, uprightness, knowledge, discernment, and orthodoxy are the Brahmin's job born from his inherent nature. Championing, energy, bearing, skill, not fleeing in battle, the gift, and lordly nature are the Kṣatriya's job born from his inherent nature. Agriculture, herding, and trade are the Vaiśya's job, born from his inherent nature, while the inherent nature born to the Śūdra has the character of service. Contented each in his own job, a man attains complete fulfillment. Engaged in his own job, hear how he finds that perfection. A man finds perfection by his own job having worshiped him by whom all this is strung, whence beings are motivated to activity. Better one's *svadharma* imperfectly performed than another's *dharma* done perfectly; doing the job regulated by his inherent nature, he does not incur fault. (18.40–47)

However one translates *karman* here, which I have rendered as "jobs," one should not obscure the distinction between the last "job" reference and the one closing instance of *svadharma,* as some have done by fudging *karman* there as "duties." Kṛṣṇa is fine-tuning a well-known *dharmaśāstra* job scheme.

Clearly, there has been movement here from one side of Ring 3 to the other. While the last verse, beginning "Better one's *svadharma,*" has the same famous first line as a verse on the near side of this ring, their second lines differ. In the earlier verse, the second line simply reinforces Kṣatriya *svadharma:* "Better death in one's *svadharma;* another's *dharma* brings danger" (3.35). In the later verse, the second line refers *svadharma* back to the two terms that govern the passage, *karma* and *svabhāva:* "doing the job regulated by his inherent nature, he does not incur fault." No longer needing to convince Arjuna to do his Kṣatriya *svadharma,* Kṛṣṇa now uses the Kṣatriya as the spiritual role model to talk about the jobs of all four social classes. More than that, he ontologizes each job in its respective inherent nature. Here Kṛṣṇa finally straightens out the issue of "class-mixture" that defined *adharma* for Arjuna (1.38–44) and paralyzed him to *his* inherent nature (2.7).

Warrior *svadharma* thus gives a certain patina to everyone else's "own job." The *Gītā* is not alone in the way it uses these terms. In the *dharmasūtras,* one begins to notice a pattern that our other texts only reinforce. When the three earliest *dharmasūtras* use the term *svadharma,* their target in prescribing it is the classes below the Brahmin—especially the Kṣatriya, and still more singularly the king.

But when the same authors speak of the privileges and occupations reserved for Brahmins, they usually use the term *svakarma,* thereby speaking of their "own jobs" rather than their "own *dharma.*" And when they speak of other classes' "own jobs" instead of their *svadharma,* they inevitably come to saying what other classes may and may not do in terms of the jobs reserved for Brahmins. *Manu* even gives the Brahmin the job of establishing "distinctions among jobs" (1.26). The overall implication is that the *svakarma* of Brahmins defines the "archetype" or default position of *dharma* implicitly, usually without mentioning the term *dharma,* for all Āryas. Half of the Brahmins' "own jobs"—studying but not teaching, sacrificing but not officiating at sacrifices, and giving but not receiving gifts—are allowed for Kṣatriyas and Vaiśyas, while Śūdras, whose usual job description is "obedience," can apply for none of the above. It is this kind of scheme, one found in all our classical Brahmanical *dharma* texts, that Kṛṣṇa is reformulating at the far side of Ring 3.

In summary, as far as I can see, the terms *svadharma* and *svakarma* get their first real workout in the *dharmasūtras*, where a kind of semantic drift between them is set in motion; the two are then further developed as governing models and overlapping discourses in *Manu* and the *Mahābhārata*. In brief, the *svakarma* of the Brahmin is an archetype that models the activities of other classes on prerogatives grounded in sacrificial ritual. And the Kṣatriya's *svadharma* is a role model for all classes to fulfill duties that uphold the Brahmanical order.

> Ring 4: a. Kṛṣṇa claims that he himself is the restorer of *dharma* (4.7–8).
>
> b. Arjuna, during his exhilarated description of Kṛṣṇa's revelation of his divine form, accepts this, seeing that Kṛṣṇa is "the unchanging protector of the everlasting *dharma*" (11.18).

So far, most of our *dharma* citations have come from the *Bhagavad Gītā*'s edges: on the near side from chapters 1 to 3, and on the far side all from chapter 18. When it comes to Kṛṣṇa's revelations at the *Gītā*'s center, things get more diffuse. But it is simple enough to appreciate that the two passages just cited define a fourth ring. On one side, we have come to the famous passage where Kṛṣṇa reveals how he provides divine intervention whenever *dharma* is negatively affected by the course of time:

> Whenever there is a waning of *dharma* and a surge of *adharma,* O Bhārata, then I create myself; for the complete rescue of the good and for the destruction of the wicked, for the sake of the establishment of *dharma* I come into being from age to age. (4.7–8)

Here we have an idea with a long future, for the theme of Viṣṇu as preserver of *dharma* comes to be associated with the *avatāra* doctrine of "incarnation" or, preferably, divine "descent." This doctrine is probably under construction in both epics from their very conception—

and I do not think that these verses would be an exception. Meanwhile, on the farther side of Ring 4, as Arjuna stands in awe before Kṛṣṇa's universal form, we hear him say,

> You are the highest syllable to be known, you are the supreme resting place of this all, you are the unchanging protector of the everlasting *dharma,* I hold you to be the eternal Puruṣa. (11.18)

Here, where Kṛṣṇa will soon reveal himself to be "Time grown old for the destruction of the worlds" and will urge Arjuna to be Time's "mere instrument" (*Bhagavad Gītā* 11.33), we again see movement. For beyond learning that Kṛṣṇa rescues *dharma* from age to age or *yuga* to *yuga,* Arjuna now sees for himself that Kṛṣṇa protects an everlasting *dharma* through the fullness of Time. Moreover, between these two moments, Arjuna twice cries out "O Viṣṇu!" (11.24, 30).

But if these verses form a powerful inner ring, what they relate to, including a few other references to *dharma,* is now strung out all over the text.

A Heart of Dharma *in the* Bhagavad Gītā?

If, nonetheless, we ask whether the *Gītā* offers a central focus on *dharma,* we should know that it will remain a question. I believe there are four choices. The first and simplest is to take Arjuna's euphoric description of Kṛṣṇa as "the protector of eternal *dharma*" to be that center. It has the merit of being the one mention of *dharma* in the famous eleventh chapter, which some would take as the acme of the *Bhagavad Gītā* in that it discloses its theophany. Another would be for the *Gītā* to have saved its deepest disclosure for the verse where Kṛṣṇa tells Arjuna he should abandon all *dharmas* since Kṛṣṇa will release him from every sin (18.66). For some Vaishnavas (sectarians of Viṣṇu), this verse is called the *Gītā*'s "summarizing verse." Yet, if our analysis has merit, either would be a disappointing conclusion, since both occur on the far sides of rings rather than at any real center. An interesting candidate nested within all four rings has been mentioned. This is the one instance where Kṛṣṇa speaks of *dharma* in the sense of his "teaching" or "doctrine": "Men who lack faith in this *dharma,* enemy-burner, having failed to reach me, return to the runaround of deaths" (9.2–3). This is a fairly powerful verse, and it has clear soteriological implications, but of a negative sort. Arjuna would have a right to expect something more positive from Kṛṣṇa, who has moved him beyond his initial fear of going to hell.

This brings us to our final candidate, which takes a little explaining as to how it could be at a heart of things. In introducing the subject of *dharma* rings within the *Bhagavad Gītā,* I have referred to the possibility that the *Gītā*'s deepest message on *dharma* may be lodged in a center that seems off-center or deferred to its twelfth to sixteenth chapters. The theory here is that these five chapters have what has been called a "barleycorn" structure, with chapter 14 as the kernel. To simplify, having resolved Arjuna's familial and class anxieties in chapters 1 to 6, and built up to his awesome theophany from chapters 7 to 11, Kṛṣṇa now pauses to tell Arjuna some of the *Gītā*'s deep implications, couching them as secrets and mysteries. Given that chapters 12 and 16, and 13 and 15, can be read as continuous discussions, chapter 14 would lie at the center of this pattern, possibly on the analogy of the fourteenth night being that of the full moon, and marking a transition from the increasingly luminous to the increasingly dark. Looked at in this fashion, after closing chapter 16 on the topic of "demonic people," Kṛṣṇa would devote chapter 17 to people of different faiths before offering the encouraging closures of chapter 18.

There are some problems with this theory, but they diminish as one works inward. Chapters 12 and 16 can be read continuously only as a discussion of the virtues and vices held by people of different natures. Kṛṣṇa mentions four types of devotees who are each dear to him in chapter 12, and briefly takes up "divine people" (who may be the same as those mentioned in chapter 12) in chapter 16 before getting to the "demonic people" just mentioned. Chapters 13 and 15, however, feel more thematically continuous: the former introduces Kṛṣṇa as the field-knower who, in the latter, plants the first seed that yields the cosmic upside-down fig tree, which Kṛṣṇa invites Arjuna to fell at its roots with the axe of detachment. This seeding theme readily relates to the kernel verses that begin chapter 14:

> Further I shall declare the supreme knowledge of knowledges knowing which all the Munis have gone from this world to supreme success. Having resorted to this knowledge, they came to have the

> same nature as me *(mama sādharmyam).* Even at the creation they do not take birth, and they are not disturbed at the dissolution. My womb is the great *Brahman.* (14.1–3)

Clearly, these words meet our criteria for being a kernel about *dharma.* Their message is positive. They seem to be centered in a ring of five chapters: albeit off-center from our other rings, yet in a ring-pattern plausibly designed for them. And their first verse is obvious about declaring its centrality as "the supreme knowledge of knowledges." But what is *dharma* here, and what is the positive message?

Most translators have found ways to translate *sādharmyam* without making obvious reference to any of the usual meanings of *dharma.* But there is no good reason to be obscure. The term derives from *sa-dharma,* which can mean either "having the same nature" or "subject to the same laws or duties." Clearly the former is preferable, as it is when *Manu* says the "delinquent-born" and Śūdras "have the same natures" (10.41). Much as when Kṛṣṇa describes himself as "Time grown old for the destruction of the worlds" (11.33), his "nature" survives the creation and dissolution of the universe. This befits a god credited with preserving not only the universe but also the eternal *dharma.* Yet the good news is more immediate. The Munis who "have gone from this world to supreme success" have the "same nature as [Kṛṣṇa]," being neither reborn nor disturbed. It is on that note that Kṛṣṇa continues to be reassuring:

> My womb is the great *Brahman.* In it I place the germ, and the origin of all beings comes about, Bhārata. In all wombs, Kaunteya, whatever forms come into being, the great *Brahman* is their womb. I am the father who bestows the seed. (14.3–4)

From this point Kṛṣṇa begins talking about the three qualities of nature and the types of bondage each incurs, though these can be transcended by attaining Kṛṣṇa's "being" *(bhāva)* (19).

We may find it surprising after all the talk about Kṣatriya *dharma,* and in particular Kṣatriya *svadharma,* to find Kṛṣṇa telling Arjuna that the model for attaining "my being" *(mad-bhāvam)*—which would have to be Kṛṣṇa's *svabhāva*—lies in the Munis who have "the same *dharma*" that he does, in that they survive creations and dissolutions of the universe unaffected and undisturbed. Yet we have had an inkling of such exemplary sages in chapter 7 in Sītā's remark on the good fortune of the Supreme Sages who would be seeing Rāma return to heaven. And Arjuna has been prepared to understand this as well in the *Gītā* itself. Earlier, he has been told how the Munis and Ṛṣis are *yogins* who attain "the felicity of *Brahman*" *(Brahma-nirvāṇa)* and "become *Brahman*" *(Brahma-bhūta)* (5.24):

> The sages obtain the felicity of *Brahman,* their sins destroyed, their doubts cleft, their selves restrained, delighted in the welfare of all beings. To ascetics detached from desire and anger, their minds tamed, who know themselves, the felicity of *Brahman* lies near. Keeping outside contacts out, centering the eye between the eyebrows, evening out inhalation and exhalation within the nostrils, controlling the senses, mind, and spirit, the Muni intent upon *mokṣa,* whose desire, fear, and anger are gone, is released forever. Knowing that I am the recipient of sacrifices and austerities, the great lord of all the world, the friend of all beings, he attains peace. (5.25–29)

Unlike such sages, however, Arjuna, when he was given the divine eye to witness Kṛṣṇa's universal form as Creator and Destroyer, *was* affected, indeed overwhelmed, left stammering and bowing in adoration, imploring Kṛṣṇa to show his grace "as a father to a son, as a friend to a friend, as a beloved to a beloved" (11.44).

Kṛṣṇa's theophany may make his case for Kṣatriya *svadharma* a slam dunk, but he is not rushing his friend Arjuna on the deeper matters. Earlier, he has told him that will take a while:

> For there is no purifier here the like of knowledge; in time, one who is perfected by *yoga* finds that in himself. The one who has faith obtains knowledge, intent upon it, his senses controlled; having obtained knowledge, in not a long time he finds the highest peace. (4.38–39; cf. 5.6)

Mindful of Kṛṣṇa's relaxed approach, let us now look at how chapter 14, proposed as a deferred center, closes after Arjuna has learned that attaining "the supreme knowledge of knowledges" has to do not only with being, like the Munis, of the "same nature" as Kṛṣṇa, but with transcending the three qualities of nature to attain Kṛṣṇa's own "being."

Arjuna wants to know the traits and conduct of one who transcends the three qualities, and how one does it. Kṛṣṇa replies:

> He does not hate illumination, activity, and even delusion when they arise, Pāṇḍava, nor wish for them when they have ceased. Sitting as one who is sitting apart, who is not agitated by the qualities, thinking only, 'The qualities are at work,' who remains firm and is not stirred; who is the same in happiness and unhappiness, self-abiding, for whom clods, stones, and gold are the same, alike to those dear and undear, steady, alike to blame and self-praise, alike to honor and dishonor, alike to the sides of friend and foe, who abandons all undertakings, he is said to have transcended the qualities. And he who serves me with unswerving *bhaktiyoga,* having transcended these qualities, is fit for becoming *Brahman.* For I am the foundation of *Brahman,* of the immortal and the unchanging, of the everlasting *dharma,* and of the absolute happiness. (14.21–27)

Kṛṣṇa not only allows that Arjuna will need time to digest what he has to say, but he also says, Don't hate what arises from the three qualities—illumination from goodness, activity from passion, or even delusion or bewilderment *(moha)* from darkness, or wish for whatever of them has ceased. This could describe how Kṛṣṇa or the sages experience the qualities, or it could be preparing Arjuna for a long, passionate, and bewildering war. The three qualities function here something like the Buddhist *dharma* theory: one should not be attached to them as they rise and fall, they are not what one really is. But to know the "knowledge of knowledges" is to know that they arise from matter that is seeded by Kṛṣṇa as the "womb of the great *Brahman*" in which all selves find their origin and their absolute happiness and highest felicity. For that knowledge to make one "fit for becoming *Brahman,*" it would also recall the earlier passage just cited, where "becoming *Brahman*" was likewise used to describe the Ṛṣis' and Munis' attainment of *Brahma-nirvāṇa,* which I have translated as "the felicity of *Brahman.*" Although it is controversial, the fact that the *Gītā* makes such a strong use of the term *Brahma-nirvāṇa* in conjunction with "becoming *Brahman,*" which is also used in early Buddhist texts to describe *nibbāna* and even the Buddha's attainment of it (see *Saṃyutta Nikāya* iv. 94–95), is probably an indication, one of many, that the *Mahābhārata* wants Kṛṣṇa to be saying something different from the Buddha.

The *Bhagavad Gītā* does not tell us what Arjuna makes of this "knowledge of knowledges" that reveals the endgame of *bhaktiyoga,* or how he factors these interludes about the Ṛṣis into his more pressing concerns with Kṣatriya *svadharma.* But these passages are suggestive for getting at what the *Mahābhārata,* and probably also the *Rāmāyaṇa,* has to say about the relation between *dharma* and *bhakti,* the topic of our next chapter. Let us anticipate a finding we shall meet there, that the *Mahābhārata* speaks of a lofty concept it calls both "the *dharma* of the Ṛṣis" and "the *dharma* of the Munis," and ask, on the hypothesis that Kṛṣṇa could be talking about it, what the *Gītā* would have told us about this unusual *dharma.* From these passages, we can start out with this. If Kṛṣṇa and the liberated sages know themselves to have "the same nature," and if Arjuna could know this too, given time (and Time), it would relate to a delight in the "welfare of all beings" and a friendship extended to "friend and foe alike."

Finally, if chapter 14 of the *Bhagavad Gītā* gives us the deferred heart of what the *Gītā* has to say about *dharma,* it is not so much a center as another ring, beginning with *dharma* in the sense of Kṛṣṇa's ultimate salvific "nature" and ending with the "everlasting *dharma*" that has its foundation in Kṛṣṇa like the *Brahman* one can become through knowledge and unswerving *bhaktiyoga.* I suggest we think of this centerless ring as centered in "becoming *Brahman*" like the perfected Ṛṣis who attain *Brahman*'s felicity, coming "to have the same nature as" Kṛṣṇa: a golden ring to catch while the merry-go-round goes round.

CHAPTER 9

Dharma and Bhakti

One of the results of making narrative central to our discussion of classical constructions of *dharma* was that we would inevitably be questioning not only the relation between *dharma* and *mokṣa*, as many have done, but that between *dharma* and *bhakti*. We have seen that the epics make bridges between these two concepts, notably in portraying the spirituality of women and warriors. And we have seen that the *Bhagavad Gītā* makes the relation between *dharma* and *bhakti* one of Kṛṣṇa's "central" teachings and modes of "knowing."

Now, if we take the two epics and *Manu* as roughly contemporary, the question of how these three ambitious poems treat this relation becomes intriguing. The most satisfactory theory posits that the epics, led by the *Mahābhārata*, navigated a *bhakti* "swerve" that *Manu* was aware of, but was obdurately opposed to mentioning. It is an advance to see *Manu* remapping traditional legal routes through a new cosmology and terrain that has fresh epic markings (eons, ages through which *dharma* declines, kings making their age, thinking kings if not queens, a hallowed land of the Kurus, not to mention disastrous ancient dice games [9.227]), but with their *bhakti* overtones unmentioned, most likely by intent.

"Avatars" and Sages

As we saw in chapter 8, the *Gītā*'s treatment of *dharma* zeroes in on a relation between time, divinity, and *dharma* that comes to be associated with the concept of *avatāra* or divine "descent." The revelation of Kṛṣṇa's world-swallowing theophany is an indication that Viṣṇu's incarnations not only restore *dharma* from age to age but, as in Kṛṣṇa's case, also have a terrifying aspect that preserves *dharma* through Time's world destructions. The *Gītā* then goes on to tell us that cosmic cycles of creation and destruction are survived by Ṛṣis and Munis who, having attained perfection, "have the same nature *(dharma)*" as Kṛṣṇa. Presumably, such sages would know what they are talking about on matters of *dharma* and *bhakti,* and we shall begin this chapter meeting two of them, Mārkaṇḍeya and Nārada, in the *Mahābhārata* (the *Rāmāyaṇa* also knows them). One way of thinking about the epics' *bhakti* swerve would be to see it as outsourcing *dharma* to such celestial and "ancient" Ṛṣis and to a descending god whose company they keep.

As with the *Gītā,* the *Mahābhārata* never uses the term *avatāra.* But it provides early accounts of all but one of the figures later named in lists of the ten avatars—the omitted one, not surprisingly, being the Buddha. For our purposes it is enough to note that both epics know Rāma as an incarnation of Viṣṇu, while the *Mahābhārata* also knows Kṛṣṇa in this way, and speaks of the future savior Kalki, a Brahmin, as "the fame of Viṣṇu." Mārkaṇḍeya tells the stories of both Kalki and Rāma to the Pāṇḍavas and Draupadī in the forest, the former while Kṛṣṇa is visiting them (*Mahābhārata* 3.180–189).

Mārkaṇḍeya drops by at the same time as the "time-knowing" Nārada, who smilingly prompts him to begin. Once, when all that remained of the triple world was the endless waters of the cosmic dissolution, Mārkaṇḍeya, swimming all alone, saw a child sleeping on a leaf of a banyan tree. Swallowed and regurgitated by this babe, he learned, to his astonishment, after wandering in the worldly byways of the child's cosmic body, that the child was none other than Viṣṇu–Nārāyaṇa sleeping through the dissolution. Awakened, the child tells Mārkaṇḍeya of his greatness as Nārāyaṇa, starting out with the same "surge" verse we heard from Kṛṣṇa in Ring 4 of the *Bhagavad Gītā,* its only other occurrence in the epic (Arjuna has yet to hear Kṛṣṇa repeat it):

> Whenever there is a waning of *dharma* and a surge of *adharma,* O sage, then I create myself. When demons bent on harm spring up invincible to the chiefs of the gods, and terrifying Rākṣasas, then I take on birth in the dwellings of the virtuous and, entering a human body, I pacify it all.

Mārkaṇḍeya then says the child was none other than this Kṛṣṇa in the Pāṇḍavas and Draupadī's company, "your ally . . . who sits here as though at play, . . . the unborn God of the beginning, Viṣṇu the Person of the yellow robe," and tells the five brothers they should "go to him for refuge; he will grant it."

When Yudhiṣṭhira soon asks Mārkaṇḍeya what will happen "with the destruction of the age," Mārkaṇḍeya tells about the upcoming Kali age or Age of Discord that will end with the coming of Kalki. One sign of the faltering of *dharma* will be that people will abandon Brahmanical sites of worship in favor of sepulchral mounds, which may refer to the Buddhist monuments called *stūpas* that Aśoka is reputed to have built all over the subcontinent. Once Kalki sets aright this topsy-turvy world, Brahmanical sanctuaries will be restored, "Brahmins will be strict, Munis will do penance, and hermitages with heretics will become firm in truth." The point to note is that the Pāṇḍavas and Draupadī have just hosted Mārkaṇḍeya, Nārada, and Kṛṣṇa in such a forest hermitage.

Mapping Dharma *and* Bhakti

What kind of cartography best suits the mapping of *dharma* and *bhakti* across this large terrain? Clearly, it will not be just a matter of mapping *bhakti* terms (although I will flag some formations from the verbal root behind avatars, meaning "descend," and the term *bhakti* itself in some passages). If one wants to get into the bones of these works, the first answer for a book on *dharma* is to keep track of the way the epics and *Manu* relate to the Veda. As noted in chapter 1, all three depict *dharma* as allegiance to the Veda, but in markedly different ways. The *Mahābhārata* identifies itself as a "fifth Veda" and fits itself out with Vedic allusions. *Manu* lists Veda as the first and foremost of its four sources of *dharma*. And the *Rāmāyaṇa* surrounds Rāma with a virtually Vedic world. Also, in contrast to the very ambiguous and capacious treatments of both *dharma* and *bhakti* in the *Mahābhārata*, *Manu* seems to screen out *bhakti* while putting an orthodox stamp on *dharma;* and the *Rāmāyaṇa* streamlines and straightens out both *bhakti* and *dharma* around its figure of a royal perfect man living in a nearly perfect Vedic time. If *Manu* refuses to accommodate a *bhakti* swerve and the *Rāmāyaṇa* seeks to disambiguate it, we have further ways to think about the politics of *bhakti* and the spiritualities it fosters in relation to *dharma*.

There is much to contrast the two epics on this score. But there are two interrelated practices or discourses where *dharma* and *bhakti* coincide that go to the heart (if not the bones) of what both epics are about: hospitality and friendship. With hospitality, if we simply ask, Who hosts Kṛṣṇa and Rāma? Who do they host in turn? What is the tone or mood created? we get into revealing segments enlivened by *bhakti* sentiments. Similarly with friendship. We have seen how Sītā and Draupadī fare in separation from Rāma and Kṛṣṇa. Devotional tones or moods can also be noticed in circumstances where Rāma or Kṛṣṇa are parting and people accompany them as far as possible and then hold them dearly in mind.

The epics are sometimes attentive to such departures in ways that are not the case for the comings and goings of other "characters." Rāma's prolonged departure from Ayodhyā is perhaps well enough known to be recalled only in a few details below. But the *Mahābhārata* has similar descriptions of Kṛṣṇa's departures. Two occur in Book 2, and one, which will be mentioned below, in Book 5. But it is fitting to highlight Kṛṣṇa's poignant last farewell, which comes after he has lingered longer than he wished to help Arjuna out of goodheartedness to remember the *Gītā*. Having mounted his chariot amid the city folk of the capital; having said his difficult goodbyes to his sister, paternal aunt Kuntī, and others close to him in the Pāṇḍavas' company, and bid them return to the city; and having told his charioteer to "urge the horses to speed," he sets out on his way.

> And while Vārṣṇeya [Kṛṣṇa] was proceeding to Dvārakā, O Bharata bull, those foe-scorchers with their retinue, having embraced, turned back. Again and again Phalguna [Arjuna] embraced Vārṣṇeya and as long as he was in eye's range, he saw him again and again. And even so, Pārtha withdrew that sight fixed on Govinda with difficulty, and the unvanquished Kṛṣṇa [withdrew his sight with difficulty from Arjuna] as well. (14.52.1–3)

As it would be in later texts, this is clearly the *bhakti* trope of *viraha* or "love in separation," and it is worth pointing out that the Buddhist poet Aśvaghoṣa, who knew both epics, already uses it in that fashion as an established idiom in his portrayal of the Buddha's Great Departure, as we shall see in chapter 10.

Practices and Idioms of Hospitality and Friendship

With the exception of the friendship of Kṛṣṇa and Arjuna, hospitality and friendship (and separation) are not the first things one thinks of regarding epic treatments of *dharma* and *bhakti.* But if a post-Aśokan Brahmanical ideology puts kingship front and center in both epics and *Manu,* and may even be said to be what their arguments are ostensibly about, this is not, in any of these texts, the grounds on which the argument was capable of being won. How society is ordered is one thing. How people get along is another. That was encouraged by invoking hospitality and friendship among the more open and flexible civilizational discourses and practices (another is the gift) familiar as custom throughout South Asian Ārya culture under countless local and regional variations. Indeed, these are *spiritual* discourses and practices that the Buddha himself relied on rather than criticized (as he did class) and could do no better than attempt to refine, as we saw in chapter 4. In reformulating hospitality and friendship as *dharma,* the *dharmasūtras* and *Manu* all sought to harmonize custom with Vedic practices and discourses, and so did the epics. But the epics could give this amalgam more complex treatment by telling stories about hallowed ancient Ṛṣis, among others, and a god among men. In making this "swerve," they could develop it in narratives that were far more nuanced than incessant top-heavy reminders that the four social classes were created from Puruṣa.

For the most part, the basic vocabularies on friendship and hospitality are shared by the epics and the legal literature. But the epics also innovate and archaize. Although several Sanskrit words are often translated as "friend," I will use that translation for only the most prominent of them, *sakhi*—the term that defines the special spiritual friendships of Kṛṣṇa with Draupadī and Arjuna. In using it, the *Mahābhārata* draws on Vedic precedents in giving it two senses, one of which we can call "pact-friendship," and the other, "intimate friendship." Other terms with sometimes overlapping meaning will be translated as "ally" and "well-wisher."

Meanwhile, *atithi* is the main old word for "guest," and *ātithyam* for "hospitality." There is no consistent term for host, that concept being more contextual. A host may be found in a house, a sacrifice, a performance, perhaps on a chariot, in a heart, and so on. A few pre-epic usages are also interesting here. Drawing on older Vedic notions of Viṣṇu as the exemplary guest in the "guest offering rites" that "call the gods to mind," *Āpastamba* 2.7.5–10 tells us,

> "Whether you hold them dear or not," it is stated, "guests lead you to heaven." When a man gives food in the morning, at noon, and in the evening, they constitute the three pressings of Soma; when he rises as his guest gets up to leave, it constitutes the final rite of the Soma sacrifice; when he addresses the guest with kind words, it constitutes the praise of the priestly fee; when he follows the guest as he leaves, it constitutes the Viṣṇu steps; and when he returns, it constitutes the final bath.

It is interesting, in the light of passages on Kṛṣṇa's and Rāma's departures, that following the guest until he leaves should "constitute the Viṣṇu steps." *Āpastamba* 2.6.3–6 is vivid in exemplifying *dharma* as hospitality:

> A guest comes like a blazing fire. When someone has studied one branch from each of the Vedas in accordance with *dharma*, he is called a "Vedic scholar." When such a man comes to the home of a householder devoted to his *svadharma*—and he comes for no other purpose than to put *dharma* first—then he is called a "guest." By paying him homage, the householder obtains peace and heaven.

The "blazing 'fire'" that is like an arriving guest is *"agni"*: it could be the god Agni visiting, or the spiritual opportunity to offer one of the five daily "great sacrifices" to feed an almsman. This brings us to a sort of touchstone-text: a surprising unit from the *Mahābhārata*'s Book 13 that closes King Yudhiṣṭhira's postwar instruction on the topic of "the law of giving" after the learned Bhīṣma has covered three prior *dharma* topics in Book 12—a curriculum that we shall seek to clarify in chapter 10.

Ṛṣidharma

At the close of chapter 8, we anticipated a *Mahābhārata* discussion on "the *dharma* of Ṛṣis." This occurs in the "Dialogue between Umā and

Maheśvara" (*Mahābhārata* 13.126–134, henceforth *Umā-Maheśvara Saṃvāda*), which comes toward the end of Yudhiṣṭhira's postwar instruction in which Bhīṣma coordinates his lawgiving with *bhakti.* It begins with Yudhiṣṭhira wanting to know more about Kṛṣṇa, who has up to now been standing by, once again the listening guest, ever since Bhīṣma began his long sermon. Bhīṣma is overjoyed to speak on this subject, and tells one story about Kṛṣṇa that leads him to a second, in which he quotes Nārada to narrate the actual *Umā-Maheśvara Saṃvāda.* As one would expect, there are threads that link the two stories. The first tells how Kṛṣṇa once undertook a twelve-year vow at some mountain to obtain a son.

When Kṛṣṇa had completed the initiation for this vow, he was visited by a "company of Ṛṣis" called a *Ṛṣisaṅgha,* a term worth tracking along with its equivalent, the "host of Munis" or *Munigaṇa.* Among the Ṛṣi visitors were Nārada, Vyāsa, and others with their disciples, and Kṛṣṇa received them all with rites of hospitality like those offered to the gods. Once he had seated them on gorgeous seats, they chatted amiably on matters of *dharma* until Kṛṣṇa released a fire from his mouth that burned the entire mountain with its living creatures and came back to him like a docile disciple, after which he brought everything back to life. Noticing that his well-travelled callers were "surprised" at this "inconceivable wonder," Kṛṣṇa explained that the fire contained his "energy of Viṣṇu." Then he asked them to tell him something "highly wonderful" that they had seen or heard on earth or in heaven. The sages appointed Nārada to tell a wonderful sequel.

Nārada leads us into an idyll of the god Śiva (the "Destroyer") and his wife Umā on Mount Himavat that is interrupted when Umā covers Śiva's eyes in jest, leaving the world in darkness and distress until Śiva's third eye opens and burns the mountain—which Umā then gets him to restore to its natural beauty. This inspires her to ask a series of questions about her husband's quirks, beginning with his third eye, followed by further questions about *dharma,* asked for the benefit of the Ṛṣis and Munis who attend them.

Umā soon wants to know about the *dharma* of Ṛṣis or Munis, using the compounds *Ṛṣidharma* and *Munidharma.* Śiva responds by describing different types of "gleaners": "foam drinkers," who "glean" or, perhaps better, "skim" their nourishment from the foam of waters left over from sacrifices; "wheel rovers," who practice the *dharma* of compassion, rove in the world of the gods, and "glean" their food from moonbeams; others, who live with their wives, practice the five "great sacrifices," and "glean" their nourishment from the flames of their fires; and thumb-sized sages, who live in the solar disc, wear deer skins or tree bark, follow an actual "gleaning" mode of life by subsisting like birds on grains left in the fields, and "attain equity with the gods in accomplishing the purpose of the gods' work."

It is with reference to this varied "gleaning" ideal that Śiva then summarizes the *dharma* of Ṛṣis and Munis in the passage that should interest us:

> In all the *Ṛṣidharmas,* selves are to be conquered, sense faculties are conquered. . . . Turning away from food prepared with cows' milk and taking pleasure in lying on the bare ground, [doing] yoga, enjoying vegetables and leaves, eating fruits and roots, partaking of wind, water, and duck weed—these are some observances of the Ṛṣis by which they conquer the way of the unsubjugated. When there is no more smoke, when the pestle is set down, when there are no more coals, when the people have eaten their meal, when the handing around of vessels is over, when the time for asking alms has passed by, surely [it is then, still] longing for a guest, [that] one eats the food left over. Delighted by the *dharma* of truth, patient, he is yoked to the *Munidharma.* Not arrogant or proud, the one who is neither heedless nor surprised, a friend alike to friend and foe, he is the foremost knower of *dharma.*

The basic hospitality practice here of waiting for the settling or setting down of the pestle, smoke, embers, and plates as four signals for when to eat occurs, sometimes partially, as a *dharmasūtra* adage at *Baudhāyana* 2.11.22 and *Vasiṣṭha* 10.7–8, as well as at *Manu* 6.56. It is also mentioned in the *Aggañña Sutta,* where the Buddha, offering a sly etymology for Brahmins by punning on the words linking fire-tending and meditation, speaks of the prelapsarian practices of the original good Brahmins (*Dīgha Nikāya* 27.22). What is striking is that, except for Śiva, everyone else describes when a begging guest gets to eat, not when the host waiting for a guest gets to eat. Achieving a startling effect, the *Mahābhārata* has transformed the adage to describe *Ṛṣidharma* as what householder hosts do themselves, longing for a guest to honor with their meager fare.

Now it is not surprising that Umā and Śiva, surrounded in their Himalayan retreat by hosts of eccentric sages, would share an interest in unusual and surprising *dharmas.* But the term *Ṛṣidharma* was a surprise to me, as I had never even considered that there was such a thing. One does not hear about *Ṛṣidharma* or *Munidharma* from *Manu,* even though the celestial sages form Manu's first audience. Nor, even though we may have found in chapter 8 that Kṛṣṇa refers to it indirectly when he tells Arjuna about Munis who "came to have the same nature *(dharma)* as" him and who "even at the creation do not take birth, and are not disturbed at the dissolution," it is not the sort of thing one would have expected in the *Bhagavad Gītā.* It shows the value of having more than one god's opinion about *dharma.* Indeed, Śiva will round off his dialogue with Umā by getting her reply to *his* question about the *dharma* of women.

The terms *Ṛṣidharma* and *Munidharma* occur five and four times, respectively, in the *Mahābhārata;* all but two of these occurrences are in the *Umā-Maheśvara Saṃvāda,* and all of them are in Bhīṣma's postwar instructions. Clearly, Mārkaṇḍeya and Nārada exemplify this "*dharma* of the sages": the first by surviving and witnessing the dissolution; the latter by narrating Śiva and Pārvatī's dialogue in the *Umā-Maheśvara Saṃvāda,* where the terms are most fully developed. Neither term is found in the *Rāmāyaṇa.* Yet, *Ṛṣidharma* is all over the place in both epics, and in them has much to do not only with *dharma* but also with *bhakti*—and, as the quote from Śiva would suggest, with hospitality and friendship. Let us begin by noting some of the ways *Ṛṣidharma* can be appreciated straight from this passage. I will first deal with practitioners of *Ṛṣidharma*—at least as Śiva describes them—and then turn to the topic of Ṛṣi companies as audiences.

It seems that despite their elemental modes of subsistence and access to higher worlds, Śiva's gleaners still lead earthly lives. As one can gather from various texts, their mode of life is a high spiritual ideal for real people. Gleaners are not necessarily Brahmins and are not evidence of bad kings. That is, they are not reduced to a starvation diet or forced to lower themselves to the jobs of other classes because a king goes bad, and they have nothing to do with class-mixing. Even a king may elevate himself by the practice; says *Manu,* should a king "eke out a living by gleaning, his fame spreads in the world like a drop of oil on water" (7.33). But as *Manu* indicates elsewhere, it is mainly Brahmins who would have this high ideal, that of a sort of liminal householder life somewhere between the second and third life-stage, enjoined to perform the five "great sacrifices" but with what seems the absolute minimum that its practitioners might offer to their own families, not to mention guests. Among those mentioned by Śiva, the foam-, moonbeam-, and fire-gleaners could be forest dwellers, but the actual grain-gleaners would have to live near agricultural fields even if they are dressed in leaves and tree bark. Yet they all "attain equity with the gods in accomplishing the purpose of the gods' work." It is indeed a high ideal in the *Mahābhārata,* where it is exalted to Yudhiṣṭhira in several sub-tales, where a god in disguise (his father Dharma), or a saint, comes as a hungry guest to test its practitioner.

Clearly, the ideal is precisely this: to live out daily, as Śiva says, the challenges of hospitality and friendship to all with patience in a world of marvels, indeed, where one is oneself one of the marvels, but as one who is surprised by nothing. It remains a living ideal in India, as I learned from my friend T. P. Mahadevan, who grew up in Kerala. He remembers that his mother thought there was no one finer than a gleaner Brahmin who lived a life beyond "the taint of the stipends [that] regular Vaidika Brahmins had to endure" and who could rise "above it all, a liberated soul squaring the circle, as it were, in the world but out of it."

As to the audiences of more celestial Ṛṣis and Munis, such as the two Ṛṣi companies that attend to Kṛṣṇa and to Umā and Śiva, here we meet variants of the widest audiences of the two epics and *Manu:* in the *Mahābhārata,* the stellar Ṛṣis who hear the epic in its outer frame; the Ṛṣis who come from Brahmaloka with Brahmā's permission to hear the rest of the *Rāmāyaṇa* once Sītā has descended into the earth; and the heavenly Ṛṣis who listen to Manu's son Bhṛgu recite *Manu.* We also find another variation in the last verses of the *Śvetāśvatara*

Upaniṣad (6.21–23), a text that has often been thought to be theologically and chronologically close to the *Bhagavad Gītā:*

> By the power of his austerities and by the grace of God, the wise Śvetāśvatara first came to know *Brahman* and then proclaimed it to those who had passed beyond their orders of life as the highest means of purification that brings delight to the company of Ṛṣis *(ṛṣisaṅgha).* This supreme secret was proclaimed during a former eon in the Vedānta. One should not disclose it to a person who is not of a tranquil disposition, or who is not one's son or pupil. Only in a man who has the deepest *bhakti* for God, and who shows the same love for his teacher as toward God, do these points declared by the Noble One shine forth.

Here, where we meet the term *Ṛṣisaṅgha* explicitly, what is interesting is how this *bhakti* text uses it to do something *bhakti* is famous for: constructing a spiritual community, and with it an audience. Such a usage of the term *saṅgha* has counterparts in the wider sense of the Buddhist second refuge "in the *saṅgha,*" which can also be an audience for texts, and in the use of the same term for the first audiences of Tamil literature. Even without the term, I think *Manu* also shows familiarity with the novel textual practice of providing a Ṛṣi audience for Manu's unbudging orthodoxy.

In our Brahmanical texts, however, such universal listeners are not only the greatest of sages, enough of them Vedic to make that part of their aura, but a model audience that listens for and with a carefully constructed and spiritually attuned "us." Indeed, in very broad terms, we can say that the Ṛṣis host the texts, and of course not just the texts but their readers, since they set the model for receiving the texts into human lives and homes and open questions of interpretation just by their aware spiritual presence, not to mention their interventions where they tell tall tales and "do the gods' work." Indeed, as we have seen, Kṛṣṇa, and indeed Rāma, too, can be listening in.

These highly reflexive and nearly metatextual considerations do point us away from the two Sanskrit epics' main stories. But as I have said, *Ṛṣidharma* is all over the place in both epics, where it has to do not only with hospitality and friendship but with a kind of intimacy and spiritual complicity in these matters that is fostered by the texts themselves, and indeed by their poets under the pen names of their Ṛṣis authors. Vālmīki composes the *Rāmāyaṇa* and imparts it to Sīta's twin boys at his hermitage as nothing less than the host of Sītā, and he comes with the twins to have them sing the *Rāmāyaṇa* at Rāma's Horse Sacrifice as a guest of Rāma before he arrives there again with Sītā for her final ordeal. Vyāsa is time and again a surprise visitor and occasional host. Through these author–sages we are party to thoughts of Rāma and Kṛṣṇa and the generations of heroes and heroines who share their time on earth.

Rāma and Kṛṣṇa as Guests, Hosts, and Friends

Let us then look at a couple of examples from each epic that show the poets' work in creating this kind of spiritual intimacy around hospitality and friendship.

If one looks at the *Rāmāyaṇa* in terms of hospitality for and by Rāma, there are two broad phases. In the first five books one meets Rāma mostly as a guest of forest sages, and as one who refuses to be hosted in the monkey capital of Kiṣkindhā. But the tables turn in Book 6, where he gives refuge to a younger brother of Rāvaṇa. And in Book 7 Rāma, as king, finally gets to host just about everybody—Rākasas, Monkeys, Ṛṣis, and kings—more than once, including, as noted, Vālmīki, and ultimately the intemperate hungry Ṛṣi whose demand for food signals Rāma and his brothers' deaths.

The first phase brings an explicitly Vedic variety of *Ṛṣidharma* right into the story. This is Vālmīki's idea, for only one of the great Ṛṣis Rāma encounters appears in the *Mahābhārata*'s version of the Rāma story. Vālmīki presents himself and Rāma as contemporaries of a set of the most hallowed Vedic Ṛṣis, those from six of the oldest families of Vedic poets. And the culmination of these meetings is with another Rigvedic Ṛṣi who is named along with the others as ancestors of the eight primary Brahmin lineages. Rāma is guided by these sages from his conception to the point where the eighth, Agastya, directs him farther south to the place where Sītā will be abducted. Four of them host Rāma in their hermitages, as do other sages, and several call him their "beloved guest." The most telling instance is the last, where Agastya says to Rāma, with joined hands:

> King of the whole world, one who fares in *dharma,* a great chariot warrior, a man offered reverence and esteem, you have come as my beloved guest. (*Rāmāyaṇa* 3.11.27)

As with the earthly gleaners described by Śiva, these *Rāmāyaṇa* sages do the gods' work and would seem to have more than an inkling of what it is. Once Agastya recognizes his "beloved guest" even in exile as the king of the world, he gives Rāma a bow of Viṣṇu. When Sītā is soon abducted, Brahmā speaks of it as something that had to be done, and the Daṇḍaka Forest Ṛṣis are "thrilled" at the sight.

As to friendship in the *Rāmāyaṇa,* it is the second book that brings the subject to the fore. Here we meet the first articulation of *sakhi* as a "friend" to "master" relation specifically focused on Rāma in his dealings with a low-class or "tribal" boatman (2.44.14; 2.78.5). Otherwise, as Rāma emerges into view in his palace life as he is about to be made heir apparent, he is not a "friend" of anyone else in this book. In departing Ayodhyā, Rāma leaves behind only "well-wishers." Although he has plenty of these, when they are around him they are impersonal, never named. For example, "As for Rāma's well-wishers, they were all bewildered: crushed by the weight of their grief, they could not rise from where they had fallen." The well-wishers are last in the run of those bidding Rāma adieu, mentioned just before the city, "Ayodhyā, with all its hosts of soldiers and herds and horses and elephants"—after which Rāma disappears from the sight of those remaining in the capital. After following Rāma's departure as far as they can, they are among the residents who return to the city and say, "Every hill and grove Rāma visits will treat him as a beloved guest and not fail to accord him hospitality" (2.36–42). Only when Sītā is abducted does Rāma make close friends, most notably with the monkey Sugrīva, through whom he also inspires the devotion of Hanumān. As befits the *Rāmāyaṇa*'s master–servant politics, it restricts the role of friend to subordinates, and separates the roles of friend and devotee, leaving the one no less a servant than the other.

As to the *Mahābhārata,* scenes of friendship and hospitality are more numerous and also harder to separate from each other. Things are also more complex in other ways: unlike Rāma, Kṛṣṇa is never a king with need for subordinates or grandiose hosting obligations; and he tends not to play things straight. Suffice it to say that if one looks at hostings of or by Kṛṣṇa, one can rarely forget that he is the special friend of Arjuna and Draupadī. With Kṛṣṇa coming and going into the *Mahābhārata* action, there are many scenes that relate hospitality and friendship to *dharma*. I choose examples from Kṛṣṇa's embassy to the Kuru court (*Mahābhārata* 5.84–141). For this, we will need to remember that Karṇa is the Pāṇḍavas' older brother and arch foe, and introduce two more *Mahābhārata* characters. One is Vidura, a paternal uncle of both the Pāṇḍavas and Kauravas who speaks as a voice of *dharma* in the Kuru court, and is the incarnation of the god Dharma, whereas Yudhiṣṭhira is Dharma's son. The other is Rāma Jāmadagnya, a potent Ṛṣi who bears a violent grudge against Kṣatriyas since one of them killed his father.

Here, for once, Kṛṣṇa is being hosted by the Kauravas. The lengthy sub-book on Kṛṣṇa's embassy—"The Coming of the Lord"—is filled with moments that could illustrate our points, including Dhṛtarāṣṭra's raptures at the thought of giving Kṛṣna fabulous gifts and displays of welcome; Vidura's advice that it would be enough to give him "a beloved's hospitality"—just a jar of water to drink, water to wash his feet, an inquiry into his health, and what he (supposedly) really wants, peace; and Duryodhana's plans to capture Kṛṣṇa. But let us focus in on the Ṛṣis.

As Kṛṣṇa leaves the Pāṇḍavas' camp, various birds circle auspiciously above him, and then some of the great Brahma-Ṛṣis and divine Ṛṣis, including Nārada and Vālmīki, circumambulate him and perform smokeless rites with mantras on his behalf. We do not hear where they have come from until he sees them standing on both sides of the road, and asks:

> Where have you reached perfection, your lordships? What path has brought you here? What is to be done for your lordships? What can I do for you? For what purpose have your lordships come down to earth?

This show of roadside hospitality to the celestial Ṛṣis now turns into a remarkable scene of friendship: Rāma Jāmadagnya, "embracing Govinda as an old friend in good conduct," speaks for them. Having witnessed the old battles of the gods and the demons, the Ṛṣis are "everywhere wishing to see the gathering of the royal warrior class, the kings sitting in the hall, and yourself speaking the truth, Janārdana. We are coming to watch this grand spectacle." He closes, "Go unhindered, hero, we shall see you in the hall." Note the depth of precedent behind this exchange: not only have the Ṛṣis witnessed the old divine–demonic wars; there is the veiled reference to an old friendship between Kṛṣṇa and Rāma Jāmadagnya. Is this an affinity in their tasks, since this Rāma brought about the "destruction of the Kṣatriyas," as Kṛṣṇa will now do as well? Is it that they are both "avatars" before the term itself gains currency?

Kṛṣṇa's welcome by the Kurus is no simple matter. He rejects Duryodhana's hospitality and spends the night at Vidura's. There at night, after Kṛṣṇa has relaxed, Vidura tells Kṛṣṇa he thinks it was a mistake for him to have come and discourages him from returning to talk to Duryodhana:

> When all those villains are huddled together, your descent *(avataraṇam)* in their midst does not please me, Kṛṣṇa.

Vidura's words are virtually identical with an earlier line, where Yudhiṣṭhira had the same reservations *before* Kṛṣṇa left on this mission:

> I do not agree, Kṛṣṇa, that you should go to the Kurus. Duryodhana will not accept your advice. The earth's assembled warrior class comes under Duryodhana's sway. Your descent *(avataraṇam)* in their midst does not please me, Kṛṣṇa. (5.70.82–83)

It can be no coincidence that Yudhiṣṭhira and Vidura, the son and incarnation of Dharma, discourage Kṛṣṇa from "descending" into what, in the epic's genealogical and incarnational terms, amounts to the camp of demons. This double usage of *avataraṇa* as "descent" resonates with the line that Kṛṣṇa overhears Mārkaṇḍeya attribute to Nārāyaṇa and then repeats to Arjuna in the *Bhagavad Gītā*, "Whenever there is a waning of *dharma* and a surge of *adharma*, then I create myself."

> Disregarding Vidura's cautions, the next day Kṛṣṇa enters Duryodhana's hall: There standing amidst the kings, the foe-

> scorcher . . . saw the Ṛṣis hovering in the sky. While watching them, headed by Nārada, Dāśārha [Kṛṣṇa] said softly to Bhīṣma, "King, the Ṛṣis have come to watch the earthly assembly, and should be invited and honored with seats and full hospitality. No one can sit before they are seated. Let homage be paid to these Munis whose souls have been perfected." Bhīṣma, seeing the Ṛṣis arrived at the gate of the hall, hurriedly ordered the servants: "Seats!"

Clearly the poets leave questions that an attentive reader or company of Ṛṣis might ask: Was the hall open to the sky? Did Bhīṣma not see the Ṛṣis until they got to the gate? How many seats did the servants provide? How many angels can dance on the head of a pin? But this is serious business. Once everyone falls silent looking at the elixir of the dark yellow-robed god in the middle of the court, Kṛṣṇa makes his first speech, beginning, "Let there be peace."

The Ṛṣis will not be silent in this assembly. Rāma Jāmadagnya will warn Duryodhana with the story of an ancient king who foolishly challenged two Ṛṣis at their Himalayan hermitage. Others, including Nārada, will tell stories to urge Duryodhana to curb his pride and make peace. Then Kṛṣṇa will address Duryodhana directly before Duryodhana tries to capture him, his guest. Kṛṣṇa then gives the Ṛṣis and a few others the divine eye to see his uncapturable divine form, and quits the court. Having met with the Pāṇḍavas' mother Kuntī, who sends words to her sons through him, his last business before leaving is with Karṇa.

This scene at the end of Kṛṣṇa's embassy illustrates our whole nexus. First, Kṛṣṇa shows a kind of hospitality by inviting Karṇa to mount his chariot. At this point Dhṛtarāṣṭra asks Sañjaya, "What consolations" did Kṛṣṇa offer Karṇa? Sañjaya replies, "Hear from me [what the two said] in the course of their conversing, in words that were smooth and gentle, dear, joined with *dharma,* truthful, helpful, and to be cherished in the heart."

Recounting Karṇa's birth from Kuntī, Kṛṣṇa tells him he is legally a Pāṇḍava—a son of Pāṇḍu through her—and offers him the kingship. The Pāṇḍavas will clasp his feet. Draupadī will make him her sixth. Hospitality indeed! Kṛṣṇa himself will consecrate him. As Karṇa rides the royal chariot, Yudhiṣṭhira, as his heir apparent, will fan him.

Arjuna will drive. Karṇa will have a whole new life, on which Kṛṣṇa concludes: "Your allies shall shudder with joy, your enemies with fear. Today let there be good brotherhood between you and your Pāṇḍava brothers!" Karṇa does not doubt that Kṛṣṇa is a well-wisher speaking from love or affection, and further, that he speaks to Karṇa's best interests "out of friendship."

The theme of these words being heartfelt is then carried through to the parting words of their meeting, where Kṛṣṇa responds to Karṇa's explanation of why he must refuse. "Kṛṣṇa said, 'Of a certainty the destruction of the earth is now near, for my words do not touch your heart, Karṇa. When the destruction of all creatures is at hand, bad policy disguised as good does not crawl off from the heart.'" Kṛṣṇa commends Karṇa for holding to good policy from his heart, despite rejecting Kṛṣṇa's offer. As they part, Karṇa "clasped Mādhava tightly." As befits the *Mahābhārata*'s *bhakti* politics of friend and foe, Kṛṣṇa and Karṇa's embrace extends the circle of the god's men and women friends to include even the sworn enemy, and, as with Arjuna, combines the roles of friend and devotee.

Now Kṛṣṇa's words in this dialogue are said to have been "smooth and gentle, dear, joined with *dharma*, truthful, helpful, and to be cherished in the heart." In *whose* heart? Karṇa's, whose words are equally heartfelt? Old blind Dhṛtarāṣṭra's, as first listener? The hearts of the seated attendees listening to the *Mahābhārata*'s first recital at the Snake Sacrifice of the Pāṇḍavas' great grandson? The hearts of the great Ṛṣis who are listening to its retelling? All listeners and readers? The phrase puts a big asterisk to these heartfelt words, which provide one of those points where we can feel that the notion of the "well-wisher" ultimately extends to the *bhakti* community of readers that the *Mahābhārata* seeks to create as its audience of aficionados; that is, what classical Indian aesthetic theory calls its *sahṛdayas*, those who appreciate a work of art because they are spiritually "with it at heart."

In conclusion, we come back to the necessities and niceties of textual discretion in portraying the hiddenness of gods among men, which constrains even Kṛṣṇa to operate within human limits, and in Rāma's case is tacitly structured into the *Rāmāyaṇa* around the fact that Rāvaṇa can be slain only by a man. *Bhakti* and *dharma* are in the bones and sinews of these texts *as we have them*. I believe that the *Mahābhārata*'s *bhakti* politics reflected a post-Aśokan and probably post-Mauryan sly and confident sense of taking over the intertextual and inter-religious game. For the *Rāmāyaṇa,* it would appear to be the same game disambiguated by adding live Vedic Brahmins to exemplify *dharma* as hosts and guests through the hero's long career. In both epics, however, *bhakti* is a trump card played discretely and not that often (though certainly more often in the *Mahābhārata*). And it is played with a deck stacked with Ṛṣis who, by "doing the gods' work," support a *new* Brahmanical *dharma,* one they now make spiritually familiar in every sense. It is this combination that could give life to a king who has listened well enough to Kṛṣṇa and even better to the Ṛṣis, as is the case with Yudhiṣṭhira the son of Dharma; or to a king who, as a hidden god himself, could be the Vedic Ṛṣis' "beloved guest." As we shall now see, the Buddhist poet Aśvaghoṣa could respond to this game from a familiarity with both epics, linking his own *bhakti* overtures to the Buddha's quest for the "true *dharma.*"

CHAPTER 10

Reimagining the Dharma Hero

The Adventure of the Buddha

Chapter 6 raised the possibility of viewing the epics' portrayals of Rāma and Yudhiṣṭhira as moral biographies. We now come to a text that may do just that: Aśvaghoṣa's *Buddhacarita,* "The Adventure of the Buddha," which offers a *dharma* biography of a prince who becomes a Buddha. This chapter argues the following: (1) that Aśvaghoṣa's likely first- or second-century CE date makes the question of his reading of the two Sanskrit epics "close" historically, and "critical" from his standpoint as a Buddhist who is reputed to have been a Brahmin convert; and (2) that he probably was familiar with both epics in much the same form as we know them today—citing from both, where it suited him, to show that they presented cases of bad precedent in *dharma.*

Aśvaghoṣa refers early to Vyāsa and Vālmīki as poet precursors (*Buddhacarita* 1.42–43). But he treats the *Mahābhārata* differently from the *Rāmāyaṇa,* being nearly silent on the *Mahābhārata*'s main story and never mentioning such chief characters as Arjuna, Yudhiṣṭhira, Draupadī, Duryodhana, or Karṇa. Given that fact, we can say that he is not really interested in touching base with any of this epic's high dramas, as he is, explicitly, with Rāma's departure from Ayodhyā. Still, he does refer to Pāṇḍu (4.79); to Bhīṣma, Rāma, and Rāma Jāmadagnya as exemplars of doing deeds to please one's fathers (9.25); and to "the entire destruction of the Kurus" (11.31). Finally, in the last canto, when seven kings are ready to go to war over the Buddha's bones and cite as epic justifications several catastrophic *Mahābhārata* episodes and Rāvaṇa's infatuation with Sītā (28.28–31), the point could not be clearer that heroic precedents from the Brahmanical epics are dangerous.

Aśvaghoṣa's stance on precedent is most vivid, however, on the crucial point of the prince's decision not to return home from the forest after his Great Departure. The prince dispenses with royal precedents for doing so, including the precedent of Rāma, by saying to one of his father's emissaries, "And as for your quoting the instances of Rāma and the others to justify my return [home], they do not prove your case; for those who have broken their vows are not competent authorities in deciding matters of *dharma*" (*Buddhacarita* 9.77). We are not told what vows Rāma may have broken, but the main point remains clear: Rāma may offer precedent, but he is not an "authority" or "standard" on *dharma!*

Aśvaghoṣa thus has a point in making epic and other Brahmanical mythological allusions. It is to bring across a realization that, no matter how illuminating heroic, sagely, and divine precedents may be as parallels, they are ultimately irrelevant to the achievement of the Buddha.

The Centrality of Dharma *in Aśvaghoṣa's* Buddhacarita

It is a surprising point to have to make that Aśvaghoṣa would be centrally concerned with *dharma,* but others seem to have missed it. Scholars have tended to focus on his virtuosity as a poet; his refutation of Brahmanical philosophical positions current in his own time; a scholastic interest in early Buddhist doctrine, including the idea of "no self"; and a use of *bhakti* idioms when emphasizing faith in the Buddha. I will argue instead that the unfolding of *dharma* from a Buddhist perspective is probably his central concern.

First, Aśvaghoṣa clearly rehearses many of the varied Buddhist and Brahmanical meanings of *dharma* likely to have been known to him. On the Brahmanical side, while giving direct reference to social class only in passing (4.18) and spinning out debates about life-stage *dharma* without ever precisely calling it that, he provides special moments for *dharma* in the Triple Set along with Wealth and Pleasure (10.28–38, 11.58); clan or family *dharma* (10.39); the three debts a man owes to his ancestors, the seers, and the gods (9.65); and criticism of the wavering of traditional authorities on custom (see 4.83, 7.14, 9.76; 13.49). On the Buddhist side, along with the "Turning of the Wheel of the Dharma" (15.54–55), Aśvaghoṣa also rehearses many of the basic Buddhist meanings of *dharma* that we noted in chapter 4. Among several references to the "true *dharma,*" a Vedic sage comes thirsting for it at the prince's birth and predicts that he will deliver it (1.49; 1.74); the demon Māra is its "enemy" (13.1); and the divine sages in their pure abodes are devoted to it (13.31). On *dharmas* plural, and probably with specific reference to the thirty-seven "*dharmas* on the side of enlightenment," the prince reflects, just before his five companions leave him and he goes to sit under the Tree of Enlightenment: "By the practice of trance those *dharmas* are obtained through which is won the highest, peaceful stage, so hard to reach, which is ageless and deathless" (12.106). For *dharma* as the "quality" or "nature" of something at the end of compounds, Aśvaghoṣa offers this from the prince's rejection of the teachings attributed to his first teacher: "For I am of the opinion that the field-knower, although liberated from the primary and secondary constituents, still possesses the quality *(dharman)* of giving birth and also the quality *(dharman)* of being seed" (12.70). Even the *dharmakāya* (the Buddha's "absolute body") seems to be mentioned (24.10), perhaps anticipated by moments to be noted where the prince prefigures *dharma* in embodied form.

Second, for its foundational importance for all that follows, I examine how Aśvaghoṣa presents the famous story of the four signs that change the prince's life (*Buddhacarita* 3–5). This story is framed by what are now familiar idioms of classical epic *bhakti* (see chapter 9). The mood sets in when the prince's father contemplates his son's first outing from the palace:

> Thereon the ruler of men, with tears in his eyes, gazed long at his son and kissed him on his head; and with his voice he bade him set forth, but out of affection he did not let him go in his mind.

Aśvaghoṣa uses the same trope of love in separation that we have noted in each epic for departures of Rāma and Kṛṣṇa.

For the first outing, the Gods of the Pure Abodes create the "illusion of an old man." The prince asks his charioteer about it: "Is this some transformation in him, or his original state, or mere chance?" Thanks to the gods' confusing the charioteer into spilling the beans about old age, the prince, having learned the truth, "started a little" and offered this first response: "Will this evil come upon me also?"—a rather shallow response compared to what he says when next confronted with signs two and three. For now, he asks to be taken back to the city; he cannot take pleasure "when the fear of old age rules" in his mind.

For the second outing, the same gods fashion a diseased man. The prince is now more reflective: "Thereupon the king's son looked at the man compassionately and spoke: 'Is this evil peculiar to him, or is the danger of disease common to all men?'" Made aware of the realities, he observes the "vast ignorance" of men "who sport under the very shadow of disease." When he has returned to the palace, his father, sensing the prince had "already abandoned" him, scolds "the officer in charge of clearing the roads," but with no severe punishment, and prepares another outing, hoping to change the prince's mood.

For the third outing, the same gods now fashion a lifeless man, arranging it so that only the prince and charioteer see it! Now the prince's question is still more sophisticated: "Is this law *(dharma)* peculiar to this man, or is such the end of all creatures?" To which the charioteer replies, "This is the last act for all creatures. Destruction is inevitable for all in the world, be he of low or middle or high degree." In short, from first asking about only himself with regard to old age to asking about whether disease is unique to one or common to all, he is now, when it comes to the dead man, still framing the question in the same way as for the diseased man. But he is also not only asking whether death applies to one or to all but is asking after the underlying "law" *(dharma)* that results in it. But whereas the prince asks about a "law," the charioteer answers him only in terms of "acts." So the discovery of such a law will remain the prince's problem. He is not handed such a law by a charioteer—I am, of course, alluding to the *Bhagavad Gītā*—or anyone else. Instead of *dharma* being revealed, it is approached through developing insight.

Now the prince suddenly becomes "faint on hearing of death," grabs the chariot rail, and then reflects "in a melodious voice" that "this is the end appointed for all creatures," and that, to appear happy, men must harden their hearts to be in good cheer as they fare along the road. He asks to return to the city as it is no time for pleasure parks, but the driver goes at the king's behest to a grove prepared in advance, a park filled with birds and beautiful women, which the prince experiences as if he were a Muni carried there by force to a place presenting "obstacles." This sylvan pause gives Aśvaghoṣa the opportunity to devote the next canto of lacy poetry to the wiles of women, and to the prince's newfound indifference to them before he is visited by the fourth sign.

The prince now heads out, again with his father's permission, to see the forests, taking a retinue of friends who are the sons of ministers. He rides his special horse, but the charioteer is not with him. Going to some distant savannah, he sees the soil being plowed and, seeing insects cut up, he mourns for them as for his own kindred. Seeking clearness of mind, he stops his well-wishers and goes to sit beneath a rose apple tree. There, "reflecting on the origin and destruction of creation" and taking "the path of mental stillness," he enters the "first trance of calmness" and attains "concentration of mind." And, having rightly perceived it, he meditates on the "course of the world." In the *Nidānakathā,* dated to the fifth century CE, which Aśvaghoṣa may have known in an earlier version, this episode occurs when the prince is a mere child with nurses. But Aśvaghoṣa's prince is now a mature young man who carries forward with this meditation from what he began to realize when he encountered the third sign:

> A pitiable thing it is indeed that a man, who is himself helpless and subject to the law *(dharma)* of old age, disease, and destruction, should in his ignorance and the blindness of his conceit, pay no heed to another who is the victim of old age, disease, or death. For if I, who am myself such, should pay no heed to another whose nature is equally such, it would not be right or fitting in me, who have knowledge of this, the ultimate law.

He is realizing that this "law" involves a recognition of "the other," with whom all are in this together, which carries forward from the progression through the first three signs. And after the next two verses further describe this insight and its neutralizing of the passions in the prince, it is now the moment for the arrival of the fourth sign, which, rather than provoking these reflections, comes in response to them. Not fabricated by the gods like the other three signs, a Śramaṇa or ascetic appears as a *bhikṣu* or mendicant, and says, "In fear of birth and death [I] have left the home life for the sake of salvation *(mokṣa).*" Whatever he means by Śramaṇa or *bhikṣu,* he says he is a homeless wanderer–seeker, "accepting any alms [he] may receive," and, moreover, a "heavenly being who in that form had seen other Buddhas, and has encountered the prince to rouse his attention," which he gets. The *Nidānakathā* notes, "When that being went like a bird to heaven, the best of men was thrilled and amazed. And he gained awareness of *dharma* and set his mind on the way to leave his home." When he returns to the palace, it is "with yearning aroused for the imperishable *dharma.*" This birdlike divine creature sets the prince to the task of unfolding this new awareness of *dharma* he has already begun discovering on his own by setting his mind on departure from home—which is clearly not the locus of the *dharma* he now seeks.

Finally, once the prince has made his Great Departure, Aśvaghoṣa brings the initial devotional mood to a climax in a *bhakti* set piece when the charioteer, about to leave the prince behind in the forest, first recalls Rāma's charioteer in the corresponding *Rāmāyaṇa* scene:

> I cannot leave you in the forest, as Sumantra did Rāghava [Rāma], and go to the city with a burning heart. (6.36)

and then gives way to a mood typical of complete *bhakti* abandon such as one finds in later stories of Kṛṣṇa and the cowherd maidens:

> Looking back once more, he wept aloud and clasped the horse, Kanthaka, with his arms. Then in despair he lamented again and again, and started for the city with his body, but not with his mind. Sometimes he brooded and sometimes he lamented, sometimes he stumbled and fell. So journeying in grief under the force of devotion *(bhakti),* he performed many actions on the road in complete abandon. (6.67–68)

Even after this Great Departure, the prince will tell the first anchorites he meets that he is still "a novice at *dharma*" (7.46).

Challenging the King of Magadha

As the traditional story tells it, it will be seven years from the Great Departure to the prince's enlightenment. During the first year he will be a disciple of two masters, and during the last six he will perform asceticism. As Aśvaghoṣa tells it, having learned from some anchorites about the first master he will train with, the prince sets off toward his hermitage in the central Indian Vindhya mountains, despite the anchorites' admonition that he should head north to pursue the highest *dharma,* and take not a step toward the south (*Buddhacarita* 7.41). It seems he heads south so as to take in the Magadha capital of

Rājagṛha, ruled by King Bimbisāra. Before he was killed by his son, Bimbisāra was the most powerful king in northeastern India for most of the Buddha's career.

We will now look at how, in telling of the prince's visit to Magadha, Aśvaghoṣa makes unspoken references to an episode in *Mahābhārata* Book 2, and in the next section at his handling of *dharma* terminologies that he would seem to draw from *Mahābhārata* Book 12.

For the rest of this section, I offer a table to allow easy navigation of the two parallel stories. I suggest readers first scan the unaccented sequence (items 1, 2, 4, 6, etc.) on the left, the *Buddhacarita* side, to see what we surmise Aśvaghoṣa would have known from other Buddhist stories, and then the whole alignment with the boldface entries included (3,5,7,etc.) to see what Aśvaghoṣa seems to have taken from the *Mahābhārata* story into his own version of the Buddha's adventure.

Buddhacarita (B)	*Mahābhārata (M)*
1. The prince enters the city of the five hills (10.2)	1. Kṛṣṇa, Bhīma, and Arjuna approach the city o five hills
2. The prince makes his first appearance dressed (or disguised) as a mendicant (*bhikṣu*) (9)	2. Following Kṛṣṇa's counsel, the three are disguised as bath-graduate (*snātaka*) Brahmin (2.18.22)
3. **He seems to onlookers like Dharma incarnate** (6)	3. In Kṛṣṇa is prudent policy (*naya, nīti*), in Bhīma strength, in Arjuna victory (14.9, 18.3). Prudent policy turns out to be tricky *dharma* (see item 14 below)
4. First amazed, onlookers then fall still and silent and have no unruly thoughts (2–6)	4. Onlookers fall to "wondering" (19.27) and are at first baffled
5. **The city's goddess Lakṣmī shows favor on the prince** (9)	5. Kṛṣṇa soon reveals that the goddess Śrī favors Kṣatriya bath-graduates who wear garlands (19.46)
6. The prince climbs Pāṇḍava Mountain (14). After receiving a report of his ascent, so does King Bimbisāra, "**in heroism equal to a Pāṇḍava**" (17)	6. The two Pāṇḍavas and Kṛṣṇa climb Caityaka Mountain
7. **There King Bimbisāra sees the tranquil cross-legged Bodhisattva "being as it were a horn of the mountain"** (18)	7. There they destroy the "horn" of Caityaka Mountain (19.18)
8. Bimbisāra thus shows deference and hospitality by coming to the mountain	8. The two Pāṇḍavas and Kṛṣṇa come to King Jarāsandha's palace, where they reject his hospitality (19.34)
9. **The prince looks to the king "like some being magically projected by Dharma"** (19)	9. Jarāsandha asks about the *dharma* of this rejection, and about the trio's disguises

Buddhacarita (B)	*Mahābhārata (M)*
10. **The king and prince debate about *dharma:* Bimbisāra links the Triple Set with aging: pleasure for youth, wealth for middle years, *dharma* for old age** (34–37); **but the prince, seeing danger in old age and death, "resorts to this *dharma* out of longing for salvation"** (11.7). **The prince should do family *dharma* and offer sacrifices** (10.39–40); **but he does "not approve of sacrifices" or of "happiness sought at the price of another's suffering"** (11.64–67), etc.	10. Kṛṣṇa and Jarāsandha air opposing views of *dharma:* Kṛṣṇa reveals they are Kṣatriya bath-graduates and hold him as enemy. Asking why, Jarāsandha protests himself a ruler by *dharma* (20.3–5). Kṛṣṇa says the trio follows *dharma* in opposing Jarāsandha's plan to sacrifice a hundred kings to Rudra (20.9), but Jarāsandha sees it as Kṣatriya *dharma* to treat captives as one pleases (20.6)
11. Bimbisāra offers the prince half his Magadha kingdom (10.25–26), which the prince explicitly rejects (11.49–56)	11. Kṛṣṇa's plan will eliminate Magadha's sovereignty so that Dharmarāja Yudhiṣṭhira can be universal monarch by performing a Rājasūya sacrifice
12. **Bimbisāra also challenges the prince to fight his foes; moved as he is by compassion at seeing him, a Kṣatriya, in the garb or guise of a mendicant (*bhikṣu*), Bimbisāra would be the prince's ally** (10.27–32)	12. Kṛṣṇa challenges Jarāsandha to fight one of the trio in the guise and garb of bath-graduates, now revealing who they are (20.23–24)
13. **The prince implicitly rejects such a fight**	13. Jarāsandha chooses to fight Bhīma (21.3), as Kṛṣṇa had devised (20.32–34)
14. The prince promises to come back as a Buddha (11.72–73), at which point he will preach the *dharma* that converts Bimbisāra and many other Magadhans.	14. Once Jarāsandha is killed, the freed kings imprisoned in Girivraja recognize that Kṛṣṇa protects the *dharma,* and that he is Viṣṇu (22.31–32).

Certain verses describing the prince's approach are immediately interesting:

> On seeing him, the gaudily-dressed felt ashamed and the chatterers on the roadside fell silent; as in the presence of Dharma incarnate none think thoughts not directed to the way of salvation, so no one indulged in improper thoughts. (*Buddhacarita* 10.6; item B3 in table)
>
> . . .
>
> And Rājagṛha's Goddess of Fortune was perturbed on seeing him, who was worthy of ruling the earth and was yet in a *bhikṣu*'s robe, with the circle of hair between his brows, with the long eyes, radiant body and hands that were beautifully webbed. (*Buddhacarita* 10.9; item *B*5).

For the very first time, Aśvaghoṣa describes the prince as "dressed," or "disguised," as a mendicant or *bhikṣu* (item *B2*), just like the Śramaṇa who appeared before him in that guise earlier as the fourth sign. Indeed, that it was a guise for the Śramaṇa is emphasized in the earlier *Nidānakathā*, which remarks that it was a sign of things to come sent from the gods, since there were no *bhikkhus* at the time. Along his way, the prince stills the improper thoughts of those who see him appear "like Dharma incarnate," thoughts not only of the city's bon vivants but of Rājagṛha's Goddess of Fortune, who understands that, despite his *bhikṣu* dress or guise, he is fit to rule the earth. When Bimbisāra, who might thus have reasons for concern, also sees him from a palace balcony, he orders an officer to report on his movements. The prince moves calmly, now begging for food apparently for the first time—that it is the first time is suggested in the *Nidānakathā*, where he has to force down some disgusting almsfood—accepting what comes to him without distinction. Taking his meal at a lonely rivulet (Aśvaghoṣa does not, like the *Nidānakathā*, have him nearly vomit), from there he climbs Mount Pāṇḍava. Hearing of this destination, Bimbisāra, who is now said to be "equal in heroism to a Pāṇḍava"—then ascends the same Pāṇḍava Mountain (item *B6*), where he sees the bodhisattva sitting "in majestic beauty and tranquility like some being magically projected by Dharma" (item *B9*).

Buddhist tradition itself thus makes one of the five peaks of Rājagṛha, or at least part of one of them, the Pāṇḍava Mountain. Mount Pāṇḍava is a stable feature in Buddhist stories of this event, with perhaps the oldest instance in the *Suttanipāta* (*Mahāvagga, Pabbajjā Sutta* 10–13), which is usually accepted as an early part of the Pāli canon and is certainly older than Aśvaghoṣa. It seems to be a basis for the more developed account mentioning the same mountain in the *Nidānakathā*, which Aśvaghoṣa may also have known in an early version. In the *Mahābhārata*, not surprisingly, there is no mountain by that name. Rather, when Kṛṣṇa, Arjuna, and Bhīma approach Magadha to kill King Jarāsandha and reach a certain Mount Goratha, they set eyes on "Magadha city" (*Mahābhārata* 2.18.30), which Kṛṣṇa describes as having "five beautiful mountains" that "stand guard over Girivraja" (19.2–3). We note that the *Mahābhārata*'s name for the city is Girivraja, not Rājagṛha. For the epic to use only Girivraja is probably an archaism. The *Mahābhārata* means by this name not just the Magadha capital but the "mountain corral" where Jarāsandha keeps eighty-six of the world's hundred kings imprisoned to be sacrificed, when he gets a full hundred of them, to Rudra-Śiva (items *M*10, *M*14 in table).

Buddhist tradition thus references the Pāṇḍavas, and one may assume the *Mahābhārata,* and in all likelihood the Jarāsandha episode, when it has the prince cross the Pāṇḍavas' tracks on Pāṇḍava Mountain. From this, the most straightforward assumption would be that the Buddhists have named as "Pāṇḍava Mountain" the mountain, or at least part of the mountain, which Kṛṣṇa, Arjuna, and Bhīma ascended: the Caityaka Peak (items *B*6, *M*6). It seems to correspond on maps with Chattha Mountain with its Vulture Peak, where the Buddha will spend many of his later days, and is in the northeast, where the Pāṇḍavas would likely have approached the city. Yet Aśvaghoṣa goes beyond other Buddhist sources in describing the Bodhisattva's trek here. And though it is not a matter one can demonstrate irrefutably, it seems from some of Aśvaghoṣa's new themes, similes, and points of emphasis that he does so not only out of a residue of folklore but with a *Mahābhārata* "textually" in view.

The first thing worth noting is that Aśvaghoṣa introduces an epic tone. Magadha's goddess of Fortune, or Lakṣmī, shows her favor on the prince (item *B*5), and Bimbisāra challenges him to take up arms against his foes with Bimbisāra as an ally (item *B*12). The challenge is particularly gratuitous, and when it is noticed that Bimbisāra makes it upon seeing the prince in the guise of a *bhikṣu,* one gets a good index that Aśvaghoṣa is taking the Pāṇḍavas' bath-graduate guises as his epic touchstone (see items *M*2, *M*5, *M*10, *M*12). In each case it is a matter of being thinly disguised Kṣatriyas: in one case three Kṣatriyas disguised as bath-graduate Brahmins, in the other a prince in mendicant garb that some texts, including some passages in the *Mahābhārata,* say should be restricted to Brahmins. Moreover, while challenging the prince to take up arms, Bimbisāra mentions the Bodhisattva's appearance precisely, calling him "lover of the mendicant life-stage" (10.33), thereby providing the one instance in the text where *āśrama* clearly means "life-stage" rather than "hermitage." Just as the prince's royal father had told his son not to go against the "proper order" of the implied life-stages (5.32–33), so Bimbisāra now seconds the point with additional unusual arguments correlating the Triple Set with the life-stages (item *B10*). Both kings are making a "legitimate" point, for they would be speaking as "protectors of the Law of Class and Life-stage," a role that even Buddhist kings come to play.

Next, as one would expect of an accomplished poet, Aśvaghoṣa tips his hand further with his similes. When the prince has climbed Mount Pāṇḍava, the *Suttanipāta* has the king's messengers report back and say, "Your majesty, the *bhikkhu* has settled down on the east side of Mount Pāṇḍava. He's sitting there in his mountain lair like a lion or a tiger or a bull" (*Pabbajjā Sutta* 12). Aśvaghoṣa may have offered this as an improvement: "On that mountain . . . he, the sun of mankind, appeared in his ochre-colored robe like the sun in the early morning above the eastern mountain" (*Buddhacarita* 10.15). To paraphrase, as he ascends Pāṇḍava mountain in his new reddish garment, the future Buddha is compared to the morning sun. That is how Aśvaghoṣa describes what Bimbisāra's officer sees (10.16), and perhaps what the officer reported back to Bimbisāra. But now, when Bimbisāra himself ascends this same mountain with the heroism of a Pāṇḍava, he sees the tranquil cross-legged bodhisattva "being as it were a horn of the mountain" (item *B7*). That is, the rising sun of mankind has become the "horn" of the very Pāṇḍava Mountain he and King Bimbisāra have just climbed. I cannot imagine that Aśvaghoṣa has any other *first* pretext for introducing this singular, surprising, and somewhat strained simile than a reference to the *Mahābhārata*'s double use of "horn" *(śṛṅga)* to describe what it is on Caityaka Mountain that the two Pāṇḍavas and Kṛṣṇa destroy (items *M6–7*). The *Mahābhārata*'s Critical Edition, which first describes this "horn" as garlanded and then has Jarāsandha mention it when he asks how the trio broke it, leaves nothing to suggest that the trio destroys anything else. Kṛṣna establishes the first meaning of "horn" for the whole passage when he describes Girivraja's five mountains as all having "great horns and cool trees" (2.19.3–41).

Aśvaghoṣa could, however, also have a second pretext for using the word "horn" to describe the tranquilly seated prince: the word's symbolic significance is brought out in the *Mahābhārata*'s so-called appendix, the *Harivaṃśa*, in a question raised about the same Jarāsandha cycle:

> To what end did Madhusūdana (Kṛṣṇa) abandon Mathurā, that [zebu bull's] hump of the Middle Country, the sole abode of Lakṣmī, easily perceived as the horn of the earth, rich in money and grain, abounding in water, rich in Āryas, the choicest of residences? (*Harivaṃśa* 1.57.2–3)

This "horn of the earth" evokes associations of Kṛṣṇa with the horn in contested situations where he uses his "Horned" bow in battles, and associations with Viṣṇu's Fish and Boar *avatāras*, where he uses the "single horn" or "single tusk" (in either case, *śṛṅga*) to rescue Manu's ark and the earth. In other words, in the Jarāsandha cycle, the horn is a symbol of unique sovereignty in contested circumstances, which makes it fitting that Kṛṣṇa and the two Pāṇḍavas break the horn of Magadha's Caityaka Mountain—no matter how difficult it is to imagine—with their bare arms. For they are intent, in the *Mahābhārata*'s terms, upon eliminating Jarāsandha as a rival of Yudhiṣṭhira for the title of universal sovereign or emperor, and, in the *Harivaṃśa*'s terms, upon restoring the unique centrality of Mathurā to the Middle Country, even in Kṛṣṇa's absence from it.

At one level, what is being contested in the *Buddhacarita* is thus royal sovereignty, which is personified in the goddess Lakṣmī, who favors the prince even though he declines royal sovereignty when Bimbisāra offers it to him. But as Aśvaghoṣa registers in further similes, by in fact doubling one simile, what is really contested is the *dharma:* the prince seems to onlookers "like Dharma incarnate" (item *B*3), and to Bimbisāra he looks "like some being magically projected by Dharma" (item *B*9). In Aśvaghoṣa's hands, it no longer has to do with a debate about the Śaiva-Vaishnava overtones of Kṣatriya *dharma,* such as occurs between Jarāsandha and Kṛṣṇa in the *Mahābhārata* (items *M*10, *M*14). Rather, it now concerns oppositions between Brahmanical royal *dharma* and Buddhist *dharma*—the latter as it is, so to speak, still taking shape in the Bodhisattva–prince's mind. Yet given the undoubtedly intended ambiguity of Caityaka Mountain's association with the term *caitya,* "sanctuary," which can have both Brahmanical and Buddhist meanings, the *Mahābhārata* story can also be taken as a story about Brahmanical–Buddhist opposition. Scholars have sensed this for over a century.

That brings us to a third pretext for Aśvaghoṣa's surprising "horn" simile. For when one takes the force of the "horn" and "Dharma incarnate" similes in conjunction with the fact that it is King Bimbisāra, not the prince, who is made "equal to a Pāṇḍava in heroism" and who sees the Bodhisattva as if he had become the horn of the mountain, one could take it that Bimbisāra sees not only Dharma incarnate but a cross-legged bodhisattva appearing as the restored horn of the mountain that the Pāṇḍavas and Kṛṣṇa broke down.

The *Mahābhārata* episode has been open to such readings because it has to do with overtones of spiritual rivalry over empire in the name of *dharma.* This is the real hinge upon which Aśvaghoṣa opens his reading of this episode. For although it may look like a weak point to align the Bodhisattva with Kṛṣṇa on the matter of the Bodhisattva's double appearance as "Dharma incarnate," we are at the deepest level at which Aśvaghoṣa engages this *Mahābhārata* scene: the level of Buddhist versus Brahmanical *dharma* and *bhakti.* The position of Kṛṣna in representing Brahmanical *dharma* in the Jarāsandha episode is decisive. For the first thing to strike one is that the *Mahābhārata*'s actual Dharma King, Dharma's son Yudhiṣṭhira, is precisely not among the trio assaulting Magadha, among whom, as Bhīma says first and Kṛṣṇa then confirms, Kṛṣṇa represents prudent policy *(naya, nīti),* Bhīma strength, and Arjuna victory (item *M*3). Yet what Yudhiṣṭhira says before the trio departs is pertinent to this train of associations. Fearing Jarāsandha's might and ready to change his mind about performing his imperial consecration, the Dharma King says, "Bhīma and Arjuna are my two eyes, Janārdana [Kṛṣṇa] I deem my mind; what kind of life shall be left for me without mind or eyes?" (*Mahābhārata* 2.15.2). Kṛṣṇa supplies "policy" that will turn out to be tricky *dharma,* or more precisely *upāyadharma* (item *M*14)—a "*dharma* of strategy" or "means," such as we have often seen Kṛṣṇa deploy. Indeed, the two verses that identify Kṛṣṇa with policy and Arjuna with victory resonate with a recurrent *Mahābhārata* formula, "Where *dharma* is there is Kṛṣṇa; where Kṛṣṇa is there is victory." In short, Aśvaghoṣa's reading of the Jarāsandha episode could be summed up as follows: where Kṛṣna was, there now is the Dharma looking like the horn of a mountain.

In closing this section, it is worth asking about the spiritual significance of these findings. What would be at stake for a Buddhist poet to take up this particular episode for such a critical and even subversive reading? I make two observations. First, it is clear that for both the Buddhist and Brahmanical traditions, Magadha remained, in Aśvaghoṣa's time, a potent symbol not only of contested imperial sovereignty but of a struggle for ascendancy between the ways the two traditions represented the very embodiment of *dharma* in two persons; whereas the *Mahābhārata* wants Kṛṣṇa to symbolically reassert Mathurā and the "Middle Country" as the spiritual heartland of "Vedic" *dharma*, the *Buddhacarita* wants to reassert the spiritual centrality of Magadha where, to the city's good fortune, the Buddha embodies "the true *dharma*." Second, the direct confrontation of the Buddha with Kṛṣṇa, who in the Jarāsandha episode is finally recognized as Viṣṇu by the eighty-six freed kings (item *M*14), makes it clear that what was at stake in both texts were remappings, literally and geographically, of the politics of *bhakti*.

Buddhist Mokṣadharma

Aśvaghoṣa thus focuses on pivotal matters bearing on Rāma and Kṛṣṇa in the second books of each epic. In a *bhakti* idiom, the *dharma* has the same spiritual appeal as the man whose life embodies it. Yet I believe Aśvaghoṣa has read even deeper into the *Mahābhārata*'s treatment of *dharma* to take stock of its didactic teachings on *mokṣa*.

Our chief question here is not what kind of *Mahābhārata* Aśvaghoṣa would have known but why teachings on *mokṣadharma* would have interested him. Let us begin with a sense that although Buddhist and Brahmanical texts do sometimes have differences they want to stress when one uses the term *nirvāṇa* and the other the term *mokṣa*, neither has any internal ban on using the other's term, and both would know they are alternate terms for what we can call spiritual freedom. Like the Buddha, Yudhiṣṭhira wishes after the *Mahābhārata* war to take up the mendicant life and praises the pursuit of *mokṣa;* but unlike the Buddha, he will not do so. Instead, he agrees to listen to Bhīṣma, knowing that he will be dissuaded from pursuing it. Bhīṣma's first order of business is thus to secure Yudhiṣṭhira's commitment to the *dharma* of kings. By the time Bhīṣma gets to *mokṣadharma*, *mokṣa* as liberation has become an interesting theoretical matter that Yudhiṣṭhira has more or less agreed to defer, perhaps to some other life. For Aśvaghoṣa, it is this tension with *rājadharma* that would make the notion of *mokṣadharma* interesting, and we can find evidence for this in the ways that he juxtaposes the two terms. Curiously, however, the *Mahābhārata*'s use, and it seems, possible invention, of the term *mokṣadharma* has an anomalous, even uncomfortable feel to it. Wasn't it one of the high points of the *Bhagavad Gītā* that Kṛṣṇa told Arjuna he should abandon all *dharmas* since Kṛṣṇa would "release" him from every sin (18.66)? How can there be "Laws on Salvation or Release" if one is to be released from all laws? It has been said that compared to older Brahmanical uses of *mokṣa* in the Upaniṣads, the *Mahābhārata*'s usage of *mokṣadharma* looks like an oxymoron. It would be tempting to translate *mokṣadharma* as "way" or "ways of salvation," but neither the *Mahābhārata* nor Aśvaghoṣa uses *dharma* to mean "way." Aśvaghoṣa clearly takes the *dharma* in *mokṣadharma* to mean "law," which means that he would be reading the *Mahābhārata*'s usages to mean "laws."

Aśvaghoṣa's interest in *rājadharma* and *mokṣadharma* is focused mainly in the *Buddhacarita*'s ninth and tenth cantos. Canto 9—"The Deputation to the Prince"—is a hinge chapter that allows Aśvaghoṣa to transition from a *Rāmāyaṇa* reading to a *Mahābhārata* reading. This means that the chaplain and the minister get to double not only for the Vedic Brahmins Rāma meets in the forest but for the postwar comforters of Yudhiṣṭhira. Yet as I have begun to demonstrate, such a *Mahābhārata* reading would not be limited to Cantos 9 and 10 but would carry over into Canto 11, where it is anchored in the *full* meeting with King Bimbisāra. Following Canto 12, in which several have long seen parallels between Aśvaghoṣa's treatment of the views of the Buddha's first teacher and certain teachings in the *Mokṣadharma* anthology, this *Mahābhārata* reading would then be concluded in the encounter with Māra in Canto 13.

To understand how Aśvaghoṣa makes Canto 9 a hinge to these unfoldings, we must note two matters. First, such a Brahmanical deputation of a chaplain and minister to find the prince in the forest seems to be an invention by Aśvaghoṣa made, in fact, for the *Buddhacarita*. In Aśvaghoṣa's earlier work, the *Saundarananda*, the events from the Great Departure to the defeat of Māra take only eight verses (3.2–9) and do not mention the deputation. Second, we must look back to a line near the end of Canto 8 where the chaplain and the minister define their mission to the prince's father: "Just let there be a war of many kinds between your son and the various prescriptions of scripture." For these two speakers, this war will be a struggle with Brahmanical scriptures, which the prince will handle rather easily; but, more than this, it sets the terms for the prince's inner struggle that carries through all these cantos to his ultimate contest with Māra.

Now, important as it is that Aśvaghoṣa knows something of the *Mahābhārata*'s *Mokṣadharma* anthology, it is even more interesting that he knows and uses the term *mokṣadharma.* Before examining the three usages that occur in the surviving Sanskrit portions of the first half of the *Buddhacarita,* all in the segment just described, there are also two likely usages in subsequent cantos, where the Tibetan and Chinese translations allow the rendering "law of salvation." Resting after his enlightenment and preparing to preach, the Buddha saw that "the law of salvation was exceedingly subtle" (*Buddhacarita* 14.96). And, just after turning the "wheel of the law" and converting his first five disciples, "the Omniscient established the law of salvation" with further preaching and more conversions (16.1). The "law of salvation" (probably *mokṣadharma*) would seem to reach its full impact as one of Aśvaghoṣa's terms for the *dharma* itself as the "law" and "teaching" of the newly enlightened Buddha.

As to the three verifiable usages, the first two occur in the exchange between the prince and the chaplain. In being the first to convey the message of the prince's father, the chaplain acknowledges that the prince's "fixed resolve with regard to *dharma*" will be realized as his "future goal," but invokes the father's massive grief that the prince is doing this "at the wrong time":

> Therefore enjoy lordship for the present over the earth and you shall go to the forest at the time approved by the scriptures. Have regard for me, your unlucky father, for *dharma* consists in compassion for all creatures. Nor is it only in the forest that this *dharma* is achieved; its achievement is certain for the self-controlled in a city too. Purpose and effort are the means in this matter; for the forest and the badges of mendicancy are the mark of the faint-hearted. The *dharma* of salvation *(mokṣadharma)* has been obtained by

> kings even though they remained at home, wearing the royal tiara, with strings of pearls hanging over their shoulders and their arms fortified by rings, as they lay cradled in the lap of imperial Fortune (Lakṣmī). (*Buddhacarita* 9.17–19)

When the prince replies "after a moment's meditation," he says that fear of the three signs left him no choice but leaving, even knowing the fatherly affections involved (*Buddhacarita* 9.30–31). However noble it is that his father wishes to hand him the kingdom, he rejects kingship as an "abode of delusion" marked by "the oppression of *dharma* through the mishandling of others." For a man of resolution who has gone to the forest out of desire for *dharma*, return to the city would be like eating one's own vomit, like reentering a burning house (39–47). And now, with precise and loaded words on our central point, comes the second usage:

> As for the revelation that kings obtained *mokṣa* while remaining as householders, this is not the case. How can the *dharma* of salvation *(mokṣadharma)* in which quietude predominates be reconciled with the *dharma* of kings *(rājadharma)* in which the rod of punishment predominates? (*Buddhacarita* 9.48)

He does not accept the chaplain's assurances on this point. And indeed, the epic's *Mokṣadharma* anthology makes it doubtful at times that royal householders obtain domiciled bliss. Going on to argue that "quietude and severity are incompatible" for a king (*Buddhacarita* 9.49), the prince now rejects the chaplain's affirmation dialectically:

> Either therefore those lords of the earth resolutely cast aside their kingdoms and obtained quietude, or, stained by kingship, they claimed to have attained liberation on the ground that their senses were under control, but in fact only reached a state that was not final. Or let it be conceded they attained quietude while holding kingship, still I have not gone to the forest with an undecided mind; for having cut through the net known as home and kindred I am freed and have no intention of re-entering that net. (*Buddhacarita* 9.50–51)

What a crystal-clear Buddhist critique of the ambiguities of the Brahmanical position! And, I think implicitly, what a subtle response to the nearly interminable indecisiveness and ultimate resignation to *rājadharma* and householder *dharma,* while putting aside *mokṣadharma,* of Yudhiṣṭhira Dharmarāja.

The third usage of *mokṣadharma* then comes from Māra, early in his determination to prevent the prince's enlightenment. Fingering an arrow as he first challenges the bodhisattva's right to sit beneath the *bodhi* tree, he says,

> Arise, Sir Kṣatriya, afraid of death. Follow your *svadharma,* give up the *dharma* of liberation *(mokṣadharma).* Subdue the world with both arrows and sacrifices, and from the world obtain the world of Indra. (*Buddhacarita* 13.9)

This is the first and only usage of *svadharma* in the first fourteen cantos of the *Buddhacarita,* and probably the only one in the entire text. Whereas in the first usage of *mokṣadharma* the chaplain says it is possible to combine *mokṣadharma* with householder *dharma,* and in the second the prince contrasts *mokṣadharma* with *rājadharma,* Māra now contrasts it with *svadharma.*

Indeed, in using such contrastive terms with a *Mahābhārata* cachet, Aśvaghoṣa might be intending to prickle Brahmanical ears with references not only to the postwar predicament of Yudhiṣṭhira, who of course wants to do something like what the Buddha does and is persuaded not to, but also the prewar muddle of Arjuna, who seems to consider these tensions fleetingly as well (see chapter 8). From the first word "Arise," Aśvaghoṣa puts Māra's insulting challenge in the simplest imperative language of the *Bhagavad Gītā.* Kṛṣṇa tells Arjuna "Arise!" four times, with the last coming more or less decisively at the full disclosure of his theophany (*Bhagavad Gītā* 11.33). Likewise, Māra uses the verb three times in his short speech (*Buddhacarita* 13.9–13), twice in the imperative. Māra's words are especially reminiscent of *Gītā* 2.31–37, where Kṛṣṇa uses this command language after urging Arjuna to do his Kṣatriya *svadharma* with some of his most insulting prods, goading him, just as Māra does the Bodhisattva, to stop looking like he is afraid of fighting. The upshot for Aśvaghoṣa is that Māra's challenge to fight and perform Kṣatriya *svadharma* rather than pursue *mokṣadharma* not only replays the *Gītā* but puts Kṛṣṇa's words into the mouth of the devil. Buddhists seem to have preferred to do without the concept of *svadharma*, probably because it implies that separate, socially ranked selves all have essentialized *dharmas* according to their "inherent natures." There is, for instance, no use of the corresponding term **sadhamma* in the Pāli canon.

But let us not lose track of the opposition between *mokṣadharma* and *rājadharma*. As mentioned above, these terms provide the title topics of the first and third of the four anthologies that comprise Yudhiṣṭhira's postwar curriculum. Through this sequence Yudhiṣṭhira learns first about kingship, then about its distresses, then about how one might pursue *mokṣa* while not doing so himself, and finally, after abandoning his wish to retreat to a hermitage, how to become a giving king. As far as I am able to discern, this fourfold sequence is unique in Indian *dharma* literature to the *Mahābhārata*, and may, I believe, be called one of its signature formulations about *dharma*. Whatever Aśvaghoṣa knows about it, it would present an outcome that the Buddha must, at least for himself, reject, but not one that he would necessarily reject for all. Indeed, Aśvaghoṣa has found it worth engaging, for I believe that his juxtaposition of *rājadharma* and *mokṣadharma*, along with his demonstrations of textual familiarity with both the *Rājadharma* and *Mokṣadharma* anthologies, show that he has the first and third units of this arc firmly in view. But what about the second and fourth, on "times of distress" and "giving"? There is no use of these anthology terms in the *Buddhacarita*, but what about their basic concerns?

There is little about royal "distress" in the first half of the *Buddhacarita*, other than as a general theme personalized over the prince's Great Departure. His father's kingdom is supposed to be suffering no other distress than this. Unless one thinks of Māra, there are no princes or kings distressed over the possibility of losing their kingdoms in these first fourteen cantos. We thus have at least a negative explanation of why Aśvaghoṣa would overlook this shortest and somewhat sandwiched topic of *Mahābhārata* Book 12.

As to the gift *(dāna)*, surprisingly there is no use of the term in the first half of the *Buddhacarita*. But it is made an important matter in Canto 18 where, not surprisingly, the Buddha is addressing not a king but one of those wealthy merchants so important to the economic support of early Buddhism. Sudatta of Kosala, "who was in the habit of giving wealth to the destitute," came at night to visit the Buddha. Having welcomed him, the Buddha turns quickly to "the fame in this world and the reward in the hereafter [that] arise from giving," and urges that "at the proper time" Sudatta should "give the treasure that is won through the law." After hearing an initial sermon mainly on impermanence, Sudatta "obtained the first fruit of practice of the law . . . [and t]hough living in the house, he realized by insight the highest good." As with Yudhiṣṭhira, somebody has to do this job of giving, and must be educated to do it in the right spirit. After a description of Sudatta's insight in terms of the Brahmanical views he now gives up, including those about a deity, we find him offering to donate a monastery. Here the Buddha praises giving at length, mentioning that it is "one of the elements of salvation," expounding on the varied virtues of giving wealth, food, clothes, abodes, vehicles, and lamps, and concluding that Sudatta's gift is of the best kind since it "has no ulterior motive." The verses on the varied merits of giving different things could be called a capsule of the fourth anthology, since they are reminiscent of a large middle stretch of it where Bhīṣma regales Yudhiṣṭhira on the merits of giving all the same things, though above all, giving food and land to Brahmins. With this fourth part of the curriculum, we have something that is not a matter of import until the Buddha must develop a post-enlightenment theory of the gift.

These four *dharma* topics are mentioned earlier in the *Mahābhārata.* So whether or not Aśvaghoṣa is conversant with the treatment of giving in Book 13, he would have had the opportunity to be familiar with all four, and with the plan and contents of at least three-fourths of Yudhiṣṭhira's postwar curriculum. The unfolding of the "laws of giving" involves weighting giving favorably over asceticism (*Mahābhārata* 3.245–247), a matter that is returned to repeatedly in the fourth anthology. Indeed, a preference for giving over asceticism would probably win Aśvaghoṣa's and the Buddha's agreement.

It is clear, though, that what counts most for Aśvaghoṣa is *mokṣadharma,* which he seems to have introduced into Buddhist literature not only as a way to reformulate the Buddha's *dharma,* but as a way to translate *nirvāṇa* that would clarify in both Buddhist and Brahmanical circles what is comparable and what is distinctive about Buddhist and Brahmanical *dharmas.* It is my impression that neither *mokṣadharma* nor a would-be Pāli equivalent have appeared in Buddhist texts before Aśvaghoṣa.

Postscript on Aśoka and Dharma *as Civil Discourse*

Toward the end of the *Buddhacarita,* Aśvaghoṣa offers three verses on Aśoka:

> In the course of time King Aśoka was born, who was devoted to the faith; he caused grief to proud enemies and removed the grief of people in suffering, being as pleasant to look on as an *aśoka* tree, laden with blossoms and fruit. The noble glory of the Maurya race, he set to work for the good of his subjects to provide the whole earth with *stūpas,* and so he who has been called Fierce Aśoka became Aśoka Dharmarāja. The Maurya took the relics of the Seer from the seven *stūpas* in which they had been deposited, and distributed them in due course in a single day over eighty thousand majestic *stūpas,* which shone with the brilliancy of autumn clouds. (*Buddhacarita* 28.63–65)

Now, one touchstone in marking a somewhat less than civil recognition of Buddhism in the *Mahābhārata* has been noted in chapter 9: Mārkaṇḍeya's prophesy about an age of discord overrun with sepulchral mounds, using an early Buddhist term for *stūpa.* One finds a Buddhist counter-prophesy where the Buddha tells King Ajātaśatru of Magadha (who had by now killed his father, Bimbisāra):

> After my decease, the masters of the world will kill each other from father to son; the *bhikṣus* will be engrossed in business affairs, and the people, victims of greed. The laity will lose their faith, will kill and spy on one another. The land will be invaded by Devas and Tīrthikas, and the population will place its faith in the Brāhmins. (*Mañjuśrīmūlakalpa,* verses 236 ff.)

Devas and Tīrthakas would seem to be divinities housed in Brahmanical temples and other holy places served by Brahmins.

Aśoka's proliferation of *stūpas,* which his legendary biography, the *Aśokāvadāna,* actually calls *dharmarājikās,* marks the transition from his being called "Aśoka the Fierce" to Dharmāśoka, "Aśoka the Righteous"—a term for which Aśvaghoṣa lets "Aśoka Dharmarāja" stand alone. This gives Aśoka the name Dharmarāja, which is also an epithet for the Buddha, in part because the building of *stūpas* reconstructs the Buddha's *dharma*-body. As we have seen, it is also a name for King Yudhiṣṭhira in the *Mahābhārata,* as Aśvaghoṣa would clearly have known.

One question we are left with is what to make of such tacit silences. Just as Aśvaghoṣa never mentions Yudhiṣṭhira Dharmarāja, so it is that the *Mahābhārata,* despite knowing about Buddhism (sepulchral mounds are but the tip of an iceberg), never mentions the Buddha. Indeed, the practice of tacit allusion to Buddhism has been suspected, and I think convincingly traced, in the *dharmasūtras* and *Manu,* and may also be suspected in the *Rāmāyaṇa,* in which, for instance, Rāvaṇa, king of Laṅkā, disguises himself as a *bhikṣu* when he comes to abduct Sītā (*Rāmāyaṇa* 3.44.3). Like his counterparts in Brahmanical and indeed earlier Buddhist literature, Aśvaghoṣa could be more arch on the level of symbols and legends, as in his treatment of the Buddha's first entry of Magadha, and his handling of precedent, than in his dialogues. Let us note that he does not miss the opportunity to lace his epic precedents with allusions to many of the great Vedic Ṛṣis and their families to make the point that descendants may surpass their ancestors. Without quite saying so, he restates the Buddha's view that tracing precedent to the great Vedic Ṛṣis is to follow a "procession of the blind."

Yet I have chosen to interpret these silences as civil ones across the board, and to view Aśvaghoṣa as electing to open this tacit practice to the possibility of real civil discourse among those of different faiths. Clearly, it is around the term *dharma* that he envisions this discourse to be possible, or at least to have been possible during the lifetime of the Buddha.

CHAPTER 11

Dharma for the Twenty-first Century

Lately, the United States has become familiar with *dharma* within a suggestive meaning-spectrum. Jack Kerouac's *Dharma Bums* described the heyday of mid-twentieth-century America's bohemian sages or Ṛṣis. The TV situation comedy *Dharma and Greg,* now in reruns, is about a free-spirited woman in the person of Dharma (in fact, Dharmā was Aśoka's mother's name!) with a husband as straight as Rāma or Manu. The television series *Lost* continues to depict the ominous dystopian "DHARMA (Department of Heuristics and Research on Material Applications) Initiative." And *The Dhamma Brothers* documentary film now portrays the experiment of bringing Buddhist meditation sessions to prisoners in an Alabama Correctional Facility as a technique of introspection, inner peace, anger management, and harmony. This says nothing about the classical Indian *dharma* texts and teachings that are making their way into college classrooms. What are we to make of *dharma* as it reaches these and other vistas at the beginning of the twenty-first century?

Here we return to some of the questions raised in chapter 1. Let us reframe them around this new question, and return especially to the topics of *dharma* in narration, women's *dharma,* and *dharma* through the lenses of two religious traditions.

Dharma *in Narration*

We have seen that certain texts, such as the Aśokan edicts, *dharmasūtras,* and *Laws of Manu* are quite declarative about *dharma.* As instruments of public policy, even if they nuance the concept and leave it a challenge to define, they identify themselves with it and do not make it hard to spot. On the other hand, since we took up the *Ambaṭṭha Sutta* in chapter 4, it would have been possible to ask of all our classical narratives, where is the *dharma* in this text? Although the term appears often enough to keep us from losing track of it, the Sanskrit epics and the *Buddhacarita* are, like the Buddhist Suttas, illustrative of *dharma* in ways that go beyond the term's appearances. With the *Buddhacarita* we had to rediscover that the text is about *dharma,* since so many had missed the point. The *Rāmāyaṇa* makes it easier to trace the concept through the narration, since it links *dharma* from the start to the question of the hero's perfection. But still it begins with the question. Yet it is the *Mahābhārata* that makes the concept the most enigmatic. At the end, even Vyāsa admits a kind of authorly anxiety that his main point will be missed. Having, out of "desire for *dharma,*" "strung (or bound) together this *Bhārata*" (implying a completed book) so that it could be proclaimed in different worlds, he told his son, who would be one of its disseminators, a verse that could be recited at dawn to obtain the text's fullest fruit, the realization of *brahman:*

> Thousands of mothers and fathers, and hundreds of sons and wives, experiencing *saṃsāra,* go. And others will go. There are a thousand situations of joy and a hundred situations of fear. They affect the ignorant daily, but not the wise. With uplifted arms I cry this aloud, but no one hears me. Wealth and Pleasure are from *dharma.* For what purpose is it not served? For the sake of neither pleasure nor fear nor greed should one ever abandon *dharma,* even for the sake of living. *Dharma* is eternal, but happiness and suffering are not eternal; the soul is eternal but its cause is not eternal. (18.5.47–50)

Just before this the *Mahābhārata* reiterates a famous claim that it also makes much earlier about itself: "Whatever is here may be found elsewhere; what is not here does not exist anywhere" (1.56.33). The claim implies that the limits of the text are coextensive with the limits of what can be known and said of the universe, and would not be limited to any place or time, land or century.

Now the *Mahābhārata*'s ambiguous treatment of *dharma* as universal yet multifaceted and opaque has inspired one author to call it "the post–9/11 epic" for a globalized century to stumble toward new moral ideas as it steps into its newfound rubble. In the Greek epics, when a hero goes awry, he gets on with it, and if the gods are involved we largely forget about it since they are no longer anyone's gods. But in the *Mahābhārata* human failings can stop the action so that everyone can have a say about *dharma,* including a devious god who can stretch the truth to new circumstances. In this view, the *Mahābhārata* is about "the difficulty of being good": something with which our sixth to eighth chapters are in full agreement.

This would not imply, of course, that the *Mahābhārata* is pertinent only to the twenty-first century. As we have just seen, it claims to be relevant to all times. But its global reach has certainly widened. During the last century, with a different trope, it was assumed that the *Mahābhārata* was India's "national epic," and there was even a rivalry between the editors of the two epics' critical editions as to which was really *the* "national epic": the *Mahābhārata* or the *Rāmāyaṇa.* By the late twentieth century, Hindu chauvinists had no trouble identifying the *Rāmāyaṇa* with anti-Muslim sentiments during the Ayodhyā controversy, which fed into the destruction of Babri Mosque on December 6, 1992, when advocates of "eternal *dharma*" politics claimed that the first Mughal emperor, Babar, had built the mosque over the site of a Hindu temple that he had destroyed at Rāma's birthplace. A few years later the *Mahābhārata* also lent itself to nationalist sentiments during the nuclear arming of India and Pakistan, when some explained that the doomsday weapons handled by various epic heroes were proof that Indians knew the secrets of nuclear weapons way back in the Vedic age. Never mind that the *Mahābhārata* says nothing about explosives, which seem to have been a Chinese invention in the thirteenth century CE.

In these examples, *dharma* was invoked quite differently. In the last century it denoted Indianness as a term of Hindu nationalism. This century we may be beginning to see it as a term by which the Indian diaspora is appreciating its heritage as a contribution not only to understanding life at home but facing difficult and real dilemmas in a conflict-ridden world.

Women's Svadharma

What can twenty-first-century women take to their homes and offices from our texts? Probably not much from Aśoka's edicts or the Brahmanical law books. Indeed, the last century saw Indian women's groups urge that *The Laws of Manu* be burned. But narrative texts offer some richer possibilities.

On the Brahmanical side, we have seen how certain epic heroines use the concept of *dharma* to open public spaces for their just treatment. But they also do so in the private sphere. As remarked in chapter 7, the topic of women's "non-independence" has narrative outlets and subversions. The term "independent," *svatantra,* resonates with two other *sva-* terms whose usage extends more typically into narrative: women's "inherent nature" or *svabhāva* and their "own *dharma*" or *svadharma.* Much has been written about women's *svadharma* based on the assumption that it would be equivalent to their "women's *dharma.*" But this is not the case.

Many stories could be said to work their way between women's "inherent nature" and their "own *dharma*" while holding their "non-independence" up to question. Yet there is a disproportionate treatment of the two terms. One hears frequently of women's "inherent nature," which, according to *Manu,* is "to corrupt men" (2.213). Indeed, *Manu* says this capacity is created into women:

> Lechery, fickleness of mind, and hard-heartedness are inherent in them; recognizing thus the inherent nature produced in them at creation by Prajāpati, a man should make the utmost effort at guarding them. (9.15–16)

The epics usually bring up this "inherent nature" when someone wants to say women are fickle or unstable.

In contrast, there are very few points where the epics mention female *svadharma,* and only one in *Manu* where it pertains to the practice of levirate, literally "the appointment" of a wife to another man. Even though *Manu* scorns the practice, he allows that a woman may be "appointed in accordance with her *svadharma*" if her husband "is dead, impotent, or sick" (9.64–66, 167). This rule, as stated, completely ignores a woman's desire or will. In several *Mahābhārata* narratives, women find this "law" disagreeable, though they never speak of it as their *svadharma.*

Epic heroines speak only rarely about their *svadharma.* Indeed, I have found only five epic instances where anyone even mentions it with reference to women. I will highlight two of these. Most delightful is the only one in the *Rāmāyaṇa.* Rāma tells Sītā it would be her *svadharma* to stay behind and not do what she wants, which is to accompany him in his forest exile. Sītā then gets her way by quoting a supposed Vedic verse on the sanctity of marriage: "When in this world a woman's father gives her to a man by means of the ritual waters and in accord with [his?] *svadharma,* she remains his even in death" (*Rāmāyaṇa* 2.26.16). It is not so clear in this second verse whether the *svadharma* in question is the father's, the groom's, or the bride's. But before this, where Rāma is talking about Sītā's *svadharma,* the most interesting thing is that she does not accept it. Moreover, Rāma accepts her nonacceptance (something inconceivable when it comes to his own *svadharma*). Rāma seems to be making her *svadharma* up, or, perhaps more fairly, he is in the position of a man having little credibility when it comes to telling a woman what is in her own best interest (to suggest a parallel idiom).

Three of the four *Mahābhārata* instances also make *svadharma* a term by which women's difficulties might be negotiated, whether by themselves or by men. But the most intriguing is an exceptional usage involving a female ascetic named Sulabhā, who tells the proverbially wise King Janaka, "Firmly devoted to my *svadharma,* I am not one who makes confusion of *dharma*" (*Mahābhārata* 12.308.185). Sulabhā is a nun, Yoga specialist, and gender philosopher who speaks from a non-dualist philosophical position. For her, all beings, whether male or female, have bodies and qualities made equally of the same matter. It is thus important that she speaks as a woman. But where she mentions her *svadharma,* it is to claim that she is "independent" or "free" from the constraints and confusions of *dharma* that Janaka would like to say she has violated by possessing his body to see if he is as free of worldly attachments as he claims. Janaka's view that Sulabhā commits "confusion of *dharma*" comes at the pinnacle of his charges that she commits confusion of class, life-stage, and Vedic lineage (59–62), all of which seems to imply to him that she must violate her *svadharma,* although he does not use the term himself. She proves him wrong on each count, and when she finally mentions her firmness in *svadharma,* she formulates it as a rather bold, unusual, and probably ironic expression of her socially untrammelled philosophical standpoint. Draupadī is not the only *Mahābhārata* woman to philosophize.

Meanwhile, there is no discussion of women's *svadharma* in passages where one might expect it. For instance, when one of Kṛṣṇa's wives asks Draupadī how she manages five husbands (*Mahābhārata* 3.222–224), Draupadī answers only in terms of women's *dharma(s)*. "The laws that forever operate in households, I have heard all from my mother-in-law [Kuntī]," by which she means the things a woman does in connection with the five daily "great sacrifices" discussed in chapter 5:

> My *dharma* rests on my husband, as, I think, it eternally does with women. He is the god, he is the path, nothing else: what woman could displease him?

Similarly, when Yudhiṣṭhira is thinking about the painful and dangerous work of childbirth and asks a Ṛṣi about this "very frightful" aspect of women's *dharma*, he does not call it *svadharma* but "their own particular job" (3.196.8, 11). There is nowhere anything biological or "self-natured" about a woman's *svadharma*. Indeed, Sulabhā makes this very point.

"Women's *dharma*" thus takes on a dynamic between an ascribed "inherent nature" that justifies their constant supervision while denying them a slice of law that one could "call their own," and a rarely mentioned *svadharma* that, where we do find it, seems to open a conceptual space for women to negotiate "their own" *dharma* in ways that are more to their liking. Women's voices and actions are indispensable to the epics' textualization of *dharma*, bringing home its nuances—whether in questioning it, interpreting it, raising questions by their silences, or even by making a slip of the tongue. Each heroine, pace *Manu*, raises the question of her spiritual and legal independence, "whether she is a child, a young woman, or an old lady."

Meanwhile, on the Buddhist side there is, above all, the story of how the Buddha's foster mother got him to change his mind about admitting nuns to the monastic life. The capital point here is twofold. The Buddha is, or perhaps I'd better be more cautious, seems to me (after many years of asking students and colleagues if they know of any other exceptions) to be the only founding religious teacher and "law giver" on record in the history of religions to have changed his mind. And he did it over "the women's question." He was not complimentary in doing so, but he did it. This glass ceiling fell to a good argument made possible by the Buddha's own teaching.

Buddhists and Hindus

Back then to our last chapter. Did Aśvaghoṣa succeed in engaging his Brahmin counterparts—whose favorite works he knew so well—in a mutual discourse on *dharma?* If so, apparently not for long. He is remembered in Brahmanical circles only for his poetic virtuosity. Did he make an elitist discourse only more elitist by composing in such erudite Sanskrit? No doubt, but did he also seek to foster a countercurrent that we have seen in some texts, most notably the Aśokan inscriptions, the Pāli Buddhist texts, *Āpastamba,* and the *Mahābhārata? Āpastamba* allows that one may learn aspects of *dharma* from women and Śūdras (2.15.9; 29.11, 15), while Yudhiṣṭhira hears a *Mahābhārata* subtale in which a Śūdra tells a Brahmin "the entire *mokṣadharma*" (3.204.1). I think Aśvaghoṣa's treatment of the Great Departure as the beginnings of the discovery of a universal *dharma* is an attempt in this same direction. Does this dialogic type of *dharma* begin to fade, thanks to texts like *Manu* and the *Rāmāyaṇa,* as *dharma* begins to emerge as a dominant and even triumphalist or hegemonic discourse of Hinduism? To some degree I think it does. In the case of Buddhism's gradual disappearance from the subcontinent in the late classical and medieval periods, it is possible to interpret some Buddhist prophesies of the decline and end of "the 'true *dharma*'" as a tacit commentary on the relation between Buddhist and Hindu *dharmas.* My impression is that from the late classical period through the medieval and modern periods, as *dharma* becomes a dominant discourse of Hinduism its greatest *textual* developments lie in the legal sphere. As a term of civil discourse in dialogical narrative it recedes from view, or, if not entirely from view, it is sustained mainly in fable literature where its best spokespersons are often animals. Yet this also shows that *dharma* had penetrated everyday life as a medium of popular discourse open to articulating a spiritual kinship among all creatures, high and low. And what happens to *dharma*'s interfaith implications? *Dharma* does not seem to reemerge as a term by which religions held conversations with each other until the modern period, and then under the very different circumstances introduced by the comparative study of religions. Yet as one moves on to British and postindependence India, one meets numerous recuperations of *dharma* as civil discourse, most memorably in Mahatma Gandhi's exchanges with Jains, with the British, and with Ambedkar.

The use of *dhamma* rather than *dharma* in the title of Ambedkar's last book and final testament, *The Buddha and His Dhamma* (1957), speaks volumes. With Ambedkar, we have a reminder that through its whole history, *dharma* has never entirely shed its propensity to profile members of "low" and "mixed" caste and humiliate the "impure," and is far from doing so in twenty-first-century India. Anthropological studies have found that Dalits—"the oppressed" (India's vast population of "untouchables")—do not have much use for the terms *dharma* and *karma,* probably because they are so readily used together to explain their own oppression. Dalits know the story of how Arjuna gained preeminence at the expense of Ekalavya's thumb all too well and have made it their epic touchstone.

Yet with Ambedkar and Gandhi, we also have reminders that even though civil discourse on *dharma* retains elite features, it also holds out lasting models for introducing cooperation around social and spiritual norms in both top-down and bottom-up processes of historical change. As I have tried to show, at a certain point *dharma* begins to be called on to commend productive restraints on the raw motives of "men to be tamed" and to envision common hospitable and friendly grounds for all, whether of high or low station, to be able to talk about what can touch the heart and spirit at the deepest levels of human experience. It is what an emperor can call on to try to right his realm. It is what a woman—even the Buddha's aunt and foster mother, when she wanted to become the first nun—can draw on when she challenges men "in a man's world" to be their better selves. It is what a Śūdra can tell a Brahmin about "the entire *mokṣadharma.*" *Dharma* is a way of imagining religion as an ethical and spiritual conversation that in principle excludes no one. Even demons and the devil get some "good" lines. It is what gods and sages, whether Buddhist or Hindu, know to be the work they share in common, which is to imagine ways to discuss what is ethically and spiritually possible in relating worldly goals to the goal of attaining human perfection, peace, and the highest spiritual felicity.

Glossary

Ārya: "Noble"; in Brahmanical circles, used to characterize the three upper classes; *see also* twice-born. In Buddhism, used to characterize the Buddha's teaching and those who follow it.

Aryan: A Western-language term derived from Sanskrit *ārya*, as used in Indo-Aryan languages.

ascetic: Anyone following a rule of self-discipline and austerity, including Brahmanical ascetics and followers of non-Brahmanical movements.

ascetic movements: Term used for *samaṇa (śramaṇa)* ascetic groups outside Brahmanism, including Buddhists and Jains. See *samaṇa, śramaṇa.*

āśrama, āśramadharma: "Life-pattern" or "stage of life"; the regulation of such patterns or stages into an ideal course of life, particularly for males. *See* caste, class, *vara. Āśrama* can also mean "hermitage."

bath-graduate: A twice-born male, especially a Brahmin, who has undergone the sacred bath that marks the completion of his Vedic education, after which he may remain in an intermediate celibate state until marriage, or can continue to be called a bath-graduate after marriage.

Brahmanical: Adjectival for the ideas, texts, and practices generated and promoted by Brahmanism.

Brahmanism: A term used to describe post-Rigvedic Hinduism (the term Hindu is not used until about the fifteenth century), and referring especially to types of Hinduism generated and promoted by Brahmins.

Brahmanization: A term used to describe historical processes that foster Brahmanism and enable Brahmanical hegemony. *See also* Sanskritic.

canon: A collection of texts accepted as authoritative by a religion's tradition: e.g., the Vedic canon composed of the four Vedas, Brāhmaṇas, Āraṇyakas, and Upaniṣads; the Buddhist Three Baskets.

caste, class, *varṇa* Brahmanism advances the idea that society should have four harmoniously interactive classes: Brahmins, Kṣatriyas, Vaiśyas, and Śūdras.

dharmas (plural): A distinctive plural Buddhist usage of the term *dharma* that generates considerable debate in various Buddhist schools.

heterodoxy: "Other opinion"; while both Brahmanism and Buddhism avoid official statements of orthodoxy or "correct opinion," both opposed various heterodoxies, including each other. In classical texts, direct or inclusive naming of the other as heterodox was, however, unusual.

Hīnayāna: "Lower Vehicle," "Inferior Vehicle"; a pejorative term coined by the Mahāyāna that is avoided in this book; *see* Nikāya Schools.

karman, karma: Act or activity; any act or activity, especially ritual activity; in Buddhism and in Upaniṣadic and later Hinduism, the basis for reincarnation.

Mahāyāna: "Great Vehicle"; a term used by a Buddhist reform movement, beginning about the first century CE, to describe its ambition to provide the conveyance or means to bring all beings, not just self-selected practitioners, to salvation. *See also* Hīnayāna, Nikāya schools.

Mīmāṃsā: The brahmanical philosophy of "Reflection," one of the six orthodox systems of classical Hindu philosophy, concerned with the interpretation of Vedic ritual and language.

Mokṣadharma: "Law(s) of salvation"; a term of mutual interest to the *Mahābhārata* and Aśvaghoṣa's *Buddhacarita,* yet one that appears anomalously in both these Brahmanical and Buddhist usages.

Muni: A sage, etymologically a silent sage.

Nikāya: (1) The main collections that comprise the Sutta Basket of the Pāli canon; (2) the schools of so-called Hīnayāna Buddhism.

Nikāya schools: The supposedly eighteen schools or sects of early Indian Buddhism that had emerged prior to the Mahāyāna, which called them collectively the Hīnāyāna. Most prominently, they include the Theravāda and the Sarvāstivādins.

orthopraxy: "Correct practice"; a term used to describe the tendency of Hinduism to define itself more by correct practice than by orthodoxy or "correct ideas." *See also* heterodoxy.

pativratā: A woman whose vow is to her husband; the ideal devoted wife in Brahmanical *dharma* texts.

Ṛṣi: A seer, typically used of Vedic seers and those who continue their ascetic traditions and have their aura.

samaṇa, śramaṇa: The Pāli and Sanskrit spellings, respectively, for "ascetic"; literally, "one who toils" in pursuing a religious path or teaching. *See also* ascetics, ascetic movements.

Sanskritic: A term used to describe uses of Sanskrit that encode Brahmanism as normative. *See* Brahmanization.

Sarvāstivādins: "Pan-realists"; those who say of *dharmas* that each one has its own "inherent nature." See *svabhāva.*

scholastic Buddhism: The tradition of scholar monks that drew both Nikāya School and Mahāyāna monks into debates about epistemic and ontological features of early Buddhist teachings, and their interface with Brahmanical teachings.

sublime attitudes: Friendship, compassion, sympathetic joy, and equanimity: the four "Sublime Attitudes" that, according to Buddhism, should be cultivated in all circumstances.

svabhāva: "Inherent nature"; said by the Sarvāstivādins to distinguish each and every *dharma,* and by some Brahmanical texts to distinguish persons and castes.

svadharma: One's "own particular duty," spelled out particularly for members of the warrior caste.

svakarma: One's "own particular activity or job," defined on the model of jobs reserved for Brahmins.

Theravāda: "School of the Elders," keepers of the Pāli canon; first lodged primarily in Sri Lanka.

Triple Set: *Dharma,* wealth *(artha),* and pleasure *(kāma):* a set of three pursuits that raise the question of their proper weighting and balance, sometimes in conjunction with a fourth, liberation *(mokṣa),* whereupon the fourfold grouping is called the four "goals of man" *(puruṣārthas).*

twice-born: One who is born a second time through Vedic sacraments; in the widest scope, any man of the upper three castes, but usually implying a male Brahmin. *See also* Ārya.

varṇa: *See* caste, class, *varṇa.*

Further Reading

CHAPTER 1

On South Asian Buddhist spirituality, see Takeyuchi Yoshinori, ed., *Buddhist Spirituality*, vol. 1: *Indian, Southern Asian, Tibetan, Early Chinese* (New York: Crossroads, 1993). On *dharma* historically, see Wilhelm Halbfass, "*Dharma* in the Self-Understanding of Traditional Hinduism," in *India and Europe: An Essay in Understanding* (Albany: State University of New York, 1988), 310–333; *Journal of Indian Philosophy* 32 (2004): 5–6; Werner F. Menski, *Hindu Law: Beyond Tradition and Modernity* (Oxford: Oxford University Press, 2005); Adam Bowles, *Dharma, Disorder and the Political in Ancient India: The Āpaddharmaparvan of the Mahābhārata* (Leiden: Brill, 2007). For background, see Karl H. Potter, *Presuppositions of India's Philosophies* (Westport, CT: Greenwood Press, 1972); Heinrich Zimmer, *Myths and Symbols in Indian Art and Civilization* (New York: Harper, 1946). For a fuller bibliography, see Alf Hiltebeitel, "Dharma," in Hinduism entries, *Oxford Bibliography Online* (New York: Oxford University Press).

CHAPTER 2

On Aśoka, see N.A.Nikam and Richard McKeon, *The Edicts of Asoka* (Chicago: University of Chicago Press, 1978); Romila Thapar, *Aśoka and the Decline of the Mauryas* (Delhi: Oxford University Press, 1997); John S. Strong, *The Legend of King Aśoka: A Study and Translation of the Aśokāvadāna* (Princeton: Princeton University Press, 1983).

CHAPTER 3

Proposing the translation "foundation," see Joel Brereton, "*Dhármanin* the *Ṛgveda*," *Journal of Indian Philosophy* 32 (2004): 449–489. Topically, see Michael Witzel, ed., *Inside the Texts—Beyond the Texts: New Approaches to the Study of the Vedas* (Cambridge, MA: Harvard University Press, 1997); Stephanie Jamison, *The Rig Veda between Two*

Worlds (Paris: Diffusion de Boccard, 2007); Charles Malamoud, *Cooking the World: Ritual and Thought in Ancient India* (Delhi: Oxford University Press, 1996); Johannes Bronkhorst, *Greater Magadha: Studies in the Culture of Early India* (Leiden: Brill, 2007). Clifford Geertz's *Interpretation of Cultures: Selected Essays* (New York: Basic Books, 1973) provides the turtles story.

CHAPTER 4

For Pāli Sutta translations, see Maurice Walshe, *The Long Discourses of the Buddha: A Translation of the Dīgha Nikāya* (1995); Bhikkhu Bodhi, *The Connected Discourses of the Buddha: A Translation of the Saṃyutta Nikāya* (2000); *In the Buddha's Words: An Anthology of Discourses from the Pāli Canon* (2005); Bhikkhu Ñāṇamoli and Bodhi, *The Middle Length Discourses of the Buddha: A Translation of the Majjhima Nikāya* (2005); Nyanaponika Thera and Bodhi, *Numerical Discourses of the Buddha: An Anthology of Suttas from the Aṅguttara Nikāya* (Walnut Creek, CA: Altamira Press, 1999); John Strong, *The Experience of Buddhism: Sources and Interpretations* (Belmont, CA: Wadsworth, 2002). For an overview, see Richard Robinson, Willard Johnson, and Thanissaro Bhikkhu, *Buddhist Religions: A Historical Introduction,* 5th ed. (Belmont, CA: Wadsworth, 2005). On Sutta literature, see Steven Collins, *Nirvāna and Other Buddhist Felicities: Utopias of the Pali Imaginaire* (New York: Cambridge, 1998); R. Tsuchida, "Two Categories of Brahmins in the Early Buddhist Period." On *dharmas* plural, see A. K. A. Warder, "Dharmas and Data," *Journal of Indian Philosophy* 1 (1971): 272–295; on *Abhidharma,* see Collett Cox, "From Category to Ontology: The Changing Role of *Dharma* in Sarvāstivāda Abhidharma," *Journal of Indian Philosophy,* 32 (2004): 543–597. On Vinaya, see Janet Gyatso, "Sex," in *Critical Terms for the Study of Buddhism,* ed. Donald S. Lopez Jr., pp. 271–291 (Chicago: University of Chicago Press, 2005); Shayne Clarke, "Monks Who Have Sex: *Pārājika* Penance in Indian Buddhist Monasticisms," *Journal of Indian Philosophy* 37 (2009): 1–43; Gregory Schopen, *Bones, Stones, and Buddhist Monuments: Collected Papers on the Archaeology, Epigraphy, and Texts of Monastic Buddhism in India* (Honolulu: University of Hawai'i Press, 1997).

CHAPTER 5

For translations, see Patrick Olivelle, *Dharmasūtras: The Law Codes of Ancient India* (Oxford: Oxford University Press, 1999); *Manu's Code of Law: A Critical Edition and Translation of the Mānava-Dharmaśāstra* (Oxford: Oxford University Press, 2005). For an overview, see Robert Lingat, *The Classical Law of India* (Berkeley: University of California Press, 1973). Topically, see Olivelle, *The Āśrama System: The History and Hermeneutics of a Religious Institution* (New York: Oxford University Press, 1993); *Language, Texts, and Society: Explorations in Ancient Indian Culture and Religion* (Florence, Italy: Florence University Press, 2005); Timothy Lubin, "The Transmission, Patronage, and Prestige of Brahmanical Piety from the Mauryas to the Guptas," in *Boundary Dynamics and Construction of Traditions in South Asia,* ed. Federico Squarcini (Florence: Florence University Press, 2005); Donald R. Davis Jr., "Hinduism as a Legal Tradition," *Journal of the American Academy of Religion* 75, 2 (2007): 241–267.

CHAPTER 6

For translations, see J. A. B. van Buitenen, Books 1–5; James L. Fitzgerald, Books 11–12 (in part), *The Mahābhārata* (Chicago: University of Chicago Press, 1973–); Robert P. Goldman, ed., *The Rāmāyaṇa,* Books 1–6 (Princeton: Princeton University Press, 1984–). Compare John and Mary Brockington, *Rāma the Steadfast: An Early Form of the Rāmāyaṇa* (London: Penguin, 2006). For the *Droṇaparvan,* see Kisari Mohan Ganguli, *The Mahābhārata* (New Delhi: Munshiram Manoharlal, 1970), vol. 6. For overviews, see Hiltebeitel, "*Mahābhārata*" and "*Rāmāyaṇa,*" in *Encyclopedia of India,* ed. Stanley Wolpert, vol. 3, pp. 82–93, 390–399 (Detroit: Thompson Gale, 2006); John Brockington, *The Sanskrit Epics* (Leiden: Brill, 1998); Bimal K. Matilal, *Ethics and Epics: The Collected Essays of Bimal Krishna Matilal* (Delhi: Oxford University Press, 2002). On Rama, see Sheldon I. Pollock, "Ātmānam mānuṣam manye: Dharmākūtam on the Divinity of Rāma," *Journal of the Oriental Institute of Baroda* 33 (1984): 505–528. On Yudhiṣṭhira's lie, compare Jonardon Ganeri, *The Concealed Art of the Soul* (New York: Oxford University Press, 2007), chapter 3.

CHAPTER 7

On "women's *dharma*," see Stephanie Jamison, *Sacrificed Wife Sacrificer's Wife: Women, Ritual, and Hospitality in Ancient India* (Oxford: Oxford University Press, 1996); Patrick Olivelle's and Stephanie Jamison's essays in Olivelle, ed., *Between the Empires: Society in India 300 BCE to 400 CE* (New York: Oxford University Press, 2006). On Sītā, see various essays in Paula Richman, ed., *Many Rāmāyaṇas: The Diversity of a Narrative Tradition in South Asia* (Berkeley: University of California Press, 1991); on Draupadī, see the various essays in *Gender and Narrative in the Mahābhārata*, eds. Simon Brodbeck and Brian Black (London: Routledge, 2007); on Sītā and Draupadī, see Hiltebeitel, *Rethinking the Mahābhārata: A Reader's Guide to the Education of the Dharma King* (Chicago: University of Chicago Press, 2001), chapters 7 and 8.

CHAPTER 8

The *Gītā* translation I recommend is J.A.B. van Buitenen's *Bhagavadgītā in the Mahābhārata: A Bilingual Translation* (Chicago: University of Chicago Press, 1981). For interpretation, see D. Dennis Hudson, "The 'Barley-Corn' Pattern of *Bhagavad-Gītā* 12–16," in *Krishna's Mandala: Bhagavata Religion and Beyond*, ed. John Stratton Hawley, ch. 8, pp. 141–153 (New Delhi: Oxford, 2010). Arvind Sharma, *The Hindu Gītā: Ancient and Classical Interpretations of the Bhagavad Gītā* (La Salle, IL: Open Court, 1986); Simon Brodbeck, "Calling Kṛṣṇa's Bluff: Non-attached Action in the *Bhagavadgītā*," *Journal of Indian Philosophy* 32 (2004): 81–103.

CHAPTER 9

On the theory of a *bhakti* "swerve," see Madeleine Biardeau, *Le Mahābhārata: Un récit fondateur du brahmanisme et son interprétation* (Paris: Seuil, 2002); on *avatāra* myths, see Deborah Soifer, *The Myths of Narasimha and Vāmana: Two Avatars in Cosmological Perspective* (Albany: State University of New York, 1991). On Viṣṇu as exemplary guest, see Laurie L. Patton, *Bringing the Gods to Mind: Mantra and Ritual in Early Indian Sacrifice* (Berkeley: University of California Press, 2005). On Rāma and the Ṛṣis, see Hiltebeitel, "Authorial Paths through the Two Sanskrit Epics, Via the *Rāmopākhyāna*," in *Epic Undertakings*, eds. Robert P. Goldman and Muneo Tokunaga, 169–214 (Delhi: Motilal Banarsidass, 2008).

CHAPTER 10

The classic translation and study of the *Buddhacarita* is E.H. Johnston's *Aśvaghoṣa's Buddhacarita or Acts of the Buddha* (Delhi: Motilal Banarsidass, [1936] 2004); see now Patrick Olivelle, *Life of the Buddha* (New York: New York University Press, 2008). On Yudhiṣṭhira's postwar *dharma* curriculum, see Hiltebeitel, "On Reading Fitzgerald's Vyāsa," *Journal of the American Oriental Society* 125, 2 (2005): 241–261; and James L. Fitzgerald's essay in Olivelle, *Between the Empires;* Bowles, *Dharma, Disorder,* 257–286.

CHAPTER 11

See Jenny Phillips, *Letters from the Dhamma Brothers: Meditation behind Bars* (Onalaska WA: Pariyati Press, 2007). On the *Mahābhārata* as "post 9/11 epic," see Gurcharan Das, *The Difficulty of Being Good: On the Subtle Art of Dharma* (New York: Knopf, 2009). On women's *svadharma,* compare Wendy Doniger O'Flaherty, *The Origins of Evil in Hindu Mythology* (Berkeley: University of California Press, 1976); Fitzgerald, "Nun Befuddles King, Shows *Karmayoga* Does Not Work: Sulabhā's Refutation of King Janaka at *Mahābhārata* 12.308," *Journal of Indian Philosophy* 30, 6 (2002): 641–677; Reiko Ohnuma, "Debt to the Mother: A Neglected Aspect of the Founding of the Buddhist Nuns' Order," *Journal of the American Oriental Society* 74, 4 (2006): 861–901. On Ambedkar, see D. C. Ahir, *Gandhi and Ambedkar* (New Delhi: Ajay Prakashan, 1969); Meera Nanda, *Breaking the Spell of Dharma and Other Essays* (New Delhi: Three Essays, 2002); Christophe Jaffrelot, *Dr. Ambedkar and Untouchability: Fighting the Indian Caste System* (New York: Columbia University Press, 2005). On *dharma* in animal lore, see Patrick Olivelle, *Pañcatantra: The Book of India's Folk Wisdom* (New York: Oxford University Press, 1997). On modern *dharma* discourse in a traditional Indian town, see Leela Prasad, *A Poetics of Virtue* (New York: Columbia University Press, 2007).

Index

DIMENSIONS OF ASIAN SPIRITUALITY

Shinto: The Way Home
Thomas P. Kasulis

Chan Buddhism
Peter D. Hershock

Korean Spirituality
Don Baker

Ancient Chinese Divination
Stephen L. Field

Socially Engaged Buddhism
Sallie B. King

Dharma
Alf Hiltebeitel

About the Author

Alf Hiltebeitel is a professor of religion, history, and human sciences at the George Washington University. He received his Ph.D. in the history of religions at the University of Chicago. He teaches courses on Hinduism, Buddhism, Indian and comparative mythologies, the Goddess, and recently on Dharma in Hinduism and Buddhism. His main research interests are in the Sanskrit epics the *Mahābhārata* and *Rāmāyaṇa,* and in ethnography on the south Indian Tamil cult of Draupadī, the *Mahābhārata*'s chief heroine. In addition to authoring many articles, he has edited or coedited three books, and translated or cotranslated four books from French: two by Georges Dumézil and one each by Mircea Eliade and Madeleine Biardeau. His own books are *The Ritual of Battle: Krishna in the Mahābhārata* (1976/1991); *The Cult of Draupadī,* vol. 1, *Mythologies: From Gingee to Kurukṣetra* (1988/1992); *The Cult of Draupadī,* vol. 2, *On Hindu Ritual and the Goddess* (1991); *Rethinking India's Oral and Classical Epics: Draupadī among Rajputs, Muslims, and Dalits* (1999/2001); and *Rethinking the Mahābhārata: A Reader's Guide to the Education of the Dharma King* (2001/2002).

Production Notes for Hiltebeitel / DHARMA

Series design by Rich Hendel; cover design by Santos Barbasa, Jr.

Composition by Lucille C. Aono

Printing and binding by The Maple-Vail Book Manufacturing Group

Printed on 55# Glat Offset D37 White, 360 ppi